"May Your Days
Be Merry and Bright"
and Other
Christmas Stories by Women

"May Your Days Be Merry and Bright" and Other Christmas Stories by Women

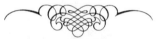

Edited and Introduced by

Susan Koppelman

WAYNE STATE UNIVERSITY PRESS   DETROIT   1988

Library of Congress Cataloging-in-Publication Data

"May your days be merry and bright" and other Christmas stories by
women / edited and introduced by Susan Koppelman.
    p. cm.
  ISBN 0–8143–2124–0
    1. Christmas stories, American—Women authors.   2. Women—Fiction.
I. Koppelman, Susan.
PS648.C45M39   1988
813′.01′0833—dc19   88–21784
                                                           CIP

Grateful acknowledgment is made for permission to reprint the following: "No Room at the
Inn" by Edna Ferber. Copyright © 1939 by Crowell-Collier Publishing Co. Copyright © 1941
by Edna Ferber. Reprinted by permission of Harriet F. Pilpel, as trustee and attorney for the
Ferber Proprietors.

To my husband,
Dennis Lee Mills,
without whom there would be no book

Contents

Acknowledgments

I thank the following for the advice, encouragement, and information that helped make this book a reality: the Reverend Janet Lutz, director of Pastoral Care, Barnes Hospital, St. Louis, Missouri; Anne Bischoff, director of Holy Communion Preschool, St. Louis, Missouri; Olivia Boyd, Lively Stone Church of God, Apostolic; Barbara J. Harman, director of Paperworks: A Print Facility for Fine Artists and vice-president of Vandermark Design; Patrick Hinkebein of Bishop Du Bourg High School, St. Louis, Missouri; W. Gail Brown Mills of the Manchester United Methodist Church Singles' Outreach; and Dr. Susan Waugh of the Church of St. Michael and St. George (Episcopal).

I am grateful to Alice Childress, Frances Gray Patton, and Wilma Shore for their cooperation. The opportunity to make their acquaintance in the process of completing the work on this manuscript has been a privilege.

My sister scholars working on the recovery of American women writers have generously shared their work with me and I am grateful for this opportunity to thank publicly, Judith Arcana, Virginia Cox, Barbara Hillyer, Carol Farley Kessler, and Abigail Keegan.

Acknowledgments

The following librarians have rendered on behalf of this project service that was courteous, good-humored, and in the very best sense professional: Bruce Collins, director, and Linda Ballard and Shirley Goldberg, reference librarians, of the University City Public Library; Rudolph Clay, social science reference librarian of Washington University Libraries, St. Louis, Missouri; Margaret Ganyard, supervisor of the Popular Library North and South and Noel Holobeck, supervisor of the History and Genealogy Department of the St. Louis Public Library.

Without the enthusiastic response to my wish to do this book by Lee Ann Schreiner, Assistant Director for Acquisitions at Wayne State University Press, and my initial and continuing contact there, this book might not have found a home so quickly. Without the unflagging and imaginative efforts of Elizabeth Davidson, reprints manager, it might have been at least another year before this collection of Christmas stories found its way into print.

My son, Edward Nathan Koppelman Cornillon, has made the completion of this work possible. He found things I lost in the mysterious memory of my personal computer (or that I had saved in the wrong file), taught me new tricks on my word-processing program, WordPerfect, and reloaded the paper into my Epson FX-80 printer each time the cats jumped in the box and attacked the moving line of paper, thinking, no doubt, that they were protecting the public welfare and promoting world peace.

My husband's unfailing and unselfish support for my work is the great blessing of my life. He read and listened to endless revisions, buoyed me up through attacks of can't-do-it-itis, and provided fun and distractions when they were the best possible road through.

My mother, Frances Bollotin Koppelman, provided me with the same loving encouragement and good advice she has given me all my life. Nothing in my life would be possible without her.

Finally, there is the inevitable tribute to the household cats: This is our formal goodbye to Mrs. Magenta Cat, Ph.D. (the degree is honorary rather than earned), who deserted us, much to our sorrow, for reason or reasons unknown, and our first public expression of affection for Pizza the Prolific, a silky half-Siamese calico; her daughter, Pepper the Loving, a generic cat; and Pizza's son, Andy the Silly, a blue-eyed, cross-eyed rag doll Siamese, who has learned in no time at all to issue not-to-be-ignored orders to his human servitors.

Introduction

American women have written hundreds of stories over the last century to be read at Christmas time. From my own collection of more than 150 of those stories, I have chosen these to share with you this year.

These Christmas stories explore the great themes of this holiday. There are joyful family reunions, reconciliations, and renewals of the spirit. There are celebrations of the miracle of hope a beloved child brings to the world. There are expressions of the belief that a time will come when faith and love will be rewarded with peace on earth. There are stories about the pain of those who are excluded or exclude themselves from the celebration. There are stories filled with the painful ironies of those who betray the meaning of the season. And there are stories about those whose holiday is *not* Christmas.

We are supposed to have strong feelings and associations about the Christmas season, and most of us do.

For some of us, Christmas means home and family, warmth, kindness, old traditions and cherished rituals to buoy us up from one year to the next. The patterns we participate in year after year give us a sense of continuity about life—and about our lives. There are gifts to choose and give, and there are gifts to receive and be responsive to. Places to go, things to do, people to see.

For some of us, Christmas is a religious celebration, rich in spiritual message and promise. A time to rededicate ourselves to our spiritual community, to feel again the message of hope and peace, joy and love that this sacred time symbolizes. It is a time to meditate on the holiness of the blessed child in our midst, whether we believe that that child came once two thousand years ago, that the spirit of that child is reborn with each new child, or that the child is in ourselves. It is a time to speculate about what the world would be like if the promise of the long waiting were to be fulfilled.

Others approach the Christmas season with heavy heart; it is a time of sorrow and despair, remembering what has been lost and will never come again, and regretting all that has never yet been and probably never will be. It is also a time when we question the decisions that led us into new and different lives, away from old fashioned, familiar, comforting Christmases.

For yet others, Christmas means alienation, feeling invisible because it is not our holiday. It is not a holiday whose public display can be avoided or ignored. For many of us it becomes a time when we are tempted to sacrifice our own culture to fit into the larger group.

Christmas is hard for some of us because it is a holiday from which we earn a frantic, seasonal living, overworked, underpaid, providing service up until the last minute, leaving no time or energy to prepare our own celebration. The commercial hysteria that was already being criticized in the middle of the nineteenth century has only intensified. The exhaustion of employees in the retail trades, whose jobs are to feed the demands of that hysteria, has become greater.

We find that we must all cultivate an attitude towards Christmas, whether it is our holiday or not and even if it is the hardest time of the year for us. Even for those richest in their expectations of happiness, the Christmas season is a time of too much work, too much rush, and too much stress.

So for all of us, here is a collection of people's stories about Christmas.

If you are one whose Christmas is a time to renew ties and share cherished traditions with loved ones, you will especially enjoy the stories about people celebrating continuity, reviving their best selves and best memories, and creating new memories to arm themselves with in the face of an uncertain future. I hope you will share these stories with those you love and that they will become part of your tradition.

If you are one whose Christmas is a time of loneliness and despair, perhaps you will be comforted by the imaginative ways some of the characters in these stories create new Christmas experiences for themselves. And if Christmas isn't your holiday but seems nevertheless inescapable, you might enjoy a sense of camaraderie with the characters in some of these stories who share your sense of alienation from all the fuss. I hope your December will be brightened and eased by meeting others who share your experience.

Relax with these stories when you have a moment here and there during the rush of the season.*

*I am completing the last headnote, the last permission check, the last acknowledgment, the last revision of the Table of Contents on April 4, 1988. Tonight is the twentieth anniversary of the murder of Dr. Martin Luther King, Jr. I cannot help but reflect on the similarity between the goals he articulated for our world and the values we find in the stories in this collection: an end to all intrafamilial warfare in the human family, the beginning of an era of peace and social justice.

Louisa May Alcott
(November 29, 1832-March 6, 1888)

Louisa May Alcott's novel about the March family, *Little Women*, opens with one of America's most beloved evocations of a family Christmas. The success of the novel, first published in 1868, surprised its thirty-five-year-old author, and transformed her into a celebrity. The characters are based on members of the author's own family and the plot is based on her family's favorite book, *Pilgrim's Progress*. The following excerpt—the first chapter and parts of the second—has been reprinted so frequently that although not originally written as a short story, it has taken on a permanent shape and life of its own as a Christmas story.

This story about sisters and their mother creating a happy holiday out of imagination, generosity, and love includes most of the traditional great themes of Christmas, themes repeated in many of the stories that follow.

A March Christmas

Louisa May Alcott

"Christmas won't be Christmas without any presents," grumbled Jo, lying on the rug.

"It's so dreadful to be poor!" sighed Meg, looking down at her old dress.

"I don't think it's fair for some girls to have plenty of pretty things, and other girls nothing at all," added little Amy, with an injured sniff.

"We've got father and mother and each other," said Beth contentedly, from her corner.

The four young faces on which the firelight shone brightened at the cheerful words, but darkened again as Jo said sadly,—

"We haven't got father, and shall not have him for a long time." She didn't say "perhaps never," but each silently added it, thinking of father far away, where the fighting was.

Nobody spoke for a minute; then Meg said in an altered tone,—

"You know the reason mother proposed not having any presents this Christmas was because it is going to be a hard winter for every one; and she thinks we ought not to spend money for pleasure, when our men are suffering so in the army. We can't do much, but we can make our little sacrifices, and ought to do it gladly. But I am afraid I don't"; and Meg shook her head, as she thought regretfully of all the pretty things she wanted.

"But I don't think the little we should spend would do any good. We've each got a dollar, and the army wouldn't be much helped by our giving that. I agree not to expect anything from mother or you, but I do want to buy Undine and Sintram for myself; I've wanted it *so* long," said Jo, who was a bookworm.

"I planned to spend mine in new music," said Beth, with a little sigh, which no one heard but the hearth-brush and kettle-holder.

"I shall get a nice box of Faber's drawing-pencils; I really need them," said Amy decidedly.

"Mother didn't say anything about our money, and she won't wish us to give up everything. Let's each buy what we want, and have a little fun; I'm sure we work hard enough to earn it," cried Jo, examining the heels of her shoes in a gentlemanly manner.

"I know *I* do,—teaching those tiresome children nearly all day, when I'm longing to enjoy myself at home," began Meg, in the complaining tone again.

"You don't have half such a hard time as I do," said Jo. "How would you like to be shut up for hours with a nervous, fussy old lady, who keeps you trotting, is never satisfied, and worries you till you're ready to fly out of the window or cry?"

"It's naughty to fret; but I do think washing dishes and keeping things tidy is the worst work in the world. It makes me cross; and my hands get so stiff, I can't practise well at all"; and Beth looked at her rough hands with a sigh that any one could hear that time.

"I don't believe any of you suffer as I do," cried Amy; "for you don't have to go to school with impertinent girls, who plague you if you don't know your lessons, and laugh at your dresses, and label your father if he isn't rich, and insult you when your nose isn't nice."

"If you mean *libel*, I'd say so, and not talk about *labels*, as if papa was a pickle-bottle," advised Jo, laughing.

"I know what I mean, and you needn't be *statirical* about it. It's proper to use good words, and improve your *vocabilary*," returned Amy, with dignity.

"Don't peck at one another, children. Don't you wish we had the money papa lost when we were little, Jo? Dear me! how happy and good we'd be, if we had no worries!" said Meg, who could remember better times.

"You said the other day, you thought we were a deal happier than the King children, for they were fighting and fretting all the time, in spite of their money."

"So I did, Beth. Well, I think we are; for, though we do have to work, we make fun for ourselves, and are a pretty jolly set, as Jo would say."

"Jo does use such slang words!" observed Amy, with a reproving look at the long figure stretched on the rug. Jo immediately sat up, put her hands in her pockets, and began to whistle.

"Don't, Jo; it's so boyish!"

"That's why I do it."

"I detest rude, unlady-like girls!"

"I hate affected, niminy-piminy chits!"

" 'Birds in their little nests agree,' " sang Beth, the peacemaker, with such a funny face that both sharp voices softened to a laugh, and the "pecking" ended for that time.

"Really, girls, you are both to be blamed," said Meg, beginning to lecture in her elder-sisterly fashion. "You are old enough to leave off boyish tricks, and to behave better, Josephine. It didn't matter so much when you were a little girl; but now you are so tall, and turn up your hair, you should remember that you are a young lady."

"I'm not! and if turning up my hair makes me one, I'll wear it in two tails till I'm twenty," cried Jo, pulling off her net, and shaking down a chestnut mane. "I hate to think I've got to grow up, and be Miss March, and wear long gowns, and look as prim as a China-aster! It's bad enough to be a girl, anyway, when I like boys' games and work and manners! I can't get over my disappointment in not being a boy; and it's worse than ever now, for I'm dying to go and fight with papa, and I can only stay at home and knit, like a poky old woman!" And Jo shook the blue army-sock till the needles rattled like castanets, and her ball bounded across the room.

"Poor Jo! It's too bad, but it can't be helped; so you must try to be contented with making your name boyish, and playing brother to us girls," said Beth, stroking the rough head at her knee with a hand that all the dish-washing and dusting in the world could not make ungentle in its touch.

"As for you, Amy," continued Meg, "you are altogether too particular and prim. Your airs are funny now; but you'll grow up an affected little goose, if you don't take care. I like your nice manners and refined ways of speaking, when you don't try to be elegant; but your absurd words are as bad as Jo's slang."

"If Jo is a tom-boy and Amy a goose, what am I, please?" asked Beth, ready to share the lecture.

"You're a dear, and nothing else," answered Meg warmly; and no one contradicted her, for the "Mouse" was the pet of the family.

As young readers like to know "how people look," we will take this moment to give them a little sketch of the four sisters, who sat knitting away in the twilight, while the December snow fell quietly without, and the fire crackled cheerfully within. It was a comfortable old room, though the carpet was faded and the furniture very plain; for a good picture or two hung on the walls, books filled the recesses, chrysanthemums and Christmas roses bloomed in the windows, and a pleasant atmosphere of home-peace pervaded it.

Margaret, the eldest of the four, was sixteen, and very pretty, being plump and fair, with large eyes, plenty of soft, brown hair, a sweet mouth, and white hands, of which she was rather vain. Fifteen-year-old Jo was very tall, thin, and brown, and reminded one of a colt; for she never seemed to know what to do with her long limbs, which were very much in her way. She had a decided mouth, a comical nose, and sharp, gray eyes, which appeared to see everything, and were by turns fierce, funny, or thoughtful. Her long, thick hair was her one beauty; but it was usually bundled into a net, to be out of her way. Round shoulders had Jo, big hands and feet, a flyaway look to her clothes, and the uncomfortable appearance of a girl who was rapidly shooting up into a woman, and didn't like it. Elizabeth—or Beth, as every one called her—was a rosy, smooth-haired, bright-eyed girl of thirteen, with a shy manner, a timid voice, and a peaceful expression, which was seldom disturbed. Her father called her "Little Tranquillity," and the name suited her excellently;

for she seemed to live in a happy world of her own, only venturing out to meet the few whom she trusted and loved. Amy, though the youngest, was a most important person,—in her own opinion at least. A regular snow-maiden, with blue eyes, and yellow hair, curling on her shoulders, pale and slender, and always carrying herself like a young lady mindful of her manners. What the characters of the four sisters were we will leave to be found out.

The clock struck six; and, having swept up the hearth, Beth put a pair of slippers down to warm. Somehow the sight of the old shoes had a good effect upon the girls; for mother was coming, and every one brightened to welcome her. Meg stopped lecturing, and lighted the lamp, Amy got out of the easy-chair without being asked, and Jo forgot how tired she was as she sat up to hold the slippers nearer to the blaze.

"They are quite worn out; Marmee must have a new pair."

"I thought I'd get her some with my dollar," said Beth.

"No, I shall!" cried Amy.

"I'm the oldest," began Meg, but Jo cut in with a decided—

"I'm the man of the family now papa is away, and *I* shall provide the slippers, for he told me to take special care of mother while he was gone."

"I'll tell you what we'll do," said Beth; "let's each get her something for Christmas, and not get anything for ourselves."

"That's like you, dear! What will we get?" exclaimed Jo.

Every one thought soberly for a minute; then Meg announced, as if the idea was suggested by the sight of her own pretty hands, "I shall give her a nice pair of gloves."

"Army shoes, best to be had," cried Jo.

"Some handkerchiefs, all hemmed," said Beth.

"I'll get a little bottle of cologne; she likes it, and it won't cost much, so I'll have some left to buy my pencils," added Amy.

"How will we give the things?" asked Meg.

"Put them on the table, and bring her in and see her open the bundles. Don't you remember how we used to do on our birthdays?" answered Jo.

"I used to be *so* frightened when it was my turn to sit in the big chair with the crown on, and see you all come marching round to give the presents, with a kiss. I liked the things and the kisses, but it was dreadful to have you sit looking at me while I opened the bundles," said Beth, who was toasting her face and the bread for tea, at the same time.

"Let Marmee think we are getting things for ourselves, and then surprise her. We must go shopping to-morrow afternoon, Meg; there is so much to do about the play for Christmas night," said Jo, marching up and down, with her hands behind her back and her nose in the air.

"I don't mean to act any more after this time; I'm getting too old for such things," observed Meg, who was as much a child as ever about "dressing-up" frolics.

"You won't stop, I know, as long as you can trail round in a white gown with your hair down, and wear gold-paper jewelry. You are the best actress we've got, and there'll be an end of everything if you quit the boards," said Jo. "We ought to rehearse to-night. Come here, Amy, and do the fainting scene, for you are as stiff as a poker in that."

"I can't help it; I never saw any one faint, and I don't choose to make myself all black and blue, tumbling flat as you do. If I can go down easily, I'll drop; if I can't, I shall fall into a chair and be graceful; I don't care if Hugo does come at me with a pistol," returned Amy, who was not gifted with dramatic power, but was chosen because she was small enough to be borne out shrieking by the villain of the piece.

"Do it this way; clasp your hands so, and stagger across the room, crying frantically, 'Roderigo! save me! save me!'" and away went Jo, with a melodramatic scream which was truly thrilling.

Amy followed, but she poked her hands out stiffly before her, and jerked herself along as if she went by machinery; and her "Ow!" was more suggestive of pins being run into her than of fear and anguish. Jo gave a despairing groan, and Meg laughed outright, while Beth let her bread burn as she watched the fun, with interest.

"It's no use! Do the best you can when the time comes, and if the audience laughs don't blame me. Come on, Meg."

Then things went smoothly, for Don Pedro defied the world in a speech of two pages without a single break; Hagar, the witch, chanted an awful incantation over her kettleful of simmering toads, with weird effect; Roderigo rent his chains asunder manfully, and Hugo died in agonies of remorse and arsenic, with a wild "Ha! ha!"

"It's the best we've had yet," said Meg, as the dead villain sat up and rubbed his elbows.

"I don't see how you can write and act such splendid things, Jo. You're a regular Shakespeare!" exclaimed Beth, who firmly believed that her sisters were gifted with wonderful genius in all things.

"Not quite," replied Jo modestly. "I do think 'The Witch's Curse, an Operatic Tragedy,' is rather a nice thing; but I'd like to try Macbeth, if we only had a trap-door for Banquo. I always wanted to do the killing part. 'Is that a dagger that I see before me?' " muttered Jo, rolling her eyes and clutching at the air, as she had seen a famous tragedian do.

"No, it's the toasting fork, with mother's shoe on it instead of the bread. Beth's stage-struck!" cried Meg, and the rehearsal ended in a general burst of laughter.

"Glad to find you so merry, my girls," said a cheery voice at the door, and actors and audience turned to welcome a tall, motherly lady, with a "can-I-help-you" look about her which was truly delightful. She was not elegantly dressed, but a noble-looking woman, and the girls thought the gray cloak and unfashionable bonnet covered the most splendid mother in the world.

"Well, dearies, how have you got on to-day? There was so much to do, getting the boxes ready to go to-morrow, that I didn't come home to dinner. Has any one called, Beth? How is your cold, Meg? Jo, you look tired to death. Come and kiss me, baby."

While making these maternal inquiries Mrs. March got her wet things off, her warm slippers on, and sitting down in the easy-chair, drew Amy to her lap, preparing to enjoy the happiest hour of her busy day. The girls flew about, trying to make things comfortable, each in her own way. Meg arranged the tea-table; Jo brought wood and set chairs, dropping, overturning, and clattering everything she touched; Beth trotted to and fro between parlor and kitchen, quiet and busy; while Amy gave directions to every one, as she sat with her hands folded.

As they gathered about the table, Mrs. March said, with a particularly happy face, "I've got a treat for you after supper."

A quick, bright smile went round like a streak of sunshine. Beth clapped her hands, regardless of the biscuit she held, and Jo tossed up her napkin, crying, "A letter! a letter! Three cheers for father!"

"Yes, a nice long letter. He is well, and thinks he shall get through the cold season better than we feared. He sends all sorts of loving wishes for Christmas, and an especial message to you girls," said Mrs. March, patting her pocket as if she had got a treasure there.

"Hurry and get done! Don't stop to quirk your little finger, and simper over your plate, Amy," cried Jo, choking in her tea, and dropping her bread, butter side down, on the carpet, in her haste to get at the treat.

Beth ate no more, but crept away, to sit in her shadowy corner and brood over the delight to come, till the others were ready.

"I think it was so splendid in father to go as a chaplain when he was too old to be drafted, and not strong enough for a soldier," said Meg warmly.

"Don't I wish I could go as a drummer, a *vivan*—what's its name? or a nurse, so I could be near him and help him," exclaimed Jo, with a groan.

"It must be very disagreeable to sleep in a tent, and eat all sorts of bad-tasting things, and drink out of a tin mug," sighed Amy.

"When will he come home, Marmee?" asked Beth, with a little quiver in her voice.

"Not for many months, dear, unless he is sick. He will stay and do his work faithfully as long as he can, and we won't ask for him back a minute sooner than he can be spared. Now come and hear the letter."

They all drew to the fire, mother in the big chair with Beth at her feet, Meg and Amy perched on either arm of the chair, and Jo leaning on the back, where no one would see any sign of emotion if the letter should happen to be touching.

Very few letters were written in those hard times that were not touching, especially those which fathers sent home. In this one little was said of the hardships endured, the dangers faced, or the home-sickness conquered; it was a cheerful, hopeful letter, full of lively descriptions of camp life, marches, and military news; and only at the end did the writer's heart overflow with fatherly love and long-ing for the little girls at home.

"Give them all my dear love and a kiss. Tell them I think of them by day, pray for them by night, and find my best comfort in their affection at all times. A year seems very long to wait before I see them, but remind them that while we wait we may all work, so that these hard days need not be wasted. I know they will re-member all I said to them, that they will be loving children to you, will do their duty faithfully, fight their bosom enemies bravely, and conquer themselves so beautifully, that when I come back to them I may be fonder and prouder than ever of my little women."

Everybody sniffed when they came to that part; Jo wasn't ashamed of the great tear that dropped off the end of her nose, and Amy never minded the rumpling of her curls as she hid her face on her mother's shoulder and sobbed out, "I *am* a selfish girl! but I'll truly try to be better, so he mayn't be disappointed in me by and by."

"We all will!" cried Meg. "I think too much of my looks, and hate to work, but won't any more, if I can help it."

"I'll try and be what he loves to call me, 'a little woman,' and not be rough and wild; but do my duty here instead of wanting to be somewhere else," said Jo, thinking that keeping her temper at home was a much harder task than facing a rebel or two down South.

Beth said nothing, but wiped away her tears with the blue army-sock, and began to knit with all her might, losing no time in doing the duty that lay nearest her, while she resolved in her quiet little soul to be all that father hoped to find her when the year brought round the happy coming home.

Mrs. March broke the silence that followed Jo's words, by saying in her cheery voice, "Do you remember how you used to play Pilgrim's Progress when you were little things? Nothing de-lighted you more than to have me tie my piece-bags on your backs for burdens, give you hats and sticks and rolls of paper, and let you travel through the house from the cellar, which was the City of

Destruction, up, up, to the house-top, where you had all the lovely things you could collect to make a Celestial City."

"What fun it was, especially going by the lions, fighting Apolylon, and passing through the Valley where the hobgoblins were!" said Jo.

"I liked the place where the bundles fell off and tumbled down stairs," said Meg.

"My favorite part was when we came out on the flat roof where our flowers and arbors and pretty things were, and all stood and sung for joy up there in the sunshine," said Beth, smiling, as if that pleasant moment had come back to her.

"I don't remember much about it, except that I was afraid of the cellar and the dark entry, and always liked the cake and milk we had up at the top. If I wasn't too old for such things, I'd rather like to play it over again," said Amy, who began to talk of renouncing childish things at the mature age of twelve.

"We never are too old for this, my dear, because it is a play we are playing all the time in one way or another. Our burdens are here, our road is before us, and the longing for goodness and happiness is the guide that leads us through many troubles and mistakes to the peace which is a true Celestial City. Now, my little pilgrims, suppose you begin again, not in play, but in earnest, and see how far on you can get before father comes home."

"Really, mother? Where are our bundles?" asked Amy, who was a very literal young lady.

"Each of you told what your burden was just now, except Beth; I rather think she hasn't got any," said her mother.

"Yes, I have; mine is dishes and dusters, and envying girls with nice pianos, and being afraid of people."

Beth's bundle was such a funny one that everybody wanted to laugh; but nobody did, for it would have hurt her feelings very much.

"Let us do it," said Meg thoughtfully. "It is only another name for trying to be good, and the story may help us; for though we do want to be good, it's hard work, and we forget, and don't do our best."

"We were in the Slough of Despond to-night, and mother came and pulled us out as Help did in the book. We ought to have our roll of directions, like Christian. What shall we do about that?" asked Jo, delighted with the fancy which lent a little romance to the very dull task of doing her duty.

"Look under your pillows, Christmas morning, and you will find your guide-book," replied Mrs. March.

They talked over the new plan while old Hannah cleared the table; then out came the four little work-baskets, and the needles flew as the girls made sheets for Aunt March. It was uninteresting sewing, but to-night no one grumbled. They adopted Jo's plan of dividing the long seams into four parts, and calling the quarters Europe, Asia, Africa, and America, and in that way got on capitally, especially when they talked about the different countries as they stitched their way through them.

At nine they stopped work, and sung, as usual, before they went to bed. No one but Beth could get much music out of the old piano; but she had a way of softly touching the yellow keys, and making a pleasant accompaniment to the simple songs they sung. Meg had a voice like a flute, and she and her mother led the little choir. Amy chirped like a cricket, and Jo wandered through the airs at her own sweet will, always coming out at the wrong place with a croak or a quaver that spoilt the most pensive tune. They had always done this from the time they could lisp "Crinkle, crinkle, 'ittle 'tar," and it had become a household custom, for the mother was a born singer. The first sound in the morning was her voice, as she went about the house singing like a lark; and the last sound at night was the same cheery sound, for the girls never grew too old for that familiar lullaby.

Jo was the first to wake in the gray dawn of Christmas morning. No stockings hung at the fireplace, and for a moment she felt as much disappointed as she did long ago, when her little sock fell down because it was so crammed with goodies. Then she remembered her mother's promise, and, slipping her hand under her pillow, drew out a little crimson-covered book. She knew it very well, for it was that beautiful old story of the best life ever lived, and Jo felt that it was a true guide-book for any pilgrim going the long journey. She woke Meg with a "Merry Christmas," and bade her see what was under her pillow. A green-covered book appeared, with the same picture inside, and a few words written by their mother, which made their one present very precious in their eyes. Presently Beth and Amy woke, to rummage and find their little books also,— one dove-colored, the other blue; and all sat looking at and talking about them, while the east grew rosy with the coming day.

In spite of her small vanities, Margaret had a sweet and pious nature, which unconsciously influenced her sisters, especially Jo, who loved her very tenderly, and obeyed her because her advice was so gently given.

"Girls," said Meg seriously, looking from the tumbled head beside her to the two little night-capped ones in the room beyond, "mother wants us to read and love and mind these books, and we must begin at once. We used to be faithful about it; but since father went away, and all this war trouble unsettled us, we have neglected many things. You can do as you please; but *I* shall keep my book on the table here, and read a little every morning as soon as I wake, for I know it will do me good, and help me through the day."

Then she opened her new book and began to read. Jo put her arm round her, and, leaning cheek to cheek, read also, with the quiet expression so seldom seen on her restless face.

"How good Meg is! Come, Amy, let's do as they do. I'll help you with the hard words, and they'll explain things if we don't understand," whispered Beth, very much impressed by the pretty books and her sisters' example.

"I'm glad mine is blue," said Amy; and then the rooms were very still while the pages were softly turned, and the winter sunshine crept in to touch the bright heads and serious faces with a Christmas greeting.

"Where is mother?" asked Meg, as she and Jo ran down to thank her for their gifts, half an hour later.

"Goodness only knows. Some poor creeter come a-beggin', and your ma went straight off to see what was needed. There never *was* such a woman for givin' away vittles and drink, clothes and firin'," replied Hannah, who had lived with the family since Meg was born, and was considered by them all more as a friend than a servant.

"She will be back soon, I think; so fry your cakes, and have everything ready," said Meg, looking over the presents which were collected in a basket and kept under the sofa, ready to be produced at the proper time. "Why, where is Amy's bottle of cologne?" she added, as the little flask did not appear.

"She took it out a minute ago, and went off with it to put a ribbon on it, or some such notion," replied Jo, dancing about the room to take the first stiffness off the new army-slippers.

"How nice my handkerchiefs look, don't they? Hannah washed and ironed them for me, and I marked them all myself," said Beth, looking proudly at the somewhat uneven letters which had cost her such labor.

"Bless the child! she's gone and put 'Mother' on them instead of 'M. March.' How funny!" cried Jo, taking up one.

"Isn't it right? I thought it was better to do it so, because Meg's initials are 'M.M.,' and I don't want any one to use these but Marmee," said Beth, looking troubled.

"It's all right, dear, and a very pretty idea,—quite sensible, too, for no one can ever mistake now. It will please her very much, I know," said Meg, with a frown for Jo and a smile for Beth.

"There's mother. Hide the basket, quick!" cried Jo, as a door slammed, and steps sounded in the hall.

Amy came in hastily, and looked rather abashed when she saw her sisters all waiting for her.

"Where have you been, and what are you hiding behind you?" asked Meg, surprised to see, by her hood and cloak, that lazy Amy had been out so early.

"Don't laugh at me, Jo! I didn't mean any one should know till the time came. I only meant to change the little bottle for a big one, and I gave *all* my money to get it, and I'm truly trying not to be selfish any more."

As she spoke, Amy showed the handsome flask which replaced

the cheap one; and looked so earnest and humble in her little effort to forget herself that Meg hugged her on the spot, and Jo pronounced her "a trump," while Beth ran to the window, and picked her finest rose to ornament the stately bottle.

"You see I felt ashamed of my present, after reading and talking about being good this morning, so I ran round the corner and changed it the minute I was up: and I'm *so* glad, for mine is the handsomest now."

Another bang of the street-door sent the basket under the sofa, and the girls to the table, eager for breakfast.

"Merry Christmas, Marmee! Many of them! Thank you for our books; we read some, and mean to every day," they cried, in chorus.

"Merry Christmas, little daughters! I'm glad you began at once, and hope you will keep on. But I want to say one word before we sit down. Not far away from here lies a poor woman with a little newborn baby. Six children are huddled into one bed to keep from freezing, for they have no fire. There is nothing to eat over there; and the oldest boy came to tell me they were suffering hunger and cold. My girls, will you give them your breakfast as a Christmas present?"

They were all unusually hungry, having waited nearly an hour, and for a minute no one spoke; only a minute, for Jo exclaimed impetuously,—

"I'm so glad you came before we began!"

"May I go and help carry the things to the poor little children?" asked Beth, eagerly.

"*I* shall take the cream and the muffins," added Amy, heroically giving up the articles she most liked.

Meg was already covering the buckwheats, and piling the bread into one big plate.

"I thought you'd do it," said Mrs. March, smiling as if satisfied. "You shall all go and help me, and when we come back we will have bread and milk for breakfast, and make it up at dinner-time."

They were soon ready, and the procession set out. Fortunately it was early, and they went through back streets, so few people saw them, and no one laughed at the queer party.

A poor, bare, miserable room it was, with broken windows, no fire, ragged bed-clothes, a sick mother, wailing baby, and a group of pale, hungry children cuddled under one old quilt, trying to keep warm.

How the big eyes stared and the blue lips smiled as the girls went in!

"Ach, mein Gott! it is good angels come to us!" said the poor woman, crying for joy.

"Funny angels in hoods and mittens," said Jo, and set them laughing.

In a few minutes it really did seem as if kind spirits had been at work there. Hannah, who had carried wood, made a fire, and stopped up the broken panes with old hats and her own cloak. Mrs. March gave the mother tea and gruel, and comforted her with promises of help, while she dressed the little baby as tenderly as if it had been her own. The girls, meantime, spread the table, set the children round the fire, and fed them like so many hungry birds,— laughing, talking, and trying to understand the funny broken English.

"Das ist gut!" "Die Engel-kinder!" cried the poor things, as they ate, and warmed their purple hands at the comfortable blaze.

The girls had never been called angel children before, and thought it very agreeable, especially Jo, who had been considered a "Sancho" ever since she was born. That was a very happy breakfast, though they didn't get any of it; and when they went away, leaving comfort behind, I think there were not in all the city four merrier people than the hungry little girls who gave away their breakfasts and contented themselves with bread and milk on Christmas morning.

"That's loving our neighbor better than ourselves, and I like it," said Meg, as they set out their presents, while their mother was upstairs collecting clothes for the poor Hummels.

Not a very splendid show, but there was a great deal of love done up in the few little bundles, and the tall vase of red roses, white chrysanthemums, and trailing vines, which stood in the middle, gave quite an elegant air to the table.

"She's coming! Strike up, Beth! Open the door, Amy! Three cheers for Marmee!" cried Jo, prancing about, while Meg went to conduct mother to the seat of honor.

Beth played her gayest march, Amy threw open the door, and Meg enacted escort with great dignity. Mrs. March was both surprised and touched; and smiled with her eyes full as she examined her presents, and read the little notes which accompanied them. The slippers went on at once, a new handkerchief was slipped into her pocket, well scented with Amy's cologne, the rose was fastened in her bosom, and the nice gloves were pronounced a "perfect fit."

There was a good deal of laughing and kissing and explaining, in the simple, loving fashion which makes these home-festivals so pleasant at the time, so sweet to remember long afterward, and then all fell to work.

Elizabeth Stuart Phelps

(August 31, 1844-January 28, 1911)

"Old Mother Goose" was first published in the January 2, 1873 issue of *The Independent*, a well-paying, widely circulated, non-denominational Christian weekly. Elizabeth Stuart Phelps (later, Ward), daughter of the writer Elizabeth Stuart Phelps and Austin Phelps, a minister and educator of ministers, was already a best-selling novelist when she wrote this powerful story of filial love and redemption.

Her 1868 novel, *The Gates Ajar*, captured the hearts of readers on two continents who longed for a more loving, forgiving God than the deity of the Calvinists. "Old Mother Goose" tells of a mother redeemed by her daughter and a daughter brought back into human community by her own forgivingness. This story about the power of loving, forgiving spirituality was written for the season during which Christians celebrate the birth of another pure child believed to be the instrument of *his* mother's salvation.

Old Mother Goose

Elizabeth Stuart Phelps

When Thamrè consented to sing for the citizens of Havermash, last year, nobody was more surprised than the citizens of Havermash themselves.

It was characteristic of Havermash to have attempted it. Nothing is too good for Havermashers. Were St. Cecilia prima donna for a season, it would appear to them quite natural to seek her services. Have they not a brown-stone post-office and a senator, a street railway and a county jail, a local newspaper, an author (the public need scarcely be reminded of the "Havermash Hand-Organ: A Tale of Love and Poverty"), and a shoe and leather trade? Transcending all, is not their city charter two years old?

When the Happy Home Handel Association, headed by little Joe Havermash (grandson of the original shoe and leather man, whose wooden cobbler's shop occupied the site of the present post-office in 1793), took upon itself the performance of an "oratorio" last Christmas eve, "We will have Thamrè," said Joe, serenely.

Still, when Joe came home from Boston, breathless and radiant, one night early in the season, with Thamrè's tiny contract (she wrote it on a card, he said, with her glove on, just in going out, and the card was as sweet now—see!—as the glove, and the glove had just the smell of one English violet, no more) to sing in the stone post-office at eight o'clock on Christmas eve, on such and such conditions (simple enough), and for such and such remuneration,—*that* was the astonishing part of it,—even Havermash was off its guard enough to be surprised.

"She'll come," said Joe. "I supposed she would. I meant she should. But the terms are *astounding*. I was prepared to offer her twice that. I'd pay a big slice of it out of my own pocket to get her here. There's no trouble about terms. Did you see what Max offered her? Do you know what she's getting a night in New York? Do you know what she asked us? Five hundred dollars, sir! Only five hundred dollars. Think of it, sir! But the conditions are the most curious thing. She scorns to take so little, maybe. I don't know. All I know is, every dollar of it is to go to old women who haven't lived as they'd ought to in this town. 'For the relief of the aged women of Havermash, who, having in their youth led questionable lives, are left friendless, needy, and perhaps repentant in their declining years.' That's the wording of the agreement. I signed it myself in her little red morocco note-book. Most curious thing all round! It's my opinion, sir, it *takes* a woman to get up an uncommon piece of work like that."

Last Christmas eve fell in Havermash wild and windy. The gusts fought furiously with each other at corners, and under fences, and over the bleak spaces in which the new little city abounded, and through which it straggled painfully away into the open country. Where the snow lay, it lay in tints of dead, sharp blue, cold as steel beneath the chilly light; where it was blown away, the dust flew fine and hard like powder. Overhead, too, there hung only shades of steel. One long, low line of corrosive red, however, had eaten its way through against the western hill-country, and looked like rust or blood upon a mighty coat of mail.

So, at least, Miss Thamrè fancied, shivering a little in her folded furs, as she watched from the car window the swooping of the night upon the bleak, outlying lands and approaching twinkle of the town.

It was a cheerless night for the prima donna to be in Havermash. Joe had been saying so all day. She thought so, it would seem, when he handed her from the cars. She scarcely spoke to him, nodding only, looking hither and thither about her, through the shriek and smoke, with that keen, baffling glance of hers, which all the world so well remembers. Joe felt rather proud of this. *He* knew what the eccentricities of genius were; was glad of a chance to show himself at ease with them. Had she bidden him stand on his head while she found her trunk, or sit on a barrel in the draught and wait for her to compose an *aria*, he would have obeyed her sweetly, thinking all the while how it would sound, told to his grandchildren on winter nights.

Half Havermash was at the station. All Havermash remembers that. It was with difficulty that Joe could get her to her carriage quietly, as befitted, to his fancy, the conduct of a lady's welcome.

"I did not expect to see so *many* people," said Miss Thamrè, in her pretty, accented, appealing way. "What are they here for?"

"I'm sure I don't know," said Joe, with a puzzled air, "unless they're here to see me."

This amused the lady, and she laughed,—a little genial laugh, which bubbled over to the ears of the people pressing nearest to her in the crowd.

"She laughs as well as she sings," said a member of the Happy Home Handel Association.

"She has the eye of a gazelle and the smile of a Sphinx," said the Author, and took out his note-book to "do" her for a religious weekly.

"She travels alone," said a mother of four daughters. (She had, indeed, come to Havermash quite alone, with neither chaperone nor maid.)

"She can wear silver seal and not look green," said a brunette, in black and garnet.

"She sees everything within a mile of her," said Joe to himself, as he held the hem of her dress back reverently from the carriage-wheels.

It would seem that she saw far and distinctly, for half within her carriage door she paused and said abruptly:—

"What is that? Let me see what that is!"

An old woman was pushing her way through the reluctant crowd; a very miserable old woman, splashed with mud. She had a blanket shawl over her head, and her unhealthy yellow gray hair blew out from under it, over her face before the wind.

A crowd of villainous urchins followed, pelting her with slush and snow, and volleys of that shrill, coarse boys' cry (one of the most pitiful sounds on earth) by which the presence of a sacred mystery or a sorrowful sin is indicated, not alone in Havermash.

"Old Mother Goose! Old Mother Goose! Hi, yi! there! Mother Goosey's out buyin' Christmas stockins for her dar-ter! Old Mother Goo-oo-ose!"

Everybody knew how old Mother Goose hated the boys (and with good reason, poor soul!); but nobody had ever seen her offer them violence before that night.

In a minute she had grown suddenly livid and awful to see, rearing her lank figure to its full height against the steel and blood-colored background of the sky, where a sudden gap in the crowd had left her alone.

"You stop *that!*" she fiercely cried; and dealt a few bad blows to right and left before she was interfered with.

Annoyed beyond measure, Joe entreated Miss Thamrè to let him take her from the scene. She hesitated, lingered, turned after a moment's thought, and sank upon the carriage seat.

"You did not tell me who it was," she said imperiously; "I asked you. I like to be answered when I ask a question. I never *saw* such a miserable old woman!"

"One of your prospective beneficiaries, madam," said Joe, humbly. "A wretched old creature. The boys call her Old Mother Goose. Do not distress yourself about her. It is no sight for you."

"You say the boys call her—I never *heard* such a poor, sad name! Has she no other name, Mr. Havermash? Oh! *there* she is again."

A sudden turn of the carriage had brought them sharply upon the miserable sight once more. Old Mother Goose was sitting stupidly in the slush beside the hack-stands. Her shawl was off, and her gray hair had fallen raggedly upon her shoulders; her teeth chattered with chill and rage; there were drops of blood about her on the snow; a few of the more undaunted spirits among the boys still hovered near her, avenging themselves for their recent defeat by furtive attempts to purloin her drabbled shawl; and a savage expression of his country's intention to preserve virtuous order, in the garb of the police, stood threatening poor Old Mother Goose with the terrors of the law.

It was a sorry sight. A sorry sight Miss Thamrè seemed to find it. She leaned forward to the window. Joe could not prevent her; she would see it all. The silver shine of her fur wrappings glittered through the dusk, as she moved; one tiny gloved and fur-bound hand hung over the window's edge; a faint sweetness, like the soul of an English violet, stirred as she stirred, and stole out upon the frosty air.

"There!" cried the old woman, mouthing a hideous oath, "there's the lady! I'll see her yet, in spite of ye!"

Old Mother Goose staggered up from the mud, staring dully; but the silver-gray picture framed in the carriage window flashed by her in an instant. For an instant only the two women looked each other in the eye.

Miss Thamrè turned white about the chin. Her hand rose to her eyes instinctively, covered them, and fell. It must have been such a miserable contrasting of life's chances to her young and happy fancy!

"I've seen enough," she said. "Never mind!"

"Her name," said Joe, thinking to divert her from the immediate disturbance of the sight, "is Peg, I believe,—Peg Mathers. You see the boys got it Old Mathers, then Old Mother, so Old Mother Goose, I suppose; and quite ingenious, too, I think, poor creature!"

Miss Thamrè made no reply. Quite weary of the subject, she wrapped herself back into the carriage corner, and, asking only how long a ride it was, drew a little silver veil she wore across her face and said no more. Quite weary still she seemed when Joe gave her his arm at the hotel steps (she had refused to accept his or any other private hospitality in the place); and very wearily she gave him to understand that she preferred to be alone till the hour of her appearance before the Havermash public should arrive.

Joe stumbled upon Old Mother Goose again, in running briskly down the hotel steps.

She was wandering in a maudlin, aimless way up and down the sidewalk at the building's front. Her shawl was gone, and her gray head was bare to the wind, which was now as sharp as high.

"What! *you* again?" said Joe. "What are you doing here, Peg? I was ashamed of you to-night, Peg! The people had come out to see a famous lady, and you must get to fighting with the boys and frighten her. You disgraced the town. Better go home, or you'll be in more mischief. Come!"

"I'm out hunting for my shawl, Mr. Havermash," said the old woman, after a moment's sly hesitation. "I've lost my shawl. Them boys took it, curse on 'em! I'd go to see the famous lady, if I had my shawl."

"Better go home; better go home!" repeated Joe. "*She* doesn't want to see *you*, Peg."

"Don't she, Mr. Havermash?"

Old Mother Goose laughed (or did she cry? She was always doing one or the other. What did it matter which?), nodding upward at the windows of the prima donna's parlors, where against the drawn shades a slight, tall shadow passed and repassed now and then, faintly, like a figure in a dream.

"Don't she? Well, I don't know as she does. How warm she looks! She must be warm in them fur tippets that she wears; don't you think she must? I like to see a famous lady well as other folks, when I have my shawl. Mr. Havermash!"

"Well, well, well!" Joe stopped impatiently in hurrying away.

"Would you rather I'd go home and say my prayers than fight the boys? I hate the boys!"

"Prayers, Peg? *Do* you say your prayers? What prayers do you say, Peg? Come!"

Mr. Havermash lingered, entertained in his own despite— thinking he would tell Miss Thamrè this; it might amuse her.

"I say my prayers," said Old Mother Goose, beating her white hair back from her face at a blow, as if she could give it pain. "I've said 'em this many years. I say: 'When the Devil forgets the world, may God remind him of the boys!' I don't feel so about girls, Mr.

Havermash. Maybe, if I hadn't had one once myself, I should. My girl ran away from me. She ran away on a Christmas eve, thirteen years ago. Did ye ever see my girl? Mr. Havermash!"

But Joe was gone. He looked back once in running up the street (he was late to supper now; his wife waited to know if Miss Thamrè would receive a call from her, and would scold a bit,— women will, it can't be helped),—he looked back across his shoulder, and saw that Old Mother Goose was still hunting for her shawl beneath the glittering, curtained windows, where a shadow passed and repassed, high above her head, like the shadow of a figure in a dream.

Thamrè took no supper. It was six o'clock when she entered into her parlors and shut her doors about her. It was five minutes before eight when Mr. Havermash called to conduct her to the concert hall in the second story of the brown-stone post-office. It is quite evident, I think, that in all the passage of the somewhat remarkable drama into which her appearance in Havermash resolved itself, no act can have equaled in intensity that comprised within those two solitary hours. Yet positively all that is known of it, even at this distant day, is that Miss Thamrè took no supper. Every boarder in the hotel knew that in half an hour. Loiterers and lion-hunters beneath the windows where the nervous shadow passed, picked it up, as loiterers and lion-hunters will. Even Old Mother Goose knew it—coming in to ask the hotel clerk if he had seen her shawl, and being for her trouble roughly shown the door.

Miss Thamrè, curtained and locked in Havermash's grand suite of rooms (of which the town is not unjustly proud, it may be said; in which the senator is always accommodated on election days; in which a Harvard professor and a Boston alderman have been known to spend a night; in which the President himself once took a private lunch, in traveling to the mountains), spent, we say, two hours alone. In all her life, perhaps, the lady never spent two hours less alone. For a year the public fancy has been a self-invited guest at the threshold of those hours. It is with reluctance that one's most reverent imagination follows the general curiosity across their sacred edge; and yet it is with something of the same inner propulsion which forces a dreamer on the seashore to keep the eyes upon the struggles of a little gala-boat wrecked by a mortal leak in calm waters on a sunny day.

One sees, in spite of one's self, the lady's soft small hands close violently on the turning key; the silver furs shine under the chandeliers as they fall, tossed hither and hither, to the floor; the little veil torn from the fine, refined, sweet face; the setness of the features and that pallor of hers about the chin.

One knows that she will pace just so across the long, unhomelike splendor of the gaudy rooms; that she will fold her hands behind her, one into the other knotted fast; that she will lift them now and then, and rub them fiercely, as if she found them in a deathly chill; that her hair will fall, perhaps, in her sharp, regardless motions, and hang about her face; that her head is bent; and that her eyes will follow that great green tulip on the Brussels carpet, from pattern to pattern, patiently, seeing only that, as the shadow of her on the curtain passes and repasses, telling only what a shadow can.

One listens, as she listens to the voices of the people passing on the pavement far below; one wonders, as she wonders what they say; if they speak of her, if they would speak of her to-morrow; and what it would happen they would say, should to-morrow bring forth what to-morrow might.

One hears, for she must hear, a Christmas carol chanted flatly by some young people in the street; the bustle of a hundred Christmas seekers coming homeward, with laden arms and empty pockets, from the little shops; one notices that she draws the shade, to see if holly is hanging in the windows, as it used to hang in Havermash, all up and down the street, by five o'clock,—and if she remembers how many times she has stolen out away in her clean hood, with some care that no one else need follow, shaming her, to see the holly herself and hear the carols sung, like happier little girls—how can one but seem to remember too? And when the church-bells ring out for Christmas prayers, melting through the obdurate mail of the welded clouds, till they seem to melt a star through, as still and clear as God's voice melting through a wrung, defiant heart,—if her set face quivers a little, can one prevent one's own from quivering as well?

Perhaps the church-bells ring in a vision with them, to the barred and curtained glitter of Miss Thamrè's rooms. Perhaps, by sheer contrast, her fancy finds the wretched creature whom she saw to-day, seated with the mud and blood about her, shut in from all the world with her, they two alone together in the dreadful, shining place.

Perhaps she seems to herself to escape it, fleeing with her eyes to the dimmest corner of the room. Perhaps she forces herself to face it, turning sharply back, and lifting her head superbly, as Thamrè can (the shadow on the curtain lifts its head just so, as a passer in the street can see). Perhaps she reasons with it, hotly, on this wise, as she walks:—

"I did not think, in coming to Havermash, you would strike across my way like this!"

"Heaven knows what restless fancy forced me here, Would to Heaven I had never come!"

"For thirteen years I have wondered what it would be like to look upon your face again. How *could* I know it would be like what it is,—so miserable, so neglected, so alone!"

Perhaps she argues sternly, now and then:—

"I have never left you to suffer, at the worst. You can not starve. The first ten-dollar bill I ever earned I sent to you. If you are too imbecile to watch the post, am I to blame? If you will have opium or rum for it, am I to blame? I've done my duty by your shameful motherhood, if ever wretched daughter did! What would you have, what will you have besides?"

Perhaps she droops and pleads at moments like a little child:—

"I have fought so hard, mother, for my name and fame! You gave me such a load of shame and ignorance and squalor to shake off! It has been such a long and bitter work! Let me be for a *little* while now, mother, *do*! Sometime before you die I'll search you out; but not just yet—*just* yet!"

Perhaps she falls to sobbing, as women will. Perhaps she flings her beautiful arms out, and slides with her face upon the stifling scarlet cushions of a little sofa, where she tossed her veil. Perhaps, in kneeling there, the bleeding, gray-haired figure stalks her by, and the quieter companionship of a troop of passive and exhausted thoughts will occupy her place.

It may be that she will think about a certain Christmas eve, windy and wild like this, and with a sky of steel and red almost like this. She thought of it in seeing the sunset from the window of the cars, remembering how a streak of red light crept into the attic corner, to help her while she packed a little bundle of her ragged clothes, thirteen years ago to-night.

It may be that she remembers counting the holly wreaths to keep her wits together as she fled, guiltily and sobbing for terror at the thing that she was doing, through the happy little town; that she saw crosses of myrtle and tuberoses in Mr. Havermash's drawing-room windows as she went by, and how grand they looked; and that a butcher's wife she knew was hanging blue tissue-paper roses in her sitting-room as she climbed the depot steps. She can even recall the butcher's name,—Jack Hash,—Mrs. Jack Hash; as well as a hot and hungry wonder that filled the soul of the desolate child that night, whether she should ever live to be as safe and clean and respectable as Mrs. Jack Hash, and how she would garland her sitting-room with blue tissue-roses on Christmas, if she did!

It may be that her fancy, being wearied, dwells more minutely upon the half comical, wholly pathetic irrelevance of these things than upon the swift and feverish history of the crowded interval between their occurrence and the fact that Helène Thamrè is kneeling in the Havermash hotel parlor, to-night, fighting all the devils that can haunt a beautiful and gifted woman's soul for her poor, old, shameful mother's sake.

Her battles for bread in factories and workshops, when first she cast herself, a little girl of fifteen bitter winters, upon the perilous chances of the world; worse contests, such as the outcast child of old Peg Mathers might not escape, being unfriended and despairing as the child had been; her desperate taxation of her only power, at last,—the voice which Heaven gave her, pure and sweet as its own summer mornings; the songs which she sang at street-corners before the twilight fell; the windows of happy people under which she chanted mournfully; the first solo which they gave her at a mission school into which she chanced; the friends who heard it, and into whose hearts God put it to stretch down their hands and draw her straightway into Paradise; her studies and struggles since in foreign lands; the death of the master who had trained her, and the falling of his great mantle upon her bewildered name,—these details, perhaps, float but mistily before her mind.

Sharp, distinct, pursuing, cruel, a single question begins to imprison her tortured thoughts. It took shapes as vague as smoke, clouds, fogs, dreams, at first; it looms as clear-cut and gigantic as a pyramid before her now.

If all the world should know next year, next week, to-morrow, at once and forever, what she knows?

If Havermash should learn, suppose, to-night, that little Nell Mathers, the unfathered and forgotten child of the creature at whose gray hairs the boys hoot on the streets, is all there is of Helène Thamrè (the very letters of the shameful name transposed to make the beautiful, false image), what would Havermash, falling at her feet this instant, do the next?

Perhaps to the woman's inner sense neither Havermash nor the world may matter much, indeed. She has kept, through deadly peril, soul and body pure as light. Not a sheltered wife, singing "Greenville" to her babies, vacant of ambitions and innocent of noisier powers, can show a hand or heart or name more spotless than her own. And now to dye them deep in the old, old hateful shame! One must have *been* little Nell Mathers and have become Thamrè, I fancy, to measure this recoil.

Perhaps it seems to her more monstrous and impossible as the thought grows more familiar to her. Perhaps a certain hardness begins to creep across the pallor of her face; or it may be only that she has wound her fallen hair back from it, and exposed the carved exactness and composure of her features. It may be that she will argue to herself again, forgetting that the gray-haired vision left her long ago:—

"I could never make you happy, if I did. It would always,

always be a curse to both of us. What have you ever done for me, that you should demand a right so cruel? You have no right, I say; you have no right!"

"And, if you speak, indeed, why, who believes you? What can your ravings do against Thamrè's denial, poor old mother!"

Perhaps she muses, half aloud: "You need a shawl, I see. You shall have a bright, warm shawl on Christmas Day. It is better for you than a daughter. Oh! a thousand times!"

Perhaps she laughs—as Thamrè does not often laugh—most bitterly; and that Joe Havermash, knocking at her door, hears, or thinks he hears, the sound, before she flashes on him, tall, serene, resplendent, in full dress and full spirit for the evening.

The Happy Home Handel Association were satisfied with the reception given by Havermash to their rendering of the oratorio of the Messiah last Christmas eve. On settees, in the aisles, on the window-sills, in the corridors, on the stairs, Havermash overflowed the brown-stone post-office.

Since the incorporation of the city (which is the Christian era of Havermash, and from which everything dates accordingly) nothing approaching such an audience had been collected for the most popular of purposes. Even Signor Blitz could not have eaten swords or played baseball with uncracked eggs before a quarter of the spectators; and the New England philosopher, it is well known, reads his lectures in Havermash to three hundred people.

In this triumph the Happy Home Handel Association felt compelled to own that Thamrè had her share, which for the H. H. H. A. was owning a great deal. When little Joe bowed the prima donna upon the somewhat uncertain (green cambric) stage, the East Havermash "orchestra" led off in a burst of applause, which threatened to shake the post-office to its foundation stone, and which fired even the leader's dignity of Joe's rotund person to ill-concealed enthusiasm. Even Mrs. Joe, gorgeous upon the front settee, in the opera dress that (it was well known) she wore in Boston, despite the ache of a secret chagrin that Miss Thamrè had received no callers, reflected the general pride and pleasure to the very links of her great gold necklace and the tiniest wrinkle of her rose-colored gloves. Even Mrs. Jack Hash, on her camp-stool, by the second left, though disposed by nature and training to be critical of anything headed by a Havermash, applauded softly with the feathered tip of her silver-paper fan upon the frill of her brown poplin upper skirt. Never had there been anything like it known in Havermash.

Like a bird, like a snow-flake, like a moonbeam, like a fancy, like nothing that the brown-stone post-office was accustomed to, Thamrè stole upon the stage. She stood for an instant poised, fluttering, as if half her mind were made to fly, then fell into her unapproachable repose, and at her leisure looked the great audience over, shooting it here and there with her nervous glance.

The packed house drew and held its breath. Women thought swiftly: Silver-gray satin, up to the throat and down to the hands. No jewelry, and a live white lily on her wrist! Young men saw her through a mist, and half turned their eyes away, as if they had seen a Madonna folded in a morning cloud. Reporters pondered, twirling a moustache end, pencil held suspended: Such severity is the superbest affectation, my lady! but it tells, as straight as a carrier-dove. Before she had opened her lips, Thamrè had conquered Havermash.

Conscious of this in an instant's flash, Thamrè grew unconscious of it in another. For an instant every detail in her house was in her grasp, even to Mrs. Jack Hash on the camp-stool and the critical attitude of the silver-paper fan; even to old Mother Goose, half fading into the shadow of the distance, quarreling with a door-keeper about her ticket. The next she cast her audience from her like a racer casting his cloak to the wind. Her face settled; her wonderful eyes dilated; the hand with the lily on it closed over the other like a seal; the soul of the music entered into her, incorporate. She grew as sacred as her theme.

"That little country house," said a critic present, who had heard her before her best houses in the great world, "was on the knees of its heart that night. She never sang like that before, nor ever will again; nor any other artist, it is my belief. She minded the jerks of that orchestra and the flats of the Havermash *prime donne* no more than she did the whistling of the wind about the post-office windows. She rendered the text like an angel sent from heaven for the purpose. When she lifted that hand with the flower on it (she did it only in the chorus, 'Surely, he hath borne our griefs,' and in the tenor, 'Behold, and see,' and at one other time) I could think of nothing but

> In the beauty of the lilies
> Christ was born across the sea.

Couldn't get it out of my head. I meant she should have been *encored*, when it was all over, to give us that itself; but for what happened, you know."

Did I say she grew as sacred as her theme? It might almost be said that its holy Personality environed and enveloped her. Reverent souls that listened to her that well-remembered night felt as if the Man of Sorrows confided to her the burden of his heart, as if he stooped to acquaint her with his grief, as if the travail of his soul fell upon her, and that with his satisfaction she was satisfied.

The sacred drama was unfolding to its solemn close, the wildness of the wind without was hushed, the Christmas stars were out, when Thamrè glided into her last solo,—that palpitating, proud, triumphant thing, in which the soul of Divine Love avenges itself against the ingenuity of human despair:—

> If God be for us, who can be against us?
> Who can be against us?
> Who shall lay anything to the charge
> Of God's elect?
> It is God that justifieth.
> Who is he that condemneth?
> It is Christ that died.

It was at this point that the interruption came.

Shrill and sharp into the thrill of the singer's liquid, clinging notes a quick cry cut:—

48

"Let me see her! Let me touch her! I can't abear it any longer! Let me see my girl!" and, forcing her way like a stream of lava through the packed and startled aisles, hot, wild, pallid, and horrible, Old Mother Goose leaped, before a hand could stay her, on the stage.

"I can't stand it any longer, Nell! It seems to craze my head! I knew you from the time I heard you laughing to the depot. I didn't mean to shame ye before so many folks, and I tried to find my shawl. They said you wouldn't want to see your poor old mother, Nelly dear. But I can't abear to hear you sing. Nell, why, Nell, you stand up like the Almighty Dead to do it!"

The shock of the shrill words and their cessation brought the house to its feet. Then came the uproar.

"Shame!" "Police!" "Order!" "Take her out!" "Arrest the hag!" "Protect the lady!" And after that the astonishment and the silence of death.

High above the wavering, peering mass, clear to the apprehension of every eye in the house, appeared a lily-bound, authoritative hand. It motioned once and dropped—as the snow drops over a grave.

By those who sat nearest her it was said that the flower trembled on the lady's wrist a little; for the rest, she stood sculptured like a statue, towering about the piteous figure at her feet. Her voice, when she spoke—for she spoke in the passing of a thought,—rang out to the remotest corner of the galleries, slipping even then, however, into Thamrè's girlish, uneven tones.

"If you *please*, do not disturb the woman at this moment. She is a very *old* woman. Let us hear what she has to say. Her hair is gray. Let us not be *rough* or *hasty* till we have *thought* of what she says."

Old Mother Goose rose from the floor, where she had fallen, half-abashed, perhaps half-dazed at that which she had done.

"I've got nothing more to say." She fumbled foolishly in the air to wrap the shawl which she had lost about her lean and tattered shoulders. "I've said as this famous lady is my daughter, that was Nell Mathers, and remembered by many folks in Havermash thirteen years ago. I wouldn't have shamed her quite so much if I'd only found my shawl. It's cold, too, without a shawl. I'll go out now, and you can sing your piece through, Nelly, without the plague of me. I wouldn't have told on you, I think, but for the music and the crazy feeling that I had. It's most too bad, Nelly, to spoil the piece. I'll go right out."

She turned, stepped off, and staggered feebly, turning her bleared eyes back to feast upon the silent, shining figure, on whose wrist the lily glittered cruelly, as only lilies can.

"What a pretty sating gown you've got, my dear!" she said.

Mr. Havermash could bear it no longer. He took Old Mother Goose by the sleeve, hurrying up, saying: "Come, come!"

"The woman is drunk, Miss Thamrè. She shall not be allowed to insult you any more like this. In the kindness of your heart, you make a mistake, I think, if you will pardon me. See! she is quite beside herself. Something is due to the audience. This disturbance should not continue. Come, Peg, come!"

But Thamrè shook her head. She had grown now deadly pale,—at least so Joe thought, letting go the woman's arm, his own face changing color sharply, the baton in his fat, white-gloved hand beginning to shake.

"If you please, Mr. Havermash, I should like to know—the people will *pardon* me a moment, I am sure—I should like to know if this poor old creature has anything *more* to say."

"Nothing more," said Old Mother Goose, shaking her gray head, "but this, maybe, Nelly dear. I says to myself, when I sits and hears you singing,—I says, when you sang them words: 'If God be for me, my girl won't be against me! My girl can't be against me!'— over and over with the music, Nelly, so I did! If God be for me, how *can* my girl be against me?"

It was said that, when Helène Thamrè stretched down her lily-guarded hand, and, lifting the lean, uncleanly fingers of Old Mother Goose, pressed them, after a moment's thought, gently and slowly to her heart, she heard the sudden break of sobs in the breathless house; and, pausing to listen to the sound, flushed fitfully like a child surprised, and smiled.

"Ladies and gentlemen,"—her great eyes stabbed the audience through and through; she lifted the old woman's hand, that all might see,—"I am *sorry* that your entertainment should be disturbed. If you will *excuse* me, I will leave you now, and take my mother home."

Home? What home was there for Old Mother Goose and her outcast child in Thamrè's hotel parlors, on that or any other night? What home was there for Thamrè in the God-forsaken cellar whence the woman of the town had crawled? Apparently, the lady had not thought of this. Joe found her standing serenely as an angel when he came into the stifling little green room. She was still smiling. She had buttoned her silver furs about the old woman's shrunken throat.

"This will be warmer than your shawl, mother, don't you see?" he heard her say. "The boys shall never bother you in this, poor old mother! There!"

Mrs. Havermash came with her husband. The Boston opera-cloak was in disorder; her rose-colored gloves were wet and spotted.

"Miss Thamrè," said Joe, "may I make you acquainted with my wife? We would not urge upon you again the acceptance of a hospitality which has been already so decidedly refused; but perhaps, considering the state of your mother's health, we can make you more comfortable now at our home than you can be elsewhere. If you will do Mrs. Havermash and myself the favor to return with us—and her—in our own carriage to-night"—

Joe's grandfather, as has been said, cobbled shoes in a wooden shop; and even Mrs. Joe to-day will drink with her spoon in her tea-cup, you will notice, if you chance to sit beside her at a supper. But show me bluer blood, if it please you, than shall flow in the veins of him and his, to preserve the existence of this most cultivated instinct and the memory of this most knightly deed.

All the world knows how Thamrè suddenly and mysteriously disappeared a year ago from public and professional life. All the world has mourned, wondered, gossiped, caught at the wings of rumors, lost them, and so mourned again at this event.

All the world does not know with what a curious development of pride in and loyalty to the personality of little Nell Mathers, Havermash has struggled, till struggle has become useless, to enforce a reticence upon the subject of Thamrè's movements and their motives.

To a few friends, familiar with her private history for the past year, its results have seemed to crown its cost, I think. At least, she herself, having proved them so, has contrived to radiate upon us the light of her own content.

"You do not know the life," she said, at the outset, shaking her beautiful, determined head, "if you would ask me to return to it while my mother lives. Even my name will not bear the scorch of hers. The world is so hard on women! Do not urge me. Let me take my way. Perhaps God and I together can make her poor old hand as white as yours or mine before she dies."

Perhaps they did. It is known that when Old Mother Goose lay dying in her daughter's quiet house in Havermash, one frosty night, not many weeks ago, and after she had fallen, as they thought, past speech or recognition, she raised herself upon her pillow, and, stretching her hands, said slowly:—

"Nell! why, Nell! It is Christ that died! If my girl was for me, Nell, *could* He be against me, do you think?"

And further it is only known that Thamrè will sing this season in the oratorio of the Messiah on Christmas eve.

Sarah Orne Jewett

(September 3, 1849-June 24, 1909)

Sarah Orne Jewett's father, a country doctor, took her to visit his patients, guided her omnivorous reading, and respected her wish to be a writer. One of her most popular novels, and her own favorite, *A Country Doctor* (1884), tells of a young woman's struggle to become a doctor. With medicine so strong an influence in her youth (her maternal grandfather was also a doctor), it is no surprise that Jewett presents portraits of spiritually and emotionally stunted people in the form of medical case histories.

"Mrs. Parkins's Christmas Eve," published in two parts in *Ladies' Home Journal* of December 1890 and January 1891, is the story of a woman whose uncharitableness has been like a disease. We read the history of her frugality; we see the symptoms. Finally, on Christmas Eve she suffers a crisis and almost dies; but she is saved by healers of souls—a minister's family—and so begins her recovery; although with Jewett's customary insistence on realism, her spiritual recovery is presented as neither painless nor easy.

Mrs. Parkins's Christmas Eve

Sarah Orne Jewett

I

One wintry-looking afternoon the sun was getting low, but still shone with cheerful radiance into Mrs. Lydia Parkins' sitting-room. To point out a likeness between the bareness of the room and the appearance of the outside world on that twenty-first of December might seem ungracious; but there was a certain leaflessless and inhospitality common to both.

The cold, gray wall-paper, and dull, thin furniture; the indescribable poverty and lack of comfort of the room were exactly like the leaflessness and sharpness and coldness of that early winter day—unless the sun shone out with a golden glow as it had done in the latter part of the afternoon; then both the room and the long hillside and frozen road and distant western hills were quite transfigured.

Mrs. Parkins sat upright in one of the six decorous wooden chairs with cane seats; she was trimming a dismal gray-and-black winter bonnet and her work-basket was on the end of the table in front of her, between the windows, with a row of spools on the window-sill at her left. The only luxury she permitted herself was a cricket, a little bench such as one sees in a church pew, with a bit of carpet to cover its top. Mrs. Parkins was so short that she would have been quite off-roundings otherwise in her cane-seated chair; but she had a great horror of persons who put their feet on chair rungs and wore the paint off. She was always on the watch to break the young of this bad habit. She cast a suspicious glance now and then at little Lucy Deems, who sat in another cane-seated chair opposite. The child had called upon Mrs. Parkins before, and was now trying so hard to be good that both her feet had gone to sleep and had come to the prickling stage of that misery. She wondered if her mother were not almost ready to go home.

Mrs. Deems sat in the rocking-chair, full in the sunlight and faced the sun itself, unflinchingly. She was a broad-faced gay-hearted, little woman, and her face was almost as bright as the winter sun itself. One might fancy that they were having a match at trying to outshine one another, but so far it was not Mrs. Deems who blinked and withdrew from the contest. She was just now conscious of little Lucy's depression and anxious looks, and bade her go out to run about a little while and see if there were some of Mrs. Parkins' butternuts left under the big tree.

The door closed, and Mrs. Parkins snapped her thread and said that there was no butternuts out there; perhaps Lucy should have a few in a basket when she was going home.

"Oh, 'taint no matter," said Mrs. Deems, easily. "She was kind of distressed sittin' so quiet; they like to rove about, children does."

"She won't do no mischief?" asked the hostess, timidly.

"Lucy?" laughed the mother. "Why you ought to be better acquainted with Lucy than that, I'm sure. I catch myself wishing she wa'n't quite so still; she takes after her father's folks, all quiet and dutiful, and ain't got the least idea how to enjoy themselves; we was all kind of noisy to our house when I was grown up, and I can't seem to sense the Deems."

"I often wish I had just such a little girl as your Lucy," said Mrs. Parkins, with a sigh. She held her gray-and-black bonnet off with her left hand and looked at it without approval.

"I shall always continue to wear black for Mr. Parkins," she said, "but I had this piece of dark-gray ribbon and I thought I had better use it on my black felt; the felt is sort of rusty, now, and black silk trimmings increase the rusty appearance."

"They do so," frankly acknowledged Mrs. Deems. "Why don't you go an' get you a new one for meeting', Mrs. Parkins? Felts ain't high this season, an' you've got this for second wear."

"I've got one that's plenty good for best," replied Mrs. Parkins, without any change of expression. "It seems best to make this do one more winter." She began to rearrange the gray ribbon, and Mrs. Deems watched her with a twinkle in her eyes; she had something to say, and did not know exactly how to begin, and Mrs. Parkins knew it as well as she did, and was holding her back which made the occasion more and more difficult.

"There!" she exclaimed at last, boldly, "I expect you know what I've come to see you for, an' I can't set here and make talk no longer. May's well ask if you can do anything about the minister's present."

Mrs. Parkins' mouth was full of pins, and she removed them all, slowly, before she spoke. The sun went behind a low snow cloud along the horizon, and Mrs. Deems shone on alone. It was not very warm in the room, and she gathered her woolen shawl closer about her shoulders as if she were getting ready to go home.

"I don't know's I feel to give you anything to-day, Mrs. Deems," said Mrs. Parkins in a resolved tone. "I don't feel much acquainted with the minister's folks. I must say *she* takes a good deal upon herself; I don't like so much of a ma'am."

"She's one of the pleasantest, best women we ever had in town, *I* think," replied Mrs. Deems. "I was tellin' 'em the other day that I always felt as if she brought a pleasant feelin' wherever she came, so sisterly and own-folks-like. They've seen a sight o' trouble and must feel pinched at times, but she finds ways to do plenty o' kindnesses. I never see a mite of behavior in 'em as if we couldn't do enough for 'em because they was ministers. Some minister's folks has such expectin' ways, and the more you do the more you may; but it ain't so with the Lanes. They are always a thinkin' what they can do for other people, an' they do it, too. You never liked 'em, but I can't see why."

"He ain't the ablest preacher that ever was," said Mrs. Parkins.

"I don't care if he ain't; words is words, but a man that lives as Mr. Lane does, is the best o' ministers," answered Mrs. Deems.

"Well, I don't owe 'em nothin' to-day," said the hostess, looking up. "I haven't got it in mind to do for the minister's folks any more than I have; but I may send 'em some apples or somethin', by'n-bye."

"Jest as you feel," said Mrs. Deems, rising quickly and looking provoked. "I didn't know but what 'twould be a pleasure to you, same's 'tis to the rest of us."

"They ain't been here very long, and I pay my part to the salary, an' 'taint no use to overdo in such cases."

"They've been put to extra expense this fall, and have been very feeling and kind; real interested in all of us, and such a help to the parish as we ain't had for a good while before. Havin' to send their boy to the hospital, has made it hard for 'em."

"Well, folks has to have their hard times, and minister's families can't escape. I am sorry about the boy, I'm sure," said Mrs. Parkins, generously. "Don't you go, Mrs. Deems; you ain't been to see me for a good while. I want you to see my bonnet in jest a minute."

"I've got to go way over to the Dilby's, and it's goin' to be dark early. I should be pleased to have you come an' see me. I've got to find Lucy and trudge along."

"I believe I won't rise to see you out o' the door, my lap's so full," said Mrs. Parkins politely, and so they parted. Lucy was hopping up and down by the front fence to keep herself warm and occupied.

"She didn't say anything about the butternuts, did she mother?" the child asked; and Mrs. Deems laughed and shook her head. Then they walked away down the road together, the big-mittened hand holding fast the little one, and the hooded heads bobbing toward each other now and then, as if they were holding a lively conversation. Mrs. Parkins looked after them two or three times, suspiciously at first, as if she thought they might be talking about her; then a little wistfully. She had come of a saving family and had married a saving man.

"Isn't Mrs. Parkins real poor, mother?" little Lucy inquired in a compassionate voice.

Mrs. Deems smiled, and assured the child that there was nobody so well off in town except Colonel Drummond, so far as money went; but Mrs. Parkins took care neither to enjoy her means herself, nor to let anybody else. Lucy pondered this strange answer for awhile and then began to hop and skip along the rough road, still holding fast her mother's warm hand.

This was the twenty-first of December, and the day of the week was Monday. On Tuesday Mrs. Parkins did her frugal ironing, and on Wednesday she meant to go over to Haybury to put some money into the bank and to do a little shopping. Goods were cheaper in Haybury in some of the large stores, than they were at the corner store at home, and she had the horse and could always get dinner at her cousin's. To be sure, the cousin was always hinting for presents for herself or her children, but Mrs. Parkins could bear that, and always cleared her conscience by asking the boys over in haying-time, though their help cost more than it came to with their growing appetites and the wear and tear of the house. Their mother came for a day's visit now and then, but everything at home depended upon her hard-working hands, as she had been early left a widow with little else to depend upon, until now, when the boys were out of school. One was doing well in the shoe factory and one in a store. Mrs. Parkins was really much attached to her cousin, but she thought if she once began to give, they would always be expecting something.

As has been said, Wednesday was the day set for the visit, but when Wednesday came it was a hard winter day, cold and windy, with an occasional flurry of snow, and Mrs. Parkins being neuralgic, gave up going until Thursday. She was pleased when she waked Thursday morning to find the weather warmer and the wind stilled. She was weather-wise enough to see snow in the clouds, but it was only eight miles to Haybury and she could start early and come home again as soon as she got her dinner. So the boy who came every morning to take care of her horse and bring in wood, was hurried and urged until he nearly lost his breath, and the horse was put into the wagon and, with rare forethought, a piece of salt-pork was wrapped up and put under the wagon-seat; then with a cloud over the re-trimmed bonnet, and a shawl over her Sunday cloak, and mittens over her woolen gloves Mrs. Parkins drove away. All her neighbors knew that she was going to Haybury to put eighty-seven dollars into the bank that the Dilby brothers had paid her for some rye planted and harvested on the halves. Very likely she had a good deal of money beside, that day; she had the best farm in that sterile neighborhood and was a famous manager.

The cousin was a hospitable, kindly soul, very loyal to her relations and always ready with a welcome. Beside, though the ears of Lydia Parkins were deaf to hints of present need and desire, it was more than likely that she would leave her farm and savings to the boys; she was not a person to speak roughly to, or one whom it was possible to disdain. More than this, no truly compassionate heart could fail to pity the thin, anxious, forbidding little woman, who behaved as if she must always be on the defensive against a plundering and begging world.

Cousin Mary Faber, as usual, begged Mrs. Parkins to spend the night; she seemed to take so little pleasure in life that the change might do her good. There would be no expense except for the horse's stabling, Mrs. Faber urged openly, and nobody would be expecting her at home. But Mrs. Parkins, as usual refused, and feared that the cellar would freeze. It had not been banked up as she liked to have it that autumn, but as for paying the Dilbys a dollar and a quarter for doing it, she didn't mean to please them so much.

"Land sakes! Why don't you feel as rich as you be, an' not mind them little expenses?" said cousin Faber, daringly. "I do declare I don't see how you can make out to grow richer an' poorer at the same time." The good-natured soul could not help laughing as she spoke, and Mrs. Parkins herself really could not help smiling.

"I'm much obliged to you for the pleasure of your company," said cousin Faber, "and it was very considerate of you to bring me that nice piece o' pork." If she had only known what an effort her guest had made to carry it into the house after she had brought it!

Twice Mrs. Parkins had pushed it back under the wagon-seat with lingering indecision, and only taken it out at last because she feared that one of those prowling boys might discover it in the wagon and tell his mother. How often she had taken something into her hand to give away and then put it back and taken it again half a dozen times, irresolutely. There were still blind movements of the heart toward generosity, but she had grown more and more skillful at soothing her conscience and finding excuses for not giving.

The Christmas preparations in the busy little town made her uncomfortable, and cheerful cousin Faber's happiness in her own pinched housekeeping was a rebuke. The boys' salaries were very small indeed, this first year or two; but their mother was proud of their steadiness, and still sewed and let rooms to lodgers and did everything she could to earn money. She looked tired and old before her time, and acknowledged to Mrs. Parkins that she should like to have a good, long visit at the farm the next summer and let the boys take their meals with a neighbor. "I never spared myself one step until they were through with their schooling; but now it will be so I can take things a little easier," said the good soul with a wistful tone that was unusual.

Mrs. Parkins felt impatient as she listened; she knew that a small present of money now and then would have been a great help, but she never could make up her mind to begin what promised to be the squandering of her carefully saved fortune. It would be the ruin of the boys, too, if they thought she could be appealed to in every emergency. She would make it up to them in the long run; she could not take her money with her to the next world, and she would make a virtue of necessity.

The afternoon was closing in cold and dark, and the snow came sifting down slowly before Mrs. Parkins was out of the street of Hayburv. She had lived too long on a hill not to be weatherwise and for a moment, as the wind buffeted her face and she saw the sky and the horizon line all dulled by the coming storm, she had a great mind to go back to cousin Faber's. If it had been any other time in the year but Christmas eve! The old horse gathered his forces and hurried along as if he had sense enough to be anxious about the weather; but presently the road turned so that the wind was not so chilling and they were quickly out of sight of the town, crossing the level land which lay between Haybury and the hills of Holton. Mrs. Parkins was persuaded that she should get home by dark, and the old horse did his very best. The road was rough and frozen and the wagon rattled and pitched along; it was like a race between Mrs. Parkins and the storm, and for a time it seemed certain that she would be the winner.

The gathering forces of the wind did not assert themselves fully until nearly half the eight miles had been passed, and the snow which had only clung to Mrs. Parkins' blanket-shawl like a white veil at first, and sifted white across the frozen grass of the lowlands, lay at last like a drift on the worn buffalo-robe, and was so deep in the road that it began to clog the wheels. It was a most surprising snow in the thickness of the flakes and the rapidity with which it gathered; it was no use to try to keep the white-knitted cloud over her face, for it became so thick with snow that it blinded and half-stifled her. The darkness began to fall, the snow came thicker and faster, and the horse climbing the drifted hills with the snow-clogged wagon, had to stop again and again. The awful thought suddenly came to Mrs. Parkins' mind that she could not reach home that night, and the next moment she had to acknowledge that she did not know exactly where she was. The thick flakes blinded her; she turned to look behind to see if any one were coming; but she might have been in the middle of an Arctic waste. She felt benumbed and stupid, and again tried to urge the tired horse, and the good creature toiled on desperately. It seemed as if they must have left the lowland far enough behind to be near some houses, but it grew still darker and snowier as they dragged slowly for another mile until it was impossible to get any further, and the horse stopped still and then gave a shake to rid himself of the drift on his back, and turned his head to look inquiringly at his mistress.

Mrs. Parkins began to cry with cold, and fear and misery. She had read accounts of such terrible, sudden storms in the west, and here she was in the night, foodless, and shelterless, and helpless.

"Oh! I'd give a thousand dollars to be safe under cover!" groaned the poor soul. "Oh, how poor I be this minute, and I come right away from that warm house!"

A strange dazzle of light troubled her eyes, and a vision of the brightly-lighted Haybury shops, and the merry customers that were hurrying in and out, and the gayety and contagious generosity of Christmas eve mocked at the stingy, little lost woman as she sat there half bewildered. The heavy flakes of snow caught her eyelashes and chilled her cheeks and melted inside the gray bonnet-strings; they heaped themselves on the top of the bonnet into a high crown that toppled into her lap as she moved. If she tried to brush the snow away, her clogged mitten only gathered more and grew more and more clumsy. It was a horrible, persistent storm; at this rate the horse and driver both would soon be covered and frozen in the road. The gathering flakes were malicious and mysterious; they were so large and flaked so fast down out of the sky.

"My goodness! How numb I be this minute," whispered Mrs. Parkins. And then she remembered that the cashier of the bank had told her that morning when she made her deposit, that everybody else was taking out their money that day; she was the only one who had come to put any in.

"I'd pay every cent of it willin' to anybody that would come along and help me get to shelter," said the poor soul. "Oh, I don't know as I've hoed so's to be worth savin'"; and a miserable sense of shame and defeat beat down whatever hope tried to rise in her heart. What had she tried to do for God and man that gave her a right to think of love and succor now?

Yet it seemed every moment as if help must come and as if this great emergency could not be so serious. Life had been so monotonous to Mrs. Parkins, so destitute of excitement and tragic situations that she could hardly understand, even now, that she was in such great danger. Again she called as loud as she could for help, and the horse whinnied louder still. The only hope was that two men who had passed her some miles back would remember that they had advised her to hurry, and would come back to look for her. The poor, old horse had dragged himself and the wagon to the side of the road under the shelter of some evergreens; Mrs. Parkins slipped down under the buffalo into the bottom of her cold, old wagon, and covered herself as well as she could. There was more than a chance that she might be found frozen under a snow-drift in the morning.

The morning! Christmas morning!

What did the advent of Christmas day hold out for her—buried in the snow-drifts of a December storm!

Anything? Yes, but she knew it not. Little did she dream what this Christmas eve was to bring into her life!

II

Lydia Parkins was a small woman of no great vigor, but as she grew a little warmer under her bed of blankets in the bottom of the old wagon, she came to her senses. She must get out and try to walk on through the snow as far as she could; it was no use to die there in this fearful storm like a rabbit. Yes, and she must unharness the horse and let him find his way; so she climbed boldly down into the knee-deep snow where a drift had blown already. She would not admit the thought that perhaps she might be lost in the snow and frozen to death that very night. It did not seem in character with Mrs. Nathan Parkins, who was the owner of plenty of money in Haybury Bank, and a good farm well divided into tillage and woodland, who had plenty of blankets and comforters at home, and firewood enough, and suitable winter clothes to protect her from the weather. The wind was rising more and more, it made the wet gray-and-black bonnet feel very limp and cold about her head, and her poor head itself felt duller and heavier than ever. She lost one glove and mitten in the snow as she tried to unharness the old horse, and her bare fingers were very clumsy, but she managed to get the good old creature clear, hoping that he would plod on and be known farther along the road and get help for her; but instead of that he only went round and round her and the wagon, floundering and whinnying, and refusing to be driven away. "What kind of a storm is this going to be?" groaned Mrs. Parkins, wading along the road and falling over her dress helplessly. The old horse meekly followed and when she gave a weak, shrill, womanish shout, old

Major neighed and shook the snow off his back. Mrs. Parkins knew in her inmost heart, that with such a wind and through such drifts she could not get very far, and at last she lost her breath and sank down at the roadside and the horse went on alone. It was horribly dark and the cold pierced her through and through. In a few minutes she staggered to her feet and went on; she could have cried because the horse was out of sight, but she found it easier following in his tracks.

Suddenly there was a faint twinkle of light on the left, and what a welcome sight it was! The poor wayfarer hastened, but the wind behaved as if it were trying to blow her back. The horse had reached shelter first and somebody had heard him outside and came out and shut the house door with a loud bang that reached Mrs. Parkins' ears. She tried to shout again but she could hardly make a sound. The light still looked a good way off, but presently she could hear voices and see another light moving. She was so tired that she must wait until they came to help her. Who lived in the first house on the left after you passed oak ridge? Why, it couldn't be the Donnells, for they were all away in Haybury, and the house was shut up; this must be the parsonage, and she was off the straight road home. The bewildered horse had taken the left-hand road. "Well," thought Mrs. Parkins, "I'd rather be most anywhere else, but I don't care where 'tis so long as I get under cover. I'm all spent and wore out."

The lantern came bobbing along quickly as if somebody were hurrying, and wavered from side to side as if it were in a fishing boat on a rough sea. Mrs. Parkins started to meet it, and made herself known to her rescuer.

"I declare, if 'taint the minister," she exclaimed. "I'm Mrs. Parkins, or what's left of her. I've come near bein' froze to death along back here a-piece. I never saw such a storm in all my life."

She sank down in the snow and could not get to her feet again. The minister was a strong man, he stooped and lifted her like a child and carried her along the road with the lantern hung on his arm. She was a little woman and she was not a person given to sentiment, but she had been dreadfully cold and frightened, and now at last she was safe. It was like the good shepherd in the Bible, and Lydia Parkins was past crying; but it seemed as if she could never speak again and as if her heart were going to break. It seemed inevitable that the minister should have come to find her and carry her to the fold; no, to the parsonage; but she felt dizzy and strange again, and the second-best gray-and-black bonnet slipped its knot and tumbled off into the snow without her knowing it.

When Mrs. Parkins opened her eyes a bright light made them shut again directly; then she discovered, a moment afterward, that she was in the parsonage sitting-room and the minister's wife was kneeling beside her with an anxious face; and there was a Christmas tree at the other side of the room, with all its pretty, shining things and gay little candles on the boughs. She was comfortably wrapped in warm blankets, but she felt very tired and weak. The minister's wife smiled with delight: "Now you'll feel all right in a few minutes," she exclaimed. "Think of your being out in this awful storm! Don't try to talk to us yet, dear," she added kindly, "I'm going to bring you a cup of good hot tea. Are you all right? Don't try to tell anything about the storm. Mr. Lane has seen to the horse. Here, I'll put my little red shawl over you, it looks prettier than the blankets, and I'm drying your clothes in the kitchen."

The minister's wife had a sweet face, and she stood for a minute looking down at her unexpected guest; then something in the thin, appealing face on the sofa seemed to touch her heart, and she stooped over and kissed Mrs. Parkins. It happened that nobody had kissed Mrs. Parkins for years, and the tears stole down her cheeks as Mrs. Lane turned away.

As for the minister's wife, she had often thought that Mrs. Parkins had a most disagreeable hard face; she liked her less than any one in the parish, but now as she brightened the kitchen fire, she began to wonder what she could find to put on the Christmas tree for her, and wondered why she never had noticed a frightened, timid look in the poor woman's eyes. "It is so forlorn for her to live all alone on that big farm," said Mrs. Lane to herself, mindful of her own happy home and the children. All three of them came close about their mother at that moment, lame-footed John with his manly pale face, and smiling little Bell and Mary, the girls.

The minister came in from the barn and blew his lantern out and hung it away. The old horse was blanketed as warm as his mistress, and there was a good supper in his crib. It was a very happy household at the parsonage, and Mrs. Parkins could hear their whispers and smothered laughter in the kitchen. It was only eight o'clock after all, and it was evident that the children longed to begin their delayed festivities. The little girls came and stood in the doorway and looked first at the stranger guest and then at their Christmas tree, and after a while their mother came with them to ask whether Mrs. Parkins felt equal to looking on at the pleasuring or whether she would rather go to bed and rest, and sleep away her fatigue.

Mrs. Parkins wished to look on; she was beginning to feel well again, but she dreaded being alone, she could not tell exactly why.

"Come right into the bedroom with me then," said Mrs. Lane, "and put on a nice warm, double gown of mine; 'twill be large enough for you, that's certain, and then if you do wish to move about by-and-by, you will be better able than in the blankets."

Mrs. Parkins felt dazed by this little excitement, yet she was strangely in the mood for it. The reaction of being in this safe and pleasant place, after the recent cold and danger, excited her, and gave her an unwonted power of enjoyment and sympathy. She felt pleased and young, and she wondered what was going to happen. She stood still and let Mrs. Lane brush her gray hair, all tangled with the snow damp, as if she were no older than the little girls themselves; then they went out again to the sitting-room. There was a great fire blazing in the Franklin stove; the minister had cleared a rough bit of the parsonage land the summer before and shown good spirit about it, and these, as Mrs. Parkins saw at once, were some of the pitch-pine roots. She had said when she heard of his hard work, that he had better put the time into his sermons, and she remembered that now with a pang at her heart, and confessed inwardly that she had been mean spirited sometimes toward the Lanes, and it was a good lesson to her to be put at their mercy now. As she sat in her corner by the old sofa in the warm double gown and watched their kindly faces, a new sense of friendliness and hopefulness stole into her heart. "I'm just as warm now as I was cold a while ago," she assured the minister.

The children sat side by side, the lame boy and the two little sisters before the fire, and Mrs. Lane sat on the sofa by Mrs. Parkins, and the minister turned over the leaves of a Bible that lay on the table. It did not seem like a stiff and formal meeting held half from superstition and only half from reverence, but it was as if the good man were telling his household news of some one they all loved and held close to their hearts. He said a few words about the birth of Christ, and of there being no room that night in the inn. Room enough for the Roman soldier and the priest and the tax-gatherer, but no room for Christ; and how we all blame that innkeeper, and then are like him too often in the busy inn of our hearts. "Room for our friends and our pleasures and our gains, and no room for Christ," said the minister sadly, as the children looked soberly into the fire and tried to understand. Then they heard again the story of the shepherds and the star, and it was a more beautiful story than ever, and seemed quite new and wonderful; and then the minister prayed, and gave special thanks for the friend who made one of their household that night, because she had come through such great danger. Afterward the Lanes sang their Christmas hymn, standing about a little old organ which the mother played: "While shepherds watched their flocks by night—"

They sang it all together as if they loved the hymn, and when they stopped and the room was still again, Mrs. Parkins could hear the wind blow outside and the great elm branches sway and creak above the little house, and the snow clicked busily against the windows. There was a curious warmth at her heart; she did not feel frightened or lonely, or cold, or even selfish any more.

They lighted the candles on the Christmas tree, and the young people capered about and were brimming over with secrets and shouted with delight, and the tree shown and glistened brave in its gay trimming of walnuts covered with gold and silver paper, and little bags sewed with bright worsteds, and all sorts of pretty homemade trifles. But when the real presents were discovered, the presents that meant no end of thought and management and secret self-denial, the brightest part of the household love and happiness shone out. One after another they came to bring Mrs. Parkins her share of the little tree's fruit until her lap was full as she sat on the sofa. One little girl brought a bag of candy, though there wasn't much candy on the tree; and the other gave her a book-mark, and the lame boy had a pretty geranium, grown by himself, with a flower on it, and came limping to put it in her hands; and Mrs. Lane brought a pretty hood that her sister had made for her a few weeks before, but her old one was still good and she did not need two. The minister had found a little book of hymns which a friend had given him at the autumn conference, and as Mrs. Parkins opened it, she happened to see these words: "Room to deny ourselves." She didn't know why the tears rushed to her eyes: "I've got to learn to deny myself of being mean," she thought, almost angrily. It was the least she could do, to do something friendly for these kind people; they had taken her in out of the storm with such loving warmth of sympathy; they did not show the least consciousness that she had never spoken a kind word about them since they came to town; that she alone had held aloof when this dear boy, their only son, had fought through an illness which might leave him a cripple for life. She had heard that there was a hope of his being cured if by-and-by his father could carry him to New York to a famous surgeon there. But all the expense of the long journey and many weeks of treatment, had seemed impossible. They were so thankful to have him still alive and with them that Christmas night. Mrs. Parkins could see the mother's eyes shine with tears as she looked at him, and the father put out a loving hand to steady him as he limped across the room.

"I wish little Lucy Deems, that lives next neighbor to me, was here to help your girls keep Christmas," said Mrs. Parkins, speaking half unconsciously. "Her mother has had it very hard; I mean to bring her over some day when the traveling gets good."

"We know Lucy Deems," said the children with satisfaction. Then Mrs. Parkins thought with regret of cousin Faber and her two boys, and was sorry that they were not all at the minister's too. She seemed to have entered upon a new life; she even thought of her dreary home with disapproval, and of its comfortable provisioning in cellar and garret, and of her money in the Haybury bank, with secret shame. Here she was with Mrs. Lane's double gown on, as poor a woman as there was in the world; she had come like a beggar to the Lanes' door that Christmas eve, and they were eagerly giving her house-room and gifts great and small; where were her independence and her riches now? She was a stranger and they had taken her in, and they did it for Christ's sake, and he would bless them, but what was there to say for herself? "Lord, how poor I be!" faltered Lydia Parkins for the second time that night.

There had not been such a storm for years. It was days before people could hear from each other along the blockaded country roads. Men were frozen to death, and cattle; and the telegraph wires were down and the safe and comfortable country side felt as if it had been in the power of some merciless and furious force of nature from which it could never again feel secure. But the sun came out and the blue-jays came back, and the crows, and the white snow melted, and the farmers went to and fro again along the highways. A new peace and good-will showed itself between the neighbors after their separation, but Mrs. Parkins' good-will outshown the rest. She went to Haybury as soon as the roads were well broken, and brought cousin Faber back with her for a visit, and sent her home again with a loaded wagon of supplies. She called in Lucy Deems and gave her a peck basketful of butternuts on New Year's Day, and told her to come for more when these were gone; and, more than all, one Sunday soon afterward, the minister told his people that he should be away for the next two Sundays. The kindness of a friend was going to put a great blessing within his reach, and he added simply, in a faltering voice, that he hoped all his friends would pray for the restoration to health of his dear boy.

Mrs. Parkins sat in her pew; she had not worn so grim an expression since before Christmas. Nobody could tell what secret pangs these gifts and others like them had cost her, yet she knew that only a right way of living would give her peace of mind. She could no longer live in a mean, narrow world of her own making; she must try to take the world as it is, and make the most of her life.

There were those who laughed and said that her stingy ways were frightened out of her on the night of the storm; but sometimes

one is taught and led slowly to a higher level of existence unconsciously and irresistibly, and the decisive upward step once taken is
seldom retraced. It was not long before Mrs. Deems said to a neighbor cheerfully: "Why, I always knew Mrs. Parkins meant well
enough, but she *didn't know how* to do for other folks; she seemed
kind of scared to use her own money, as if she didn't have any right
to it. Now she is kind of persuaded that she's got the whole responsibility, and just you see how pleased she behaves. She's just a
beginnin' to live; she never heard one word o' the first prayer
yesterday mornin'; I see her beamin' an' smilin' at the minister's boy
from the minute she see him walk up the aisle straight an' well as
anybody."

"She goin' to have one of her cousin Faber's sons come over
and stop awhile, I hear. He got run down workin' in the shoe factory
to Haybury. Perhaps he may take hold and she'll let him take the
farm by-an'-by. There, we musn't expect too much of her," said the
other woman compassionately. "I'm sure 'tis a blessed change as far
as she's got a'ready. Habits'll live sometimes after they're dead.
Folks don't find it so easy to go free of ways they've settled into;
life's truly a warfare, ain't it?"

"It is, so," answered Mrs. Deems, soberly. "There comes Mrs.
Parkins this minute, in the old wagon, and my Lucy settin' up 'long
side of her as pert as Nathan! Now ain't Mrs. Parkins' countenance
got a pleasanter look than it used to wear? Well, the more she does
for others, and the poorer she gets, the richer she seems to feel."

"It's a very unusual circumstance for a woman o' her age to
turn right about in her tracks. It makes us believe that Heaven takes
hold and helps folks," said the neighbor; and they watched the thin,
little woman out of sight along the hilly road with a look of pleased
wonder on their own faces. It was mid-spring, but Mrs. Parkins still
wore her best winter bonnet; as for the old rusty one trimmed with
gray, the minister's little girls found it when the snow drifts melted,
and carefully hid it away to deck the parsonage scarecrow in the
time of corn-planting.

Mary E. Wilkins (Freeman)
(October 31, 1852-March 13, 1930)

Mary E. Wilkins has long been considered one of the greatest writers of the late nineteenth-century United States, both beloved by
general readers and admired by critics and scholars. Although she
has been quoted as saying that she was never driven to write a story
except by the desire for a new French bonnet and although it is true
that writers are exceptionally well paid for Christmas occasional
stories, she must have had a love for Christmas that transcended
such considerations. I have discovered twenty-five of her Christmas
stories so far, and more wait in never-indexed late-nineteenth- and
early-twentieth-century periodicals and newspapers.

The eerie atmosphere in "The Twelfth Guest" is similar to that
of her many ghost stories. First published in the 1889 Christmas
issue of *Harper's New Monthly Magazine*, it was collected two years
later in *A New England Nun*, her second of more than a dozen
volumes of short stories.

The Twelfth Guest

Mary E. Wilkins (Freeman)

"I don't see how it happened, for my part," Mrs. Childs said. "Paulina, you set the table."

"You counted up yesterday how many there'd be, and you said twelve; don't you know you did, mother? So I didn't count to-day. I just put on the plates," said Paulina, smilingly defensive.

Paulina had something of a helpless and gentle look when she smiled. Her mouth was rather large, and the upper jaw full, so the smile seemed hardly under her control. She was quite pretty; her complexion was so delicate and her eyes so pleasant.

"Well, I don't see how I made such a blunder," her mother remarked further, as she went on pouring the tea.

On the opposite side of the table were a plate, a knife and fork, and a little dish of cranberry sauce, with an empty chair before them. There was no guest to fill it.

"It's a sign somebody's comin' that's hungry," Mrs. Childs' brother's wife said, with soft effusiveness which was out of proportion to the words.

The brother was carving the turkey. Caleb Childs, the host, was an old man, and his hands trembled. Moreover, no one, he himself least of all, ever had any confidence in his ability in such directions.

Whenever he helped himself to gravy, his wife watched anxiously lest he should spill it, and he always did. He spilled some to-day. There was a great spot on the beautiful clean table-cloth. Caleb set his cup and saucer over it quickly, with a little clatter because of his unsteady hand. Then he looked at his wife. He hoped she had not seen, but she had.

"You'd better have let John give you the gravy," she said, in a stern aside.

John, rigidly solicitous, bent over the turkey. He carved slowly and laboriously, but everybody had faith in him. The shoulders to which a burden is shifted have the credit of being strong. His wife, in her best black dress, sat smilingly, with her head canted a little to one side. It was a way she had when visiting. Ordinarily she did not assume it at her sister-in-law's house, but this was an extra occasion. Her fine manners spread their wings involuntarily. When she spoke about the sign, the young woman next her sniffed.

"I don't take any stock in signs," said she, with a bluntness which seemed to crash through the other's airiness with such force as to almost hurt itself. She was a distant cousin of Mr. Childs. Her husband and three children were with her.

Mrs. Childs' unmarried sister, Maria Stone, made up the eleven at the table. Maria's gaunt face was unhealthily red about the pointed nose and the high cheek-bones; her eyes looked with a steady sharpness through her spectacles.

"Well, it will be time enough to believe the sign when the twelfth one comes," said she, with a summary air. She had a judicial way of speaking. She had taught school ever since she was sixteen, and now she was sixty. She had just given up teaching. It was to celebrate that, and her final home-coming, that her sister was giving a Christmas dinner instead of a Thanksgiving one this year. The school had been in session during Thanksgiving week.

Maria Stone had scarcely spoken when there was a knock on the outer door, which led directly into the room. They all started. They were a plain, unimaginative company, but for some reason a thrill of superstitious and fantastic expectation ran through them. No one arose. They were all silent for a moment, listening and looking at the empty chair in their midst. Then the knock came again.

"Go to the door, Paulina," said her mother.

The young girl looked at her half fearfully, but she rose at once, and went and opened the door. Everybody stretched around to see. A girl stood on the stone step looking into the room. There she stood, and never said a word. Paulina looked around at her mother, with her innocent, half-involuntary smile.

"Ask her what she wants," said Mrs. Childs.

"What do you want?" repeated Paulina, like a sweet echo.

Still the girl said nothing. A gust of north wind swept into the room. John's wife shivered, then looked around to see if any one had noticed it.

"You must speak up quick an' tell what you want, so we can shut the door; it's cold," said Mrs. Childs.

The girl's small sharp face was sheathed in an old worsted hood; her eyes glared out of it like a frightened cat's. Suddenly she turned to go. She was evidently abashed by the company.

"Don't you want somethin' to eat?" Mrs. Childs asked, speaking up louder.

"It ain't—no matter." She just mumbled it.

"What?"

She would not repeat it. She was quite off the step by this time.

"You make her come in, Paulina," said Maria Stone, suddenly. "She wants something to eat, but she's half scared to death. You talk to her."

"Hadn't you better come in, and have something to eat?" said Paulina, shyly persuasive.

"Tell her she can sit right down here by the stove, where it's warm, and have a good plate of dinner," said Maria.

Paulina fluttered softly down to the stone step. The chilly snow-wind came right in her sweet, rosy face. "You can have a chair by the stove, where it's warm, and a good plate of dinner," said she.

The girl looked at her.

"Won't you come in?" said Paulina, of her own accord, and always smiling.

The stranger made a little hesitating movement forward.

"Bring her in, quick! and shut the door," Maria called out then. And Paulina entered with the girl stealing timidly in her wake.

"Take off your hood an' shawl," Mrs. Childs said, "an' sit down here by the stove, an' I'll give you some dinner." She spoke kindly. She was a warm-hearted woman, but she was rigidly built, and did not relax too quickly into action.

But the cousin, who had been observing, with head alertly raised, interrupted. She cast a mischievous glance at John's wife— the empty chair was between them. "For pity's sake!" cried she; "you ain't goin' to shove her off in the corner? Why, here's this chair. She's the twelfth one. Here's where she ought to sit." There was a mixture of heartiness and sport in the young woman's manner. She pulled the chair back from the table. "Come right over here," said she.

There was a slight flutter of consternation among the guests. They were all narrow-lived country people. Their customs had made deeper grooves in their roads; they were more fastidious and jealous of their social rights than many in higher positions. They eyed this forlorn girl, in her faded and dingy woollens which fluttered airily and showed their pitiful thinness.

Mrs. Childs stood staring at the cousin. She did not think she could be in earnest.

But she was. "Come," said she; "put some turkey in this plate, John."

"Why, it's jest as the rest of you say," Mrs. Childs said, finally, with hesitation. She looked embarrassed and doubtful.

"Say! Why, they say just as I do," the cousin went on. "Why shouldn't they? Come right around here." She tapped the chair impatiently.

The girl looked at Mrs. Childs. "You can go an' sit down there where she says," she said, slowly, in a constrained tone.

"Come," called the cousin again. And the girl took the empty chair, with the guests all smiling stiffly.

Mrs. Childs began filling a plate for the new-comer.

Now that her hood was removed, one could see her face more plainly. It was thin, and of that pale brown tint which exposure gives to some blond skins. Still there was a tangible beauty which showed through all that. Her fair hair stood up softly, with a kind of airy roughness which caught the light. She was apparently about sixteen.

"What's your name?" inquired the school-mistress sister, suddenly.

The girl started. "Christine," she said, after a second.

"What?"

"Christine."

A little thrill ran around the table. The company looked at each other. They were none of them conversant with the Christmas legends, but at that moment the universal sentiment of them seemed to seize upon their fancies. The day, the mysterious appearance of the girl, the name, which was strange to their ears—all startled them, and gave them a vague sense of the supernatural. They, however, struggled against it with their matter-of-fact pride, and threw it off directly.

"Christine what?" Maria asked further.

The girl kept her scared eyes on Maria's face, but she made no reply.

"What's your other name? Why don't you speak?"

Suddenly she rose.

"What are you goin' to do?"

"I'd—ruther—go, I guess."

"What are you goin' for? You ain't had your dinner."

"I—can't tell it," whispered the girl.

"Can't tell your name?"

She shook her head.

"Sit down, and eat your dinner," said Maria.

There was a strong sentiment of disapprobation among the company. But when Christine's food was actually before her, and she seemed to settle down upon it, like a bird, they viewed her with more toleration. She was evidently half starved. Their discovery of that fact gave them at once a fellow-feeling toward her on this feast-day, and a complacent sense of their own benevolence.

As the dinner progressed the spirits of the party appeared to rise, and a certain jollity which was almost hilarity prevailed. Beyond providing the strange guest plentifully with food, they seemed to ignore her entirely. Still nothing was more certain than the fact that they did not. Every outburst of merriment was yielded to with the most thorough sense of her prsence, which appeared in some subtle way to excite it. It was as if this forlorn twelfth guest were the foreign element needed to produce a state of nervous effervescence in those staid, decorous people who surrounded her. This taste of mystery and unusualness, once fairly admitted, although reluctantly, to their unaccustomed palates, served them as wine with their Christmas dinner.

It was late in the afternoon when they arose from the table. Christine went directly for her hood and shawl, and put them on. The others, talking among themselves, were stealthily observant of her. Christine began opening the door.

"Are you goin' home now?" asked Mrs. Childs.

"No, marm."

"Why not?"

"I ain't got any."

"Where did you come from?"

The girl looked at her. Then she unlatched the door.

"Stop!" Mrs. Childs cried, sharply. "What are you goin' for? Why don't you answer?"

She stood still, but did not speak.

"Well, shut the door up, an' wait a minute," said Mrs. Childs.

She stood close to a window, and she stared out scrutinizingly. There was no house in sight. First came a great yard, then wide stretches of fields; a desolate gray road curved around them on the left. The sky was covered with still, low clouds; the sun had not shone out that day. The ground was all bare and rigid. Out in the yard some gray hens were huddled together in little groups for warmth; their red combs showed out. Two crows flew up, away over on the edge of the field.

"It's goin' to snow," said Mrs. Childs.

"I'm afeard it is," said Caleb, looking at the girl. He gave a sort of silent sob, and brushed some tears out of his old eyes with the back of his hands.

"See here a minute, Maria," said Mrs. Childs.

The two women whispered together; then Maria stepped in front of the girl, and stood, tall and stiff and impressive.

"Now, see here," said she; "we want you to speak up and tell us your other name, and where you came from, and not keep us waiting any longer."

"I—*can't*." They guessed what she said from the motion of her head. She opened the door entirely then and stepped out.

Suddenly Maria made one stride forward and seized her by her shoulders, which felt like knife-blades through the thin clothes. "Well," said she, "we've been fussing long enough; we've got all these dishes to clear away. It's bitter cold, and it's going to snow, and you ain't going out of this house one step to-night, no matter what you are. You'd ought to tell us who you are, and it ain't many folks that would keep you if you wouldn't; but we ain't goin' to have you found dead in the road, for our own credit. It ain't on your account. Now you just take those things off again, and go and sit down in that chair."

Christine sat in the chair. Her pointed chin dipped down on her neck, whose poor little muscles showed above her dress, which sagged away from it. She never looked up. The women cleared off the table, and cast curious glances at her.

After the dishes were washed and put away, the company were all assembled in the sitting-room for an hour or so; then they went home. The cousin, passing through the kitchen to join her husband, who was waiting with his team at the door, ran hastily up to Christine.

"You stop at my house when you go to-morrow morning," said she. "Mrs. Childs will tell you where 'tis—half a mile below here."

When the company were all gone, Mrs. Childs called Christine into the sitting-room. "You'd better come in here and sit now," said she. "I'm goin' to let the kitchen fire go down; I ain't goin' to get another regular meal; I'm jest goin' to make a cup of tea on the sittin'-room stove by-an'-by."

The sitting-room was warm, and restrainedly comfortable with its ordinary village furnishings—its ingrain carpet, its little peaked clock on a corner of the high black shelf, its red-covered card-table, which had stood in the same spot for forty years. There was a little newspaper-covered stand, with some plants on it, before a window. There was one red geranium in blossom.

Paulina was going out that evening. Soon after the company went she commenced to get ready, and her mother and aunt seemed to be helping her. Christine was alone in the sitting-room for the greater part of an hour.

Finally the three women came in, and Paulina stood before the sitting-room glass for a last look at herself. She had on her best red cashmere, with some white lace around her throat. She had a red geranium flower with some leaves in her hair. Paulina's brown hair, which was rather thin, was very silky. It was apt to part into little soft strands on her forehead. She wore it brushed smoothly back. Her mother would not allow her to curl it.

The two older women stood looking at her. "Don't you think she looks nice, Christine?" Mrs. Childs asked, in a sudden overflow of love and pride, which led her to ask sympathy from even this forlorn source.

"Yes, marm." Christine regarded Paulina, in her red cashmere and geranium flower, with sharp, solemn eyes. When she really looked at any one, her gaze was as unflinching as that of a child.

There was a sudden roll of wheels in the yard.

"Willard's come!" said Mrs. Childs. "Run to the door an' tell him you'll be right out, Paulina, an' I'll get your things ready."

After Paulina had been helped into her coat and hood, and the wheels had bowled out of the yard with a quick dash, the mother turned to Christine.

"My daughter's gone to a Christmas tree over to the church," said she. "That was Willard Morris that came for her. He's a real nice young man that lives about a mile from here."

Mrs. Childs' tone was at once gently patronizing and elated.

When Christine was shown to a little back bedroom that night, nobody dreamed how many times she was to occupy it. Maria and Mrs. Childs, who after the door was closed set a table against it softly and erected a tiltlish pyramid of milkpans, to serve as an alarm signal in case the strange guest should try to leave her room with evil intentions, were fully convinced that she would depart early on the following morning.

"I dun know but I've run an awful risk keeping her," Mrs. Childs said. "I don't like her not tellin' where she come from.

Nobody knows but she belongs to a gang of burglars, an' they've kind of sent her on ahead to spy out things an' unlock the doors for 'em."

"I know it," said Maria. "I wouldn't have had her stay for a thousand dollars if it hadn't looked so much like snow. Well, I'll get up an' start her off early in the morning."

But Maria Stone could not carry out this resolution. The next morning she was ill with a sudden and severe attack of erysipelas. Moreover, there was a hard snow-storm, the worst of the season; it would have been barbarous to have turned the girl out-of-doors on such a morning. Moreover, she developed an unexpected capacity for usefulness. She assisted Pauline about the housework with timid alacrity, and Mrs. Childs could devote all her time to her sister.

"She takes right hold as if she was used to it," she told Maria. "I'd rather keep her a while than not, if I only knew a little more about her."

"I don't believe but what I could get it out of her after a while if I tried," said Maria, with her magisterial air, which illness could not subdue.

However, even Maria, with all her well-fostered imperiousness, had no effect on the girl's resolution; she continued as much of a mystery as ever. Still the days went on, then the weeks and months, and she remained in the Childs family.

None of them could tell exactly how it had been brought about. The most definite course seemed to be that her arrival had apparently been the signal for a general decline of health in the family. Maria had hardly recovered when Caleb Childs was laid up with the rheumatism; then Mrs. Childs had a long spell of exhaustion from overwork in nursing. Christine proved exceedingly useful in these emergencies. Their need of her appeared to be the dominant, and only outwardly evident, reason for her stay; still there was a deeper one which they themselves only faintly realized—this poor young girl, who was rendered almost repulsive to these honest downright folk by her persistent cloak of mystery, had somehow, in a very short time, melted herself, as it were, into their own lives. Christine asleep of a night in her little back bedroom, Christine of a day stepping about the house in one of Paulina's old

81

gowns, became a part of their existence, and a part which was not far from the nature of a sweetness to their senses.

She still retained her mild shyness of manner, and rarely spoke unless spoken to. Now that she was warmly sheltered and well fed, her beauty became evident. She grew prettier every day. Her cheeks became softly dimpled; her hair turned golden. Her language was rude and illiterate, but its very uncouthness had about it something of a soft grace.

She was really prettier than Paulina.

The two girls were much together, but could hardly be said to be intimate. There were few confidences between them, and confidences are essential for the intimacy of young girls.

Willard Morris came regularly twice a week to see Paulina, and everybody spoke of them as engaged to each other.

Along in August Mrs. Childs drove over to town one afternoon and bought a piece of cotton cloth and a little embroidery and lace. Then some fine sewing went on, but with no comment in the household. Mrs. Childs had simply said, "I guess we may as well get a few things made up for you, Paulina, you're getting rather short." And Paulina had sewed all day long, with a gentle industry, when the work was ready.

There was a report that the marriage was to take place on Thanksgiving Day. But about the first of October Willard Morris stopped going to the Childs house. There was no explanation. He simply did not come as usual on Sunday night, nor the following Wednesday, nor the next Sunday. Paulina kindled her little parlor fire, whose sticks she had laid with maiden preciseness; she arrayed herself in her best gown and ribbons. When at nine o'clock Willard had not come, she blew out the parlor lamp, shut up the parlor stove, and went to bed. Nothing was said before her, but there was much talk and surmise between Mrs. Childs and Maria, and a good deal of it went on before Christine.

It was a little while after the affair of Cyrus Morris's note, and they wondered if it could have anything to do with that. Cyrus Morris was Willard's uncle, and the note affair had occasioned much distress in the Childs family for a month back. The note was for twenty-five hundred dollars, and Cyrus Morris had given it to Caleb

Childs. The time, which was two years, had expired on the first of September, and then Caleb could not find the note.

He had kept it in his old-fashioned desk, which stood in one corner of the kitchen. He searched there a day and half a night, pulling all the soiled, creasy old papers out of the drawers and pigeon-holes before he would answer his wife's inquiries as to what he had lost.

Finally he broke down and told. "I've lost that note of Morris's," said he. "I dun know what I'm goin' to do."

He stood looking gloomily at the desk with its piles of papers. His rough old chin dropped down on his breast.

The women were all in the kitchen, and they stopped and stared.

"Why, father," said his wife, "where have you put it?"

"I put it here in this top drawer, and it ain't there."

"Let *me* look," said Maria, in a confident tone. But even Maria's energetic and self-assured researches failed. "Well, it ain't here," said she. "I don't know what you've done with it."

"I don't believe you put it in that drawer, father," said his wife.

"It was in there two weeks ago. I see it."

"Then you took it out afterwards."

"I ain't laid hands on't."

"You must have; it couldn't have gone off without hands. You know you're kind of forgetful, father."

"I guess I know when I've took a paper out of a drawer. I know a leetle somethin' yit."

"Well, I don't suppose there'll be any trouble about it, will there?" said Mrs. Childs. "Of course he knows he give the note, an' had the money."

"I dun know as there'll be any trouble, but I'd ruther give a hundred dollar than had it happen."

After dinner Caleb shaved, put on his other coat and hat, and trudged soberly up the road to Cyrus Morris's. Cyrus Morris was an elderly man, who had quite a local reputation for wealth and business shrewdness. Caleb, who was lowly-natured and easily impressed by another's importance, always made a call upon him quite a formal affair, and shaved and dressed up.

He was absent about an hour to-day. When he returned he went into the sitting-room, where the women sat with their sewing. He dropped into a chair, and looked straight ahead, with his forehead knitted.

The women dropped their work and looked at him, and then at each other.

"What did he say, father?" Mrs. Childs asked at length.

"Say! He's a rascal, that's what he is, an' I'll tell him so, too."

"Ain't he goin' to pay it?"

"No, he ain't."

"Why, father, I don't believe it! You didn't get hold of it straight," said his wife.

"You'll see."

"Why, what did he say?"

"He didn't say anything."

"Doesn't he remember he had the money and gave the note, and has been paying interest on it?" queried Maria.

"He jest laughed, an' said 'twa'n't accordin' to law to pay unless I showed the note an' give it up to him. He said he couldn't be sure but I'd want him to pay it over ag'in. *I know where that note is!*"

Caleb's voice had deep meaning in it. The women stared at him.

"Where?"

"*It's in Cyrus Morris's desk—that's where it is.*"

"Why, father, you're crazy!"

"No, I ain't crazy, nuther. I know what I'm talkin' about. I—"

"It's just where you put it," interrupted Maria, taking up her sewing with a switch; "and I wouldn't lay the blame onto anybody else."

"You'd ought to ha' looked out for a paper like that," said his wife. "I guess I should if it had been me. If you've gone an' lost all that money through your carelessness, you've done it, that's all I've got to say. I don't see what we're goin' to do."

Caleb bent forward and fixed his eyes upon the women. He held up his shaking hand impressively. "*If* you'll stop talkin' just a minute," said he, "I'll tell you what I was goin' to. Now I'd like to know just one thing: *Wa'n't Cyrus Morris alone in that kitchen as* much as fifteen minutes a week ago to-day? Didn't you leave him there while you went to look arter me? Wa'n't the key in the desk? Answer me *that*!"

His wife looked at him with cold surprise and severity. "I wouldn't talk in any such way as that if I was you, father," said she. "It don't show a Christian spirit. It's jest layin' the blame of your own carelessness onto somebody else. You're all the one that's to blame. An' when it comes to it, you'd never ought to let Cyrus Morris have the money anyhow. I could have told you better. I knew what kind of a man he was."

"He's a rascal," said Caleb, catching eagerly at the first note of foreign condemnation in his wife's words. "He'd ought to be put in state's-prison. I don't think much of his relations nuther. I don't want nothin' to do with 'em, an' I don't want none of my folks to."

Paulina's soft cheeks flushed. Then she suddenly spoke out as she had never spoken in her life.

"It doesn't make it out because he's a bad man that his relations are," said she. "You haven't any right to speak so, father. And I guess you won't stop me having anything to do with them, if you want to."

She was all pink and trembling. Suddenly she burst out crying, and ran out of the room.

"You'd ought to be ashamed of yourself, father," exclaimed Mrs. Childs.

"I didn't think of her takin' on it so," muttered Caleb, humbly. "I didn't mean nothin.'"

Caleb did not seem like himself through the following days. His simple old face took on an expression of strained thought, which made it look strange. He was tottering on a height of mental effort and worry which was almost above the breathing capacity of his innocent and placid nature. Many a night he rose, lighted a candle, and tremulously fumbled over his desk until morning, in the vain hope of finding the missing note.

One night, while he was so searching, some one touched him softly on the arm.

He jumped and turned. It was Christine. She had stolen in silently.

"Oh, it's you!" said he.

"Ain't you found it?"

"Found it? No; an' I sha'n't, nuther." He turned away from her and pulled out another drawer. The girl stood watching him wistfully. "It was a big yellow paper," the old man went on—"a big yellow paper, an' I'd wrote on the back on't, 'Cyrus Morris's note.' An' the interest he'd paid was set down on the back on't, too."

"It's too bad you can't find it," said she.

"It ain't no use lookin'; it ain't here, an' that's the hull on't. It's in *his* desk. I ain't got no more doubt on't than nothin' at all."

"Where—does he keep his desk?"

"In his kitchen; it's jest like this one."

"Would this key open it?"

"I dun know but 'twould. But it ain't no use. I s'pose I'll have to lose it." Caleb sobbed silently and wiped his eyes.

A few days later he came, all breathless, into the sitting-room. He could hardly speak; but he held out a folded yellow paper, which fluttered and blew in his unsteady hand like a yellow maple-leaf in an autumn gale.

"Look-a-here!" he gasped—"look-a-here!"

"Why, for goodness' sake, what's the matter?" cried Maria. She and Mrs. Childs and Paulina were there, sewing peacefully.

"Jest look-a-*here*!"

"Why, for mercy's sake, what is it, father? Are you crazy?"

"Its—the *note*!"

"What note? Don't get so excited, father."

"Cyrus Morris's note. That's what note 'tis. Look-a-here!"

The women all arose and pressed around him, to look at it.

"Where *did* you find it, father?" asked his wife, who was quite pale.

"I suppose it was just where you put it," broke in Maria, with sarcastic emphasis.

"No, it wa'n't. No, it wa'n't, nuther. Don't you go to crowin' too quick, Maria. That paper was just where I told you 'twas. What do you think of that, hey?"

"Oh, father, you didn't!"

"It was layin' right there in his desk. That's where 'twas. Jest where I knew—"

"Father, you didn't go over there an' take it!"

The three women stared at him with dilated eyes.

"No, I didn't."

"Who did?"

The old man jerked his head towards the kitchen door. "She."

"Who?"

"Christiny."

"How did she get it?" asked Maria, in her magisterial manner, which no astonishment could agitate.

"She saw Cyrus and Mis' Morris ride past, an' then she run over there, an' she got in through the window an' got it; that's how." Caleb braced himself like a stubborn child, in case any exception were taken to it all.

"It beats everything I ever heard," said Mrs. Childs, faintly.

"Next time you'll believe what I tell you!" said Caleb.

The whole family were in a state of delight over the recovery of the note; still Christine got rather hesitating gratitude. She was sharply questioned, and rather reproved than otherwise.

This theft, which could hardly be called a theft, aroused the old distrust of her.

"It served him just right, and it wasn't stealing, because it didn't belong to him; and I don't know what you would have done if she hadn't taken it," said Maria; "but, for all that, it went all over me."

"So it did over me," said her sister. "I felt just as you did, an' I felt as if it was real ungrateful too, when the poor child did it just for us."

But there were no such misgivings for poor Caleb, with his money, and his triumph over iniquitous Cyrus Morris. He was wholly and unquestioningly grateful.

"It was a blessed day when we took that little girl in," he told his wife.

"I hope it'll prove so," said she.

Paulina took her lover's desertion quietly. She had just as many soft smiles for every one; there was no alteration in her gentle, obliging ways. Still her mother used to listen at her door, and she knew that she cried instead of sleeping many a night. She was not able to eat much, either, although she tried to with pleasant willingness when her mother urged her.

After a while she was plainly grown thin, and her pretty color had faded. Her mother could not keep her eyes from her.

"Sometimes I think I'll go an' ask Willard myself what this kind of work means," she broke out with an abashed abruptness one afternoon. She and Paulina happened to be alone in the sitting-room.

"You'll kill me if you do, mother," said Paulina. Then she began to cry.

"Well, I won't do anything you don't want me to, of course," said her mother. She pretended not to see that Paulina was crying.

Willard had stopped coming about the first of October; the time wore on until it was the first of December, and he had not once been to the house, and Paulina had not exchanged a word with him in the meantime.

One night she had a fainting-spell. She fell heavily while crossing the sitting-room floor. They got her on to the lounge, and she soon revived; but her mother had lost all control of herself. She came out into the kitchen and paced the floor.

"Oh, my darlin'!" she wailed. "She's goin' to die. What shall I do? All the child I've got in the world. An' he's killed her! That *scamp*! I wish I could get my hands on him. Oh, Paulina, Paulina, to think it should come to this!"

Christine was in the room, and she listened with eyes dilated and lips parted. She was afraid that shrill wail would reach Paulina in the next room.

"She'll hear you," she said, finally.

Mrs. Childs grew quieter at that, and presently Maria called her into the sitting-room.

Christine stood thinking for a moment. Then she got her hood and shawl, put on her rubbers, and went out. She shut the door softly, so nobody should hear. When she stepped forth she plunged knee-deep into snow. It was snowing hard, as it had been all day. It was a cold storm, too; the wind was bitter. Christine waded out of the yard and down the street. She was so small and light that she staggered when she tried to step firmly in some tracks ahead of her. There was a full moon behind the clouds, and there was a soft white light in spite of the storm. Christine kept on down the street, in the direction of Willard Morris's house. It was a mile distant. Once in a while she stopped and turned herself about, that the terrible wind might smite her back instead of her face. When she reached the house she waded painfully through the yard to the side-door and knocked. Pretty soon it opened, and Willard stood there in the entry, with a lamp in his hand.

"Good-evening," said he, doubtfully, peering out.

"Good-evenin'." The light shone on Christine's face. The snow clung to her soft hair, so it was quite white. Her cheeks had a deep, soft color, like roses; her blue eyes blinked a little in the lamp-light, but seemed rather to flicker like jewels or stars. She panted softly through her parted lips. She stood there, with the snow-flakes driving in light past her, and "She looks like an angel," came swiftly into Willard Morris's head before he spoke.

"Oh, it's you," said he.

Christine nodded.

Then they stood waiting. "Why, won't you come in?" said Willard, finally, with an awkward blush. "I declare I never thought. I ain't very polite."

She shook her head. "No, thank you," said she.

"Did—you want to see mother?"

"No."

The young man stared at her in increasing perplexity. His own fair, handsome young face got more and more flushed. His forehead wrinkled. "Was there anything you wanted?"

"No, I guess not," Christine replied, with a slow softness.

Willard shifted the lamp into his other hand and sighed. "It's a pretty hard storm," he remarked, with an air of forced patience.

"Yes."

"Didn't you find it terrible hard walking?"

"Some."

Willard was silent again. "See here, they're all well down at your house, ain't they?" said he, finally. A look of anxious interest had sprung into his eyes. He had begun to take alarm.

"I guess so."

Suddenly he spoke out impetuously. "Say, Christine, I don't know what you came here for; you can tell me afterwards. I don't know what you'll think of me, but—Well, I want to know something. Say—well, I haven't been 'round for quite a while. You don't—suppose—they've cared much, any of them?"

"I don't know."

"Well, I don't suppose you do, but—you might have noticed. Say, Christine, you don't think she—you know whom I mean—cared anything about my coming, do you?"

"I don't know," she said again, softly, with her eyes fixed warily on his face.

"Well, I guess she didn't; she wouldn't have said what she did if she had."

Christine's eyes gave a sudden gleam. "What did she say?"

"Said she wouldn't have anything more to do with me," said the young man, bitterly. "She was afraid I would be up to just such tricks as my uncle was, trying to cheat her father. That was too much for me. I wasn't going to stand that from any girl." He shook his head angrily.

"She didn't say it."

"Yes, she did; her own father told my uncle so. Mother was in the next room and heard it."

"No, she didn't say it," the girl repeated.

"How do you know?"

"I heard her say something different." Christine told him.

"I'm going right up there," cried he, when he heard that. "Wait a minute, and I'll go along with you."

"I dun know as you'd better—to-night," Christine said, looking out towards the road, evasively. "She—ain't been very well to-night."

"Who? Paulina? What's the matter?"

"She had a faintin'-spell jest before I came out," answered Christine, with stiff gravity.

"Oh! Is she real sick?"

"She was some better."

"Don't you suppose I could see her just a few minutes? I wouldn't stay to tire her," said the young man, eagerly.

"I dun know."

"I must, anyhow."

Christine fixed her eyes on his with a solemn sharpness. "What makes you want to?"

"What makes me want to? Why, I'd give ten years to see her five minutes."

"Well, mebbe you could come over a few minutes."

"Wait a minute," cried Willard. "I'll get my hat."

"I'd better go first, I guess. The parlor fire'll be to light."

"Then had I better wait?"

"I guess so."

"Then I'll be along in about an hour. Say, you haven't said what you wanted."

Christine was off the step. "It ain't any matter," murmured she.

"Say—she didn't send you?"

"No, she didn't."

"I didn't mean that. I didn't suppose she did," said Willard, with an abashed air. "What did you want, Christine?"

"There's somethin' I want you to promise," said she, suddenly.

"What's that?"

"Don't you say anything about Mr. Childs."

"Why, how can I help it?"

"He's an old man, an' he was so worked up he didn't know what he was sayin'. They'll all scold him. Don't say anything."

"Well, I won't say anything. I don't know what I'm going to tell her, though."

Christine turned to go.

"You didn't say what 'twas you wanted," called Willard again.

But she made no reply. She was pushing through the deep snow out of the yard.

It was quite early yet, only a few minutes after seven. It was eight when she reached home. She entered the house without any one seeing her. She pulled off her snowy things, and went into the sitting-room.

Paulina was alone there. She was lying on the lounge. She was very pale, but she looked up and smiled when Christine entered.

Christine brought the fresh out-door air with her. Paulina noticed it. "Where have you been?" whispered she.

Then Christine bent over her, and talked fast in a low tone.

Presently Paulina raised herself and sat up. "To-night?" cried she, in an eager whisper. Her cheeks grew red.

"Yes; I'll go make the parlor fire."

"It's all ready to light." Suddenly Paulina threw her arms around Christine and kissed her. Both girls blushed.

"I don't think I said one thing to him that you wouldn't have wanted me to," said Christine.

"You didn't—ask him to come?"

"No, I didn't, honest."

When Mrs. Childs entered, a few minutes later, she found her daughter standing before the glass.

"Why, Paulina!" cried she.

"I feel a good deal better, mother," said Paulina.

"Ain't you goin' to bed?"

"I guess I won't quite yet."

"I've got it all ready for you. I thought you wouldn't feel like sittin' up."

"I guess I will; a little while."

Soon the door-bell rang with a sharp peal. Everybody jumped— Paulina rose and went to the door.

Mrs. Childs and Maria, listening, heard Willard's familiar voice, then the opening of the parlor door.

"It's *him!*" gasped Mrs. Childs. She and Maria looked at each other.

It was about two hours before the soft murmur of voices in the parlor ceased, the outer door closed with a thud, and Paulina came into the room. She was blushing and smiling, but she could not look in any one's face at first.

"Well," said her mother, "who was it?"

"Willard. It's all right."

It was not long before the fine sewing was brought out again, and presently two silk dresses were bought for Paulina. It was known about that she was to be married on Christmas Day. Christine assisted in the preparation. All the family called to mind afterwards the obedience so ready as to be loving which she yielded to their biddings during those few hurried weeks. She sewed, she made cake, she ran of errands, she wearied herself joyfully for the happiness of this other young girl.

About a week before the wedding, Christine, saying good-night when about to retire one evening, behaved strangely. They remembered it afterwards. She went up to Paulina and kissed her when saying good-night. It was something which she had never before done. Then she stood in the door, looking at them all. There was a sad, almost a solemn, expression on her fair girlish face.

"Why, what's the matter?" said Maria.

"Nothin'," said Christine. "Good-night."

That was the last time they ever saw her. The next morning Mrs. Childs, going to call her, found her room vacant. There was a great alarm. When they did not find her in the house nor the neighborhood, people were aroused, and there was a search instigated. It was prosecuted eagerly, but to no purpose. Paulina's wedding evening came, and Christine was still missing.

Paulina had been married, and was standing beside her husband, in the midst of the chattering guests, when Caleb stole out of the room. He opened the north door, and stood looking out over the dusky fields. "Christiny!" he called, "Christiny!"

Presently he looked up at the deep sky, full of stars, and called again—"Christiny! Christiny!" But there was no answer save in light. When Christine stood in the sitting-room door and said good-night, her friends had their last sight and sound of her. Their Twelfth Guest had departed from their hospitality forever.

Willa Cather
(December 7, 1873-April 24, 1947)

"The Burglar's Xmas" was first published under the pseudonym "Elizabeth L. Seymour" in the December 1896 issue of *Home Monthly*, the family magazine Cather managed and edited in Pittsburgh that year. It was not reprinted until 1965 when it was included in Cather's *Collected Short Fiction: 1892–1912*.

This allegorical retelling of the parable of the prodigal son from the perspective of his mother, rather than his father, is a brilliant portrayal of the mood of nineteenth-century Christian women involved in reclaiming the spiritual and theological world for women and women's values. It shares the attitude towards spirituality that prompted great numbers of women to reject infant damnation and to create a new vision of the deity as a god of love. It is "motherly" rather than "fatherly" love that is celebrated; it is the salvation by female rather than male figures that is heralded.

The Burglar's Christmas

Willa Cather

Two very shabby looking young men stood at the corner of Prairie Avenue and Eightieth Street, looking despondently at the carriages that whirled by. It was Christmas Eve, and the streets were full of vehicles; florists' wagons, grocers' carts and carriages. The streets were in that half-liquid, half-congealed condition peculiar to the streets of Chicago at that season of the year. The swift wheels that spun by sometimes threw the slush of mud and snow over the two young men who were talking on the corner.

"Well," remarked the elder of the two, "I guess we are at our rope's end, sure enough. How do you feel?"

"Pretty shaky. The wind's sharp tonight. If I had had anything to eat I mightn't mind it so much. There is simply no show. I'm sick of the whole business. Looks like there's nothing for it but the lake."

"O, nonsense, I thought you had more grit. Got anything left you can hock?"

"Nothing but my beard, and I am afraid they wouldn't find it worth a pawn ticket," said the younger man ruefully, rubbing the week's growth of stubble on his face.

"Got any folks anywhere? Now's your time to strike 'em if you have."

"Never mind if I have, they're out of the question."

"Well, you'll be out of it before many hours if you don't make a move of some sort. A man's got to eat. See here, I am going down to Longtin's saloon. I used to play the banjo in there with a couple of coons, and I'll bone him for some of his free-lunch stuff. You'd better come along, perhaps they'll fill an order for two."

"How far down is it?"

"Well, it's clear downtown, of course, 'way down on Michigan Avenue."

"Thanks, I guess I'll loaf around here. I don't feel equal to the walk, and the cars—well, the cars are crowded." His features drew themselves into what might have been a smile under happier circumstances.

"No, you never did like street cars, you're too aristocratic. See here, Crawford, I don't like leaving you here. You ain't good company for yourself tonight."

"Crawford? O, yes, that's the last one. There have been so many I forget them."

"Have you got a real name, anyway?"

"O, yes, but it's one of the ones I've forgotten. Don't you worry about me. You go along and get your free lunch. I think I had a row in Longtin's place once. I'd better not show myself there again." As he spoke the young man nodded and turned slowly up the avenue.

He was miserable enough to want to be quite alone. Even the crowd that jostled by him annoyed him. He wanted to think about himself. He had avoided this final reckoning with himself for a year now. He had laughed it off and drunk it off. But now, when all those artificial devices which are employed to turn our thoughts into other channels and shield us from ourselves had failed him, it must come. Hunger is a powerful incentive to introspection.

It is a tragic hour, that hour when we are finally driven to reckon with ourselves, when every avenue of mental distraction has been cut off and our own life and all its ineffaceable failures closes about us like the walls of that old torture chamber of the Inquisition. Tonight, as this man stood stranded in the streets of the city, his hour came. It was not the first time he had been hungry and desperate and alone. But always before there had been some out-look, some chance ahead, some pleasure yet untasted that seemed worth the effort, some face that he fancied was, or would be, dear. But it was not so tonight. The unyielding conviction was upon him that he had failed in everything, had outlived everything. It had been near him for a long time, that Pale Spectre. He had caught its shadow at the bottom of his glass many a time, at the head of his bed when he was sleepless at night, in the twilight shadows when some great sunset broke upon him. It had made life hateful to him when he awoke in the morning before now. But now it settled slowly over him, like night, the endless Northern nights that bid the sun a long farewell. It rose up before him like granite. From this brilliant city with its glad bustle of Yuletide he was shut off as completely as though he were a creature of another species. His days seemed numbered and done, sealed over like the little coral cells at the bottom of the sea. Involuntarily he drew that cold air through his lungs slowly, as though he were tasting it for the last time.

Yet he was but four and twenty, this man—he looked even younger—and he had a father some place down East who had been very proud of him once. Well, he had taken his life into his own hands, and this was what he had made of it. That was all there was to be said. He could remember the hopeful things they used to say about him at college in the old days, before he had cut away and begun to live by his wits, and he found courage to smile at them now. They had read him wrongly. He knew now that he never had the essentials of success, only the superficial agility that is often mistaken for it. He was tow without the tinder, and he had burnt himself out at other people's fires. He had helped other people to make it win, but he himself—he had never touched an enterprise that had not failed eventually. Or, if it survived his connection with it, it left him behind.

His last venture had been with some ten-cent specialty com-pany, a little lower than all the others, that had gone to pieces in Buffalo, and he had worked his way to Chicago by boat. When the boat made up its crew for the outward voyage, he was dispensed with as usual. He was used to that. The reason for it? O, there are so many reasons for failure! His was a very common one.

As he stood there in the wet under the street light he drew up his reckoning with the world and decided that it had treated him as well as he deserved. He had overdrawn his account once too often. There had been a day when he thought otherwise; when he had said he was unjustly handled, that his failure was merely the lack of proper adjustment between himself and other men, that some day he would be recognized and it would all come right. But he knew better than that now, and he was still man enough to bear no grudge against any one—man or woman.

Tonight was his birthday, too. There seemed something particularly amusing in that. He turned up a limp little coat collar to try to keep a little of the wet chill from his throat, and instinctively began to remember all the birthday parties he used to have. He was so cold and empty that his mind seemed unable to grapple with any serious question. He kept thinking about gingerbread and frosted cakes like a child. He could remember the splendid birthday parties his mother used to give him, when all the other little boys in the block came in their Sunday clothes and creaking shoes, with their ears still red from their mother's towel, and the pink and white birthday cake, and the stuffed olives and all the dishes of which he had been particularly fond, and how he would eat and eat and then go to bed and dream of Santa Claus. And in the morning he would awaken and eat again, until by night the family doctor arrived with his castor oil, and poor William used to dolefully say that it was altogether too much to have your birthday and Christmas all at once. He could remember, too, the royal birthday suppers he had given at college, and the stag dinners, and the toasts, and the music, and the good fellows who had wished him happiness and really meant what they said.

And since then there were other birthday suppers that he could not remember so clearly; the memory of them was heavy and flat, like cigarette smoke that has been shut in a room all night, like champagne that has been a day opened, a song that has been too often sung, an acute sensation that has been overstrained. They seemed tawdry and garish, discordant to him now. He rather wished he could forget them altogether.

Whichever way his mind now turned there was one thought that it could not escape, and that was the idea of food. He caught the scent of a cigar suddenly, and felt a sharp pain in the pit of his abdomen and a sudden moisture in his mouth. His cold hands clenched angrily, and for a moment he felt that bitter hatred of wealth, of ease, of everything that is well fed and well housed that is common to starving men. At any rate he had a right to eat! He had demanded great things from the world once: fame and wealth and admiration. Now it was simply bread—and he would have it! He looked about him quickly and felt the blood begin to stir in his veins. In all his straits he had never stolen anything, his tastes were above it. But tonight there would be no tomorrow. He was amused at the way in which the idea excited him. Was it possible there was yet one more experience that would distract him, one thing that had power to excite his jaded interest? Good! he had failed at everything else, now he would see what his chances would be as a common thief. It would be amusing to watch the beautiful consistency of his destiny work itself out even in that role. It would be interesting to add another study to his gallery of futile attempts, and then label them all: "the failure as a journalist," "the failure as a lecturer," "the failure as a business man," "the failure as a thief," and so on, like the titles under the pictures of the Dance of Death. It was time that Childe Roland came to the dark tower.

A girl hastened by him with her arms full of packages. She walked quickly and nervously, keeping well within the shadow, as if she were not accustomed to carrying bundles and did not care to meet any of her friends. As she crossed the muddy street, she made an effort to lift her skirt a little, and as she did so one of the packages slipped unnoticed from beneath her arm. He caught it up and overtook her. "Excuse me, but I think you dropped something."

She started, "O, yes, thank you, I would rather have lost any-thing than that."

The young man turned angrily upon himself. The package must have contained something of value. Why had he not kept it? Was this the sort of thief he would make? He ground his teeth together. There is nothing more maddening than to have morally consented to crime and then lack the nerve force to carry it out.

A carriage drove up to the house before which he stood. Several richly dressed women alighted and went in. It was a new house, and must have been built since he was in Chicago last. The front door was open and he could see down the hallway and up the staircase. The servant had left the door and gone with the guests. The first floor was brilliantly lighted, but the windows upstairs were dark. It looked very easy, just to slip upstairs to the darkened chambers where the jewels and trinkets of the fashionable occupants were kept.

Still burning with impatience against himself he entered quickly. Instinctively he removed his mud-stained hat as he passed quickly and quietly up the stair case. It struck him as being a rather superfluous courtesy in a burglar, but he had done it before he had thought. His way was clear enough, he met no one on the stairway or in the upper hall. The gas was lit in the upper hall. He passed the first chamber door through sheer cowardice. The second he entered quickly, thinking of something else lest his courage should fail him, and closed the door behind him. The light from the hall shone into the room through the transom. The apartment was furnished richly enough to justify his expectations. He went at once to the dressing case. A number of rings and small trinkets lay in a silver tray. These he put hastily in his pocket. He opened the upper drawer and found, as he expected, several leather cases. In the first he opened was a lady's watch, in the second a pair of old-fashioned bracelets; he seemed to dimly remember having seen bracelets like them before, somewhere. The third case was heavier, the spring was much worn, and it opened easily. It held a cup of some kind. He held it up to the light and then his strained nerves gave way and he uttered a sharp exclamation. It was the silver mug he used to drink from when he was a little boy.

The door opened, and a woman stood in the doorway facing him. She was a tall woman, with white hair, in evening dress. The light from the hall streamed in upon him, but she was not afraid. She stood looking at him a moment, then she threw out her hand and went quickly toward him.

"Willie, Willie! Is it you?"

He struggled to loose her arms from him, to keep her lips from his cheek. "Mother—you must not! You do not understand! O, my God, this is worst of all!" Hunger, weakness, cold, shame, all came back to him, and shook his self-control completely. Physically he was too weak to stand a shock like this. Why could it not have been an ordinary discovery, arrest, the station house and all the rest of it. Anything but this! A hard dry sob broke from him. Again he strove to disengage himself.

"Who is it says I shall not kiss my son? O, my boy, we have waited so long for this! You have been so long in coming, even I almost gave you up."

Her lips upon his cheek burnt him like fire. He put his hand to his throat, and spoke thickly and incoherently: "You do not understand. I did not know you were here. I came here to rob—it is the first time—I swear it—but I am a common thief. My pockets are full of your jewels now. Can't you hear me? I am a common thief!"

"Hush, my boy, those are ugly words. How could you rob your own house? How could you take what is your own? They are all yours, my son, as wholly yours as my great love—and you can't doubt that, Will, do you?"

That soft voice, the warmth and fragrance of her person stole through his chill, empty veins like a gentle stimulant. He felt as though all his strength were leaving him and even consciousness. He held fast to her and bowed his head on her strong shoulder, and groaned aloud.

"O, mother, life is hard, hard!"

She said nothing, but held him closer. And O, the strength of those white arms that held him! O, the assurance of safety in that warm bosom that rose and fell under his cheek! For a moment they stood so, silently. Then they heard a heavy step upon the stair. She led him to a chair and went out and closed the door. At the top of the staircase she met a tall, broad-shouldered man, with iron gray hair, and a face alert and stern. Her eyes were shining and her cheeks on fire, her whole face was one expression of intense determination.

"James, it is William in there, come home. You must keep him at any cost. If he goes this time, I go with him. O, James, be easy with him, he has suffered so." She broke from a command to an entreaty, and laid her hand on his shoulder. He looked questioningly at her a moment, then went in the room and quietly shut the door.

She stood leaning against the wall, clasping her temples with her hands and listening to the low indistinct sound of the voices within. Her own lips moved silently. She waited a long time, scarcely breathing. At last the door opened, and her husband came out. He stopped to say in a shaken voice,

"You go to him now, he will stay. I will go to my room. I will see him again in the morning."

She put her arm about his neck, "O, James, I thank you, I thank you! This is the night he came so long ago, you remember? I gave him to you then, and now you give him back to me!"

"Don't, Helen," he muttered. "He is my son, I have never forgotten that. I failed with him. I don't like to fail, it cuts my pride. Take him and make a man of him." He passed on down the hall.

She flew into the room where the young man sat with his head bowed upon his knee. She dropped upon her knees beside him. Ah, it was so good to him to feel those arms again!

"He is so glad, Willie, so glad! He may not show it, but he is as happy as I. He never was demonstrative with either of us, you know."

"O, my God, he was good enough," groaned the man. "I told him everything, and he was good enough. I don't see how either of you can look at me, speak to me, touch me." He shivered under her clasp again as when she had first touched him, and tried weakly to throw her off.

But she whispered softly,

"This is my right, my son."

Presently, when he was calmer, she rose. "Now, come with me into the library, and I will have your dinner brought there."

As they went downstairs she remarked apologetically, "I will not call Ellen tonight; she has a number of guests to attend to. She is a big girl now, you know, and came out last winter. Besides, I want you all to myself tonight."

When the dinner came, and it came very soon, he fell upon it savagely. As he ate she told him all that had transpired during the years of his absence, and how his father's business had brought them there. "I was glad when we came. I thought you would drift West. I seemed a good deal nearer to you here."

There was a gentle unobtrusive sadness in her tone that was too soft for a reproach.

"Have you everything you want? It is a comfort to see you eat."

He smiled grimly, "It is certainly a comfort to me. I have not indulged in this frivolous habit for some thirty-five hours."

She caught his hand and pressed it sharply, uttering a quick remonstrance.

"Don't say that! I know, but I can't hear you say it—it's too terrible! My boy, food has choked me many a time when I have thought of the possibility of that. Now take the old lounging chair by the fire, and if you are too tired to talk, we will just sit and rest together."

He sank into the depths of the big leather chair with the lions' heads on the arms, where he had sat so often in the days when his feet did not touch the floor and he was half afraid of the grim monsters cut in the polished wood. That chair seemed to speak to him of things long forgotten. It was like the touch of an old familiar friend. He felt a sudden yearning tenderness for the happy little boy who had sat there and dreamed of the big world so long ago. Alas, he had been dead many a summer, that little boy!

He sat looking up at the magnificent woman beside him. He had almost forgotten how handsome she was; how lustrous and sad were the eyes that were set under that serene brow, how impetuous and wayward the mouth even now, how superb the white throat and shoulders! Ah, the wit and grace and fineness of this woman! He remembered how proud he had been of her as a boy when she came to see him at school. Then in the deep red coals of the grate he saw the faces of other women who had come since then into his vexed, disordered life. Laughing faces, with eyes artificially bright, eyes without depth or meaning, features without the stamp of high sensibilities. And he had left this face for such as those!

He sighed restlessly and laid his hand on hers. There seemed refuge and protection in the touch of her, as in the old days when he was afraid of the dark. He had been in the dark so long now, his confidence was so thoroughly shaken, and he was bitterly afraid of the night and of himself.

"Ah, mother, you make other things seem so false. You must feel that I owe you an explanation, but I can't make any, even to myself. Ah, but we make poor exchanges in life. I can't make out the riddle of it all. Yet there are things I ought to tell you before I accept your confidence like this."

"I'd rather you wouldn't, Will. Listen: Between you and me there can be no secrets. We are more alike than other people. Dear boy, I know all about it. I am a woman, and circumstances were different with me, but we are of one blood. I have lived all your life before you. You have never had an impulse that I have not known, you have never touched a brink that my feet have not trod. This is your birthday night. Twenty-four years ago I foresaw all this. I was a young woman then and I had hot battles of my own, and I felt your likeness to me. You were not like other babies. From the hour you were born you were restless and discontented, as I had been before you. You used to brace your strong little limbs against mine and try to throw me off as you did tonight. Tonight you have come back to me, just as you always did after you ran away to swim in the river that was forbidden you, the river you loved because it was forbidden. You are tired and sleepy, just as you used to be then, only a little older and a little paler and a little more foolish. I never asked you where you had been then, nor will I now. You have come back to me, that's all in all to me. I know your every possibility and limitation, as a composer knows his instrument."

He found no answer that was worthy to give to talk like this. He had not found life easy since he had lived by his wits. He had come to know poverty at close quarters. He had known what it was to be gay with an empty pocket, to wear violets in his buttonhole when he had not breakfasted, and all the hateful shams of the poverty of idleness. He had been a reporter on a big metropolitan daily, where men grind out their brains on paper until they have not one idea left—and still grind on. He had worked in a real estate office, where ignorant men were swindled. He had sung in a comic opera chorus and played Harris in an *Uncle Tom's Cabin* company, and edited a socialist weekly. He had been dogged by debt and hunger and grinding poverty, until to sit here by a warm fire without concern as to how it would be paid for seemed unnatural.

He looked up at her questioningly. "I wonder if you know how much you pardon?"

"O, my poor boy, much or little, what does it matter? Have you wandered so far and paid such a bitter price for knowledge and not yet learned that love has nothing to do with pardon or forgiveness, that it only loves, and loves—and loves? They have not taught you well, the women of your world." She leaned over and kissed him, as no woman had kissed him since he left her.

He drew a long sigh of rich content. The old life, with all its bitterness and useless antagonism and flimsy sophistries, its brief delights that were always tinged with fear and distrust and unfaith, that whole miserable, futile, swindled world of Bohemia seemed immeasurably distant and far away, like a dream that is over and done. And as the chimes rang joyfully outside and sleep pressed heavily upon his eyelids, he wondered dimly if the Author of this sad little riddle of ours were not able to solve it after all, and if the Potter would not finally mete out his all comprehensive justice, such as none but he could have, to his Things of Clay, which are made in his own patterns, weak or strong, for his own ends; and if some day we will not awaken and find that all evil is a dream, a mental distortion that will pass when the dawn shall break.

Zona Gale

(August 26, 1874-December 27, 1938)

The coming and adoration of the precious Child is the occasion celebrated in " 'Not As the World Giveth': A Friendship Story," one of Zona Gale's many Christmas stories. Originally published in the December 1907 and January 1908 issues of *The Delineator*, a mass market women's magazine, it was included the following year in her collection, *Friendship Village*, the first of four volumes about the citizens of a small town based on her hometown of Portage, Wisconsin.

Calliope's Christmas party, although not a formal religious occasion, is a sacred event nonetheless. The old women welcome this child with love and through her they are able to recapture the essence of all the childhoods that have mattered in their lives: their children's, their grandchildren's, and their own. The spirituality celebrated here is based on a belief that people, by their behavior towards each other, create either a heaven or a hell in *this* world.

"Not As the World Giveth": A Friendship Story

Zona Gale

Two weeks before Christmas Friendship was thrown into a state of holiday delight. Mrs. Proudfit and her daughter, Miss Clementina, issued invitations to a reception to be given on Christmas Eve at Proudfit House, on Friendship Hill. The Proudfits, who had rarely entertained since Miss Linda went away, lived in Europe and New York and spent little time in the village, but, for all that, they remained citizens in absence, and Friendship always wrote out invitations for them whenever it gave "companies." The invitations the postmaster duly forwarded to some Manhattan bank, though I think the village had a secret conviction that these were never received— "sent out wild to a bank in the City, so." However, now that old courtesies were to be so magnificently returned, every one believed and felt a greater respect for the whole financial world.

The invitations enclosed the card of Mrs. Nita Ordway, and the name sounded for me a note of other days when, before my coming to Friendship Village, we two had, in the town, belonged to one happy circle of friends.

"I thought at first mebbe the card'd got shoved in the envelope by mistake," said Mis' Holcomb-that-was-Mame-Bliss. "I know once I got a Christmas book from a cousin o' mine in the City, an' a strange man's card fell out o' the leaves. I sent the card right straight back to her, an' Cousin Jane seemed rill cut up, so I made up my mind I'd lay low about this card. But I hear everybody's got 'em. I s'pose it's a sign that it's some Mis' Ordway's party too—only not enough hers to get her name on the invite. Mebbe she chipped in o on the expenses. Give a third, like enough."

However that was, Friendship looked on the Christmas party as on some unexpected door about to open in its path, and it woke in the morning conscious of expectation before it could remember what to expect. Proudfit House! A Christmas party! It touched every one as might some giant Santa Claus, for grown-ups, with a pack of heart'sease on his back.

When Mrs. Ordway arrived in the village, the excitement mounted. Mrs. Nita Ordway was the first exquisitely beautiful woman of the great world whom Friendship had ever seen— "beautiful like in the pictures of when noted folks was young," the village breathlessly summed her up. To be sure, when she and her little daughter, Viola, rode out in the Proudfits' motor, nobody in the street appeared to look at them. But Friendship knew when they rode, and when they walked, and what they wore, and when they returned.

It was a happiness to me to see Mrs. Ordway again, and I sat often with her in the music room at Proudfit House and listened to her glorious voice in just the songs that I love. Sometimes she would send for her little Viola, so that I might sit with the child in my arms, for she was one of those rare children who will let you love them.

"I like be made some 'tention to," Viola sometimes said shyly. She was not afraid, and she would stay with me hour-long, as if she loved to be loved. She was like a little come-a-purpose spirit, to let one pretend.

A day or two after the invitations had been received, I was in my guest room going over my Christmas list. Just before Christmas I delight in the look of a guest room, for then the bed is spread with a brave array of pretty things, and when one arranges and wraps them, the stitches of rose and blue on flowered fabrics, the flutter of crisp ribbons, and the breath of sachets make one glad. I was lingering at my task when I heard some one below, and I recognized her voice.

"Calliope!" I called gladly from the stairs, and bade her come up to me.

Calliope is one of the women in whose presence one can wrap one's Christmas gifts. She came into the room, bringing a breath of Winter, and she laid aside her tan ulster and her round straw hat, and straightway sat down on the rug by the open fire.

"Well said!" she cried contentedly, "a grate fire upstairs! It's one of the things that never seems real to me, like a tower on a house. I'd as soon think o' havin' a grate fire up a tree an' settin' there, as in my chamber. Anyway, when it comes Winter, upstairs in Friendship is just a place where you go after something in the bureau draw' an' come down again as quick as you can. I s'pose you got an invite to the party?"

"Yes," I said, "and you will go, Calliope?"

But instead of answering me:—

"My land!" she said, "think of it! A party like that, an' not a low-necked waist in town, nor a swallow-tail! An' only two weeks to do anything in, an' only Liddy Ember for dressmaker, an' it takes her two weeks to make a dress. I guess Mis' Postmaster Sykes has got her. They say she read her invite in the post-office with one hand an' snapped up that tobacco-brown net in the post-office store window with the other, an' out an' up to Liddy's an' hired her before she was up from the breakfast table. So she gets the town new dress. Mis' Sykes is terrible quick-moved."

"What will you wear, Calliope?" I asked.

"Me—I never wear anything but henriettas," she said. "I think the plainer-faced you are, the simpler you'd ought to be dressed. I use' to fix up terrible ruffled, but when I see I was reg'lar plain-faced I stuck to henriettas, mostly gray—"

"Calliope," I said resolutely, "you don't mean you're not going to the Proudfit party?"

She clasped her hands and held them, palms outward, over her mouth, and her eyes twinkled above them.

"No, sir," she said, "I can't go. You'll laugh at me!" she defended. "Don't you tell!" she warned. And finally she told me.

"Day after yesterday," she said, "I went into the City. An' I come out on the trolley. An' I donno what possessed me,—I ain't done it for months,—but when we crossed the start of the Plank Road, I got off an' went up an' visited the Old Ladies' Home. You know I've always thought," she broke off, "—well, you know I ain't a rill lot to do with, an' I always had an i-dee that mebbe sometime, when I got older, I might—"

I nodded, and she went on.

"Well, I walked around among 'em up there—canary birds an' plants an' footstools—an' the whole thing fixed up so cheerful that it's pitiful. Red wall-paper an' flowered curtains an' such, all fair yellin' at you, 'We're cheerful—cheerful—cheerful!' till I like to run. An' it comes over me, bein' so near Christmas an' all, what would they do on Christmas? So I asked a woman in a navy-blue dress, seein' she flipped around like she was the flag o' the place.

"'The south corridor,' she answers,—them's the highest payin'"—Calliope threw in, "'chipped in an' got up a tree, an' there's gifts for all,' s'she. 'The west corridor'—them's the local city ones—'all has friends to take 'em away for the day. The east corridor'—they're from farther away an' middlin' well-to-do—'all has boxes comin' to 'em from off. But the north corridor,' s'she, scowlin' some, 'is rather a trial to us.'

"An' I was waitin' for that. The north corridor is all charity old ladies, paid for out o' the fund; an' the president o' the home has just died, an' the secretary's in the old country on a pleasure trip, an' the board's in a row over the policy o' the home, an' the navy-blue matron dassent act, an' altogether it looked like the north corridor was goin' to get a regular mid-week Wednesday instead of a Christmas. An' I up an' ast' her to take me down to see 'em."

It was easy to see what Calliope had done, I thought: she had promised to spend Christmas Eve over there in the north corridor, reading aloud.

"They was nine of 'em," she went on, "nice old grandma ladies, with hands that looked like they'd ought to 'a' been tyin' little aprons an' cuttin' out cookies an' squeezin' somebody else's hand. There they set, with the wall-paper doin' its cheerfulest, loud as an insult,—one of 'em with lots o' white hair, one of 'em singin' a little, some of 'em tryin' to sew or knit some. My land!" said Calliope, "when we think of 'em sittin' up an' down the world—with their arms all empty—an' Christmas comin' on—ain't it a wonder— Well, I stayed 'round an' talked to 'em," she went on, "while the navy-blue lady whisked her starched skirts some. She seemed too busy 'tendin' to 'em to give 'em much attention. An' they looked rill pleased when I talked to 'em about their patchwork an' knittin', an' did they get the sun all day, an' didn't the canary sort o' shave somethin' off'n the human ear-drum, on his tiptop notes? An' when I said that, Grandma Holly—her with lots o' white hair—says:—

"'I donno but it does,' she says, 'but I don't mind; I'm so thankful to see somethin' around that's *little an' young.*'

"That sort o' landed in my heart. It's just what I'd been thinkin' about 'em.

"'Little, young things,' s'I, sort o' careless, 'make a lot o' racket, you know.'

"At that old Mis' Burney pipes up—her that brought up her daughter's children an' er son-in-law married again an' turned her out:—

"'I use' to think so,' she says quiet, 'the noise o' the children use' to bother me terrible. When they reely got to goin' I use' to think I couldn't stand it, my head hurt me so. But now,' s'she, 'I get to thinkin' sometimes I wouldn't mind a horse-fiddle if some of 'em played it.'

"'They're lots o' company, the little things,' says old Mis' Norris—she'd kep' mislayin' her teeth an' the navy-blue lady had took 'em away from her that day for to teach her, so I couldn't hardly understand what she said. 'Mine was named Ellen an' Nancy,' I made out.

"'Some o' you remember my Sam,'—Mis' Ailing speaks up then, an' she begun windin' up her yarn an' never noticed she was ravellin' out her mitten,—'he was an alderman,' she was goin' on, but old Mis' Winslow cuts in on her:—

"'It don't matter what he was when he was man-grown,' s'she. 'Man-grown can get along themselves. It's when they're little bits o' ones,' she says.

"'Little!' says Grandma Holly. 'Is it little you mean? Well, my Amy's two little feet use' to be swallowed up in my hand—so,' she says, shuttin' her hand over to show us.

"Well, so they went on. I give you my word I stood there sort o' grippin' up on my elbows. I'd always known it was so—like you do know things are so. But somehow when you come to *feel* they're so, that's another thing. And I was feelin' this in my throat 'bout as big as an orange. I'd thought their hands looked like they'd ought to be tyin' up little aprons, but I never thought o' the hands bein' rill lonesome to do the tyin', an' thinkin' about it, too. An' now I understood 'em like I see 'em for the first time, rill face to face. Somehow, we ain't any too apt to look at people that way," said Calliope. "You see how I mean it.

"Then comes the navy-blue woman an' says it's time for their hot milk, an' they all looked up, kind o' hopeful. An' I see that the navy-blue one had got 'em trained into the i-dee that hot milk was an event. She didn't like to hev 'em talk much about the past, she told me, when she see what we was speakin' of, because it gener'lly made some of 'em cry, an' the i-dee was to keep the spirit of the home bright an' cheerful. 'So I see,' s'I, dry. An' there was Christmas comin' on, an' nothin' to break the general cheerfulness but hot milk. Well," Calliope said, "I s'pose you'll think I'm terrible foolish, but I couldn't help what I done—"

"I don't wonder at it," said I, warmly; "you promised to spend Christmas Eve with them and read aloud to them, didn't you, Calliope?"

"No!" Calliope cried; "I didn't do that. I should think they'd be sick to death o' bein' read aloud to. I should think they'd be sick to death bein' cheered up by their surroundin's. No—I invited the whole nine of 'em to come over an' spend Christmas Eve with me."

"Calliope!" I cried, "but how—"

"I know it," she exclaimed, "I know it. But they're all well an' hardy. The charity corridor ain't expected in the infirmary much. An' Jimmy Sturgis is goin' to bring 'em over free in the closed 'bus—I'll fill it with hot bricks an' hot flat-irons an' bed-quilts. An' my land! you'd ought to see 'em when I ask' 'em. I don't s'pose they'd had an invite out in years. The navy-blue lady looked like I'd nipped a mountain off'n her shoulders, too. An' now," said Calliope, "what on top o' this earth will I do with 'em when I get 'em here?"

What indeed? I left my task and sat by her on the rug before the fire, and we talked it over. But all the while we talked, I could see that she was keeping something back—some plan of which she was doubtful.

"I ain't no money to spend, you know," she said, "an' I won't let anybody else spend any for me, for this. Folks has plans enough o' their own without mine. But I kep' sayin' to myself, all the way home when my knees give down at the i-dee of what I was goin' to do: 'Calliope, the Lord says, *"Give."* An' He meant you to give, same's those that hev got. He didn't say, "Everybody give but Calliope, an' she ain't got much, so she'd ought to be let off." He said, *"Give."*' An' He didn't mention all nice things, same's I'd like to give, an' most everybody does give—" she nodded toward my bed, brave with its Christmas array. "He didn't mention givin' *things* at all. An' so," said Calliope, "I thought o' somethin' else."

She sat with brooding eyes on the fire, her hands clasped about her knees.

"The Lord Christ," said Calliope, "didn't hev nothin' of His own. An' yet He just give an' give an' give. An' somehow I got the *i*-dee," she finished, glancing up at me shyly, "that mebbe Christmas ain't really all in your stocking foot, after all. I ain't much to spend, and mebbe that sounds some like sour grapes. But it seems like a good many beautiful things is free to all, an' that they's ways to do. Well, I've thought of a way—"

"Calliope," I said, "tell me what you have really planned for the old-lady party. You *have* planned?"

"Well, yes," she said, "I hev. But mebbe you'll think it ain't anything. First I thought o' tea, an' thin bread-an'-butter sandwiches—it seems some like a party when you get your bread thin. An' I've got apples in the house we could roast, an' corn to pop over the kitchen fire. But then I come to a stop. For I ain't nothin' else, an' I've spent every cent I *can* spend a'ready. But yet I did want to show 'em somethin' lovely—an' differ'nt from what they see, so's it'd seem as if somebody cared, an' as if they'd been *in Christmas*, too. An' all of a sudden it come to me, why not invite in a few little children o' somebody's here in Friendship? So's them old grandma ladies—"

She shook her head and turned away.

"I expec'," she said, "you think I'm terrible foolish. But wouldn't that be givin', don't you think? *Would* that be anything?"

I have planned, as will fall to us all, many happy ways of keeping festival; but I think that never, even in days when I myself was happiest, have I so delighted in any event as in this of Calliope's proposing. And when at last she had gone, and the dusk had fallen and I lighted candles and went back to my pleasant task, some way the stitches of pink and blue on flowered fabrics, the flutter of crisp ribbons, and the breath of the sachets were not greatly in my thoughts; and that which made me glad was a certain shining in the room, but this was not of candle-light, or firelight, or winter starlight.

With the days the plans for the Proudfit party—or rather the plans of the Proudfit guests—went merrily forward. It was, they said, like "in the Oldmoxon days," when the house in which I was now living had been the Friendship fairyland. Some take their parties solemnly, some joyously, some feverishly; but Friendship takes them vitally, as it takes a project or the breath of being. Like the rest of the world, the village sank Christmas in festivity. It could not see Christmas for the Christmas plans.

Speculation was the delight of meetings, and every one conspired in terms of toilettes.

"Likely," said Mis' Holcomb-that-was-Mame-Bliss, "Mis' Banker Mason'll wear her black-an'-white foulard. Them foulards are wonderful durable—you can't muss 'em. She got hers when Gramma Mason first hurt her back, so's if anything happened she'd be part mournin', an' if anything didn't, she'd have a nice dress to wear out places. Ain't it real convenient,—white standin' for both companies an' the tomb, so?"

And "Mis' Photographer Sturgis has the best of it, bein' an invalid, till a party comes up," said Libbie Liberty. "She gets plenty enough food sent in, an' flowers, an' such things, an' she's got nails hung full o' what I call sympathy clo'es, to wear durin' sympathy calls. But when it comes to a real what you might say dress-up dress, I guess she'll hev to be took worse with her side an' stay in the house."

Abigail Arnold contributed:—

"Seems Mis' Doctor Helman had a whole wine silk dress put away with her dyin' things. She always thought it sounded terrible fine to hear about the dead havin' dress-pattern after dress-pattern laid away that hadn't never been made up. So she'd got together the one, but now she an' Elzabella are goin' to work an' make it up. I guess Mis' Helman thinks her stomach is so much better 't mebbe she'll be spared till after the holidays when the sales begin."

Even Liddy Ember had promised to go and to take Ellen, and Ellen went up and down the winter streets singing sane little songs about the party, save on days when she "come herself again," and then she planned, as wildly as anybody, what she meant to wear. And Liddy, whose dream had always been to do "reg'lar city dress-makin'," with helpers an' plates an' furnish the findin's at the shop," and whose lot instead had been to cut and fit "just the durable kind," was blithely at work night and day on Mis' Postmaster Sykes's tobacco-brown net. We understood that there were to be brown velvet butterflies stitched down the skirt, and if her Lady Washington geranium flowered in time,—Mis' Sykes was said to lay bread and milk nightly about the roots to encourage it,—she was to wear the blossom in her hair. ("She'll be gettin' herself talked about, wearin' a wreath o' flowers on her head, so," said some.) But then, Mis' Sykes was recognized to be "one that picks her own steps."

"Mis' Sykes always dresses for company accordin' to the way she gets her invite," Calliope observed. "A telephone invite, she goes in somethin' she'd wear home afternoons. Word o' mouth at the front door, she wears what she wears on Sundays. Written invites, she rags out in her rill *best* dress, for parties. But *engraved*," Calliope mounted to her climax, "a bran' new dress an' a wreath in her hair is the least she'll stop at."

But I think that, in the wish to do honour to so distinguished an occasion, the temper of Mis' Sykes, and perhaps of Ellen Ember too, was the secret temper of all the village.

I daresay that excitement followed excitement when news of Calliope's party got abroad. But of this I knew little, for I spent those next days at the Proudfits' with Nita Ordway and little Viola, and though I thought often of Calliope, I chanced not to see her again until the holidays were almost upon us. In the late afternoon, two days before Christmas, I dropped in at her cottage to learn how pleasantly the plans for her party matured.

To my amazement I found her all dejection.

"Why, Calliope," I said, "can't the grandma ladies come, after all?"

Yes, they could come; they were coming.

"You are never sorry you asked them?" I pressed her.

No, Oh, no; she was glad she had asked them.

"Something is wrong, though," I said sadly—thinking what a blessed thing it is to be so joyous a spirit that one's dejections are bound to be taken seriously.

"Well," said Calliope, then, "it's the children. No it ain't, it's Friendship. The town's about as broad as a broom straw an' most as deep. Anything differ'nt scares 'em like something wore out'd ought to. Friendship's got an i-dee that Christmas begins in a stocking an' ends off in a candle. It thinks the rest o' the days are reg'lar, self-respecting days, but it looks on Christmas like an extry thing, thrown in to please 'em. It acts as if the rest o' the year was plain cake an' the holidays was the frostin' to be et, an' everybody grab the best themselves, give or take."

"Calliope!" I cried—for this was as if the moon had objected to the heavens.

"Oh, I know I'd ought not to," she said sadly; "but don't folks act as if time was give to 'em to run around wild with, as best suits 'em? Three hundred an' 'leven days a year to use for themselves, an' Sundays an' Christmas an' Thanksgivin' to give away looks to me a rill fair division. But, no. Some folks act like Sundays an' holidays was not only the frostin', but the nuts an' candy an' ice-cream o' things—*their* ice-cream, to eat an' pass to their own, an' scrape the freezer."

And then came the heart of the matter.

"'T seems," said Calliope, "there's that children's Christmas tree at the new minister's on Christmas Eve. But that ain't till ha'-past seven, an' I done my best to hev some o' the children stop in here on their way, for *my* little party. An' with one set o' lungs their mas says no, they'd get mussed for the tree if they do. I offered to hev 'em bring their white dresses pinned in papers, an' we'd dress 'em here—I think the grandma ladies'd like that. But their mas says no, pinned in papers'd take the starch out an' their hair'd get all over their heads. An' some o' the mothers says indignant: 'Old ladies from the poor-house end o' the home—well, I should think not! Children is very easy to take things. If you'd hed young o' your own, you'd think more, Calliope,' they says witherin'."

Her little wrinkled hands were trembling at the enormity.

"I donno," she added, "but I was foolish to try it. But I did want to get a-hold o' somethin' beautiful for them old ladies to see. An', my mind, they ain't much so rilly lovely as young children, together in a room."

"But, Calliope," I said in distress, "isn't there even one child you can get?"

"No, sir," she said. "Not a one. I been everywhere. You know they ain't any poor in Friendship. We're all comfortable enough off to be overparticular."

"But wouldn't you think," I said, "at Christmas time—"

"Yes, you would," Calliope said, "you would. You'd think Christmas'd make everything kind o' softened up an' differ'nt. Every time I look at the holly myself, I feel like I'd just shook hands with somebody cordial."

None the less—for Calliope had drunk deep of the wine of doing and she never gave up any project—at four o'clock on the day before Christmas I saw the closed 'bus driven by Jimmy Sturgis fare briskly past my house on its way to the "start of the Plank Road," to the Old Ladies' Home. Within, I knew, were quilts and hot stones of Calliope's providing; and Jimmy had hung the 'bus windows with cedar, and two little flags fluttered from the door. It all had a merry, holiday air as Jimmy shook the lines and drew on swiftly through the snow to those wistful nine guests, who at last were to be "in Christmas," too.

"If they can't do nothin' else," Calliope had said, "they can talk

over old times, without hot milk interferin'. But I wish, an' I wish—
seem's though there'd ought always to be a child around on Star o'
Bethlehem night, don't it?"

I dined alone that Star of Bethlehem night, and to dine alone
under Christmas candles is never a cheerful business. The Proudfit
car was to come for me soon after eight, and at eight I stood waiting
at the window of my little living room, saying to myself that if I were
to drop from the air to a deserted country road, I should be certain
that it was Christmas Eve. You can tell Christmas Eve anywhere, like
a sugarplum, with your eyes shut. It is not the lighted houses, or the
close-curtained windows behind which Christmas trees are fruiting;
nor yet, in Friendship, will it be the post-office store or the home
bakery windows, gay with Christmas trappings. But there is in the
world a subdued note of joyful preparation, as if some spirit whom
one never may see face to face had on this night a gift of perceptible
life. And in spite of my loneliness, my heart upleaped to the note of
a distant sleigh-bell jingling an air of "Home, Going Home, Christmas Eve and Going Home."

Then when the big Proudfit car came flashing to my door, I
had a sweet surprise. For from it, through the snowy dark, came
running a little fairy thing, and Viola Ordway danced to my door
with her mother, muffled in furs.

"We've been close in the house all day," Mrs. Ordway cried,
"and now we've run away to get you. Come!"

As for me, I took Viola in my arms and lifted her to my hall
table and caught off her cloak and hood. I can never resist doing
this to a child. I love to see the little warm, plump body in its fine
white linen emerge rose-wise, from the calyx cloak; and I love that
shy first gesture, whatever it may be, of a child so emerging. The
turning about, the freeing of soft hair from the neck, the smoothing
down of the frock, the half-abashed upward look. Viola did more.
She laid her hand on my cheek and held it so, looking at me quite
gravely, as if that were some secret sign of brotherhood in the
unknown, which she remembered and I, alas! had forgotten. But I
perfectly remembered how to kiss her. If only, I thought, all the
empty arms could know a Viola. If only all the empty arms, up and

down the world, could know a Viola even just at Christmas time. If only—

Over the top of Viola's head I looked across at Nita Ordway, and a sudden joyous purpose lighted all the air about me—as a joyous purpose will. Oh, if only— And then I heard myself pouring out a marvellous jumble of sound and senselessness.

"Nita!" I cried, "you are not a Friendship Village mother! You are not afraid. Viola is not going to the new minister's Christmas tree. Oh, don't you see? It's still early—surely we have time! The grandma ladies *must* see Viola!"

I remember how Nita Ordway laughed, and her answer made me love her the more—as is the way of some answers.

"I don't catch it—I don't," she said, "but it sounds delicious. All courage, and old ladies, and ample time for everything! If I said, 'Of course,' would that do?"

Already I was tying Viola's hood, and next to taking off a child's hood I love putting one on—surely every one will have noticed how their mouths bud up for kissing. While we sped along the Plank Road toward Calliope's cottage, I poured out the story of who were at her house that night, and why, and all that had befallen. In a moment the great car, devouring its own path of light, set us down at Calliope's gate, and Calliope herself, trim in her gray henrietta, her wrinkled face flushed and shining, came at our summons. And I pushed Viola in before us—little fairy thing in a fluff of white wraps and white furs.

"Look, Calliope!" I cried.

Calliope looked down at her, and I think she can hardly have seen Mrs. Ordway and me at all. She smote her hands softly together.

"Oh," she said, "if it isn't! Oh—a child for Star o' Bethlehem night, after all!"

She dropped to her knees before Viola, touching the little girl's hand almost shyly. There was in Calliope's face when she looked at any child a kind of nakedness of the woman's soul; and she, who was so deft, was curiously awkward in such a presence.

"They're out there in the dinin' room," she whispered, "settin' round the cook stove. I saw they felt some better out there. Le's us leave her go out alone by herself, just the way she is."

And that was what we did. We said something to Viola softly about "the poor old grandma ladies, with no little girl to love," and then Calliope opened the door and let her through.

We peeped for a moment at the lamp-lit crack. The dining room was warm and bright, its table covered with red cotton and set with tea-cups, shelves of plants blooming across the windows, cedar green on the walls. The odour of pop-corn was in the air, and above an open griddle hole apples bobbed on strings tied to the stove-pipe wing. And there about the cooking range, with its cheery opened hearth, Calliope's Christmas guests were gathered.

They were exquisitely neat and trim, in black and brown cloth dresses, with a brooch, or a white apron, or a geranium from a window plant worn for festival. I recognized Grandma Holly, with her soft white hair, and I thought I could tell which were Mis' Ailing and Mis' Burney and Mis' Norris. And the faces of them all, the gentle, the grief-marked, even the querulous, were grown kindly with the knowledge that somebody had cared about their Christmas.

The child went toward them as simply as if they had been friends. They looked at her with some murmuring of surprise, and at one another questioningly. Viola went straight to the knee of Grandma Holly, who was nearest.

" 'At lady tied my hood too tight," she referred unflatteringly to me, "p'eas do it off."

Grandma Holly looked down over her spectacles, and up at the other grandma ladies, and back to Viola. The others gathered nearer, hitching forward rocking-chairs, rising to peer over shoulders—breathlessly, with a manner of fearing to touch her. But because of the little uplifted face, waiting, Grandma Holly must needs untie the white hood and reveal all the shining of the child's hair.

"Nen do my toat off," Viola gravely directed.

At that Grandma Holly crooned some single indistinguishable syllable in her throat, and then off came the cloak. The little warm, plump body in its fine linen emerged, rose-wise, and Viola smoothed down her frock, and freed her hair from her neck, and glanced up shyly. By the stir and flutter among them I understood that they were feeling just as I feel when a little hood and cloak come off.

Viola stood still for a minute.

"I like be made some 'tention to," she suggested gently.

Ah—and they understood. How they understood! Grandma Holly swept the little girl in her arms, and I know the others closed about them with smiles and vague, unimportant words. Viola sat quietly and happily, like a little come-a-purpose spirit to let them pretend. And it was with them all as if something long pent up went free.

Calliope left the door and turned toward us.

"Seems like my throat couldn't stand it," she said, . . . and it seemed to me, as we three sat together in the dim little parlor, that Nita Ordway must cherish Viola for us all—for the grandma ladies and Calliope and me.

Half an hour later we three went out to the dining room. Viola ran to her mother when she entered. Nita took her in her arms and sat beside the stove, her cloak slipping from her shoulders, the soft peach tints of her gown shot through with shining lines and the light caught in her collar of gems. "I did want to get a-hold o' somethin' beautiful for them old ladies to see," Calliope had said.

"Oh," said Grandma Holly, and she laid her brown hand on Viola's hand, "ain't she *dear an' little an' young?*"

"I wish't she'd talk some," begged old Mis' Norris.

"Ain't she good, though, the little thing?" Mis' Ailing said. "Look at how still she sets. Not wigglin' 'round same as some. It was just that way with Sam when he was small—he'd set by the hour an' leave me hold him—"

A little bent creature, whose name I never learned, sat patting Viola's skirt.

"Seems like I'd gone back years," we heard her say.

Grandma Holly held up one half-closed hand.

"Like that," she told them, "my Amy's feet was so little I could hold 'em like that, an' I see hers is the same way. She's wonderful like Amy was, her age."

I cannot recall half the sweet, trivial things that they said. But I remember how they told us stories of their own babies, and we laughed with them over treasured sayings of long-ago lips, or grieved with them over silences, or rejoiced at glad things that had been. Regardless of the Proudfit party, we let them talk as they would, and remember. Then of her own accord Nita Ordway hummed some haunting air, and sang one of the songs that we all loved—the grandma ladies and Calliope and I. It was a sleepy song, whose words I have forgotten, but it was in a kind of universal tongue which I think that no one can possibly mistake. And out of the lullaby came all the little spirits, freed in babyhood or "man-grown," and stood at the knees of the grandma ladies, so that I was afraid that they could not bear it.

When the song was done, Viola suddenly sat up very straight.

"I got a litty box," she announced, "an' I had a parasol. An' once a boy div me a new nail. An' once I didn' feel berry well, but now I am. An' once—"

Their laughter was like a caress. Before it was done, we heard a stamping without, and there was Jimmy Sturgis, with a spray of holly in his old felt hat and the closed 'bus at the door.

We helped Calliope to get their wraps and to fill the 'bus with hot stones from the oven and with many quilts, and we made ready a basket of pop-corn and apples and of the cedar hung around the little room. They stood about us to say good-by, or to tell us some last bit of the news of their long-past youth—dear, wrinkled faces framed in broad lines of bonnet or hood, and smiling, every one.

"This gray shawl I got on me is the very one I used to wrap Amy in to carry her through the cold hall," said Grandma Holly. "My land-a-livin'! seems's if I'd been with her to-night, over again!"

Their way of thanks lay among stumbling words and vague repetitions, but there was a kind of glory in their grateful faces, and one always remembers that.

"Merry Prismas, gramma ladies!" Viola cried shrilly at the 'bus door, and within they laughed like mothers as they answered. And Jimmy Sturgis cracked his whip, and the sleigh-bells jingled.

Nita Ordway and Viola and I stood for a moment with Calliope at her gate.

"Come!" we begged her, "now go with us. We are all late together. There is no reason why you should not go with us to the Christmas party."

But Calliope shook her head.

"I'm ever so much obliged to you," she said, "but oh, I couldn't. I've hed too rilly a Christmas to come down to a party anywheres."

When Nita and Viola and I reached Proudfit House, the guests were all assembled, but we knew that Mrs. Proudfit and Miss Clementina would be the first to forgive us when they understood.

The big colonial home was bright with scarlet-shaded candles and holly-hung walls; there was mistletoe on the sconces, and in the great hall there were tuneful strings. On the landing of the stairs stood Mrs. Proudfit and Miss Clementina, charmingly pretty in their delicate frocks, and wholly gay and gracious. ("They seem lively like in pictures where folks don't make a loud sound a-talkin'," said Friendship. "I s'pose it's somethin' you learn in the City.") And Friendship wore its loyalty like a mantle. Twelve years had passed, and yet one and another said under breath and sighed, "If only Miss Linda could 'a' been here, too."

All Friendship Village was there, save Abel Halsey, who was at the Good Shepherd's Home Christmas tree in the City, and, perhaps one would say, Delia More, who had begged to be allowed to help in the kitchen "an' be there that way." Even Peleg Bemus was in his place in the orchestra, sitting with closed eyes, playing his flute, and keeping audible time with his wooden leg,—quite as he did when he played his flute at night, on Friendship streets. And there was Mis' Postmaster Sykes, in the tobacco-brown net, with butterflies stitched down the skirt and the Lady Washington geranium in her hair—and forever near her went little Miss Liddy Ember with an almost passionate creative pride in the gown of her hand, so that she would murmur her patron an occasional warning: "Mis' Sykes, throw back your shoulders, you hev to, to bring out the real set o' the basque;" or, "Don't forget you want to give a little hitch to the back when you stand up, Mis' Sykes." And to one and another Liddy said proudly, "I declare if I didn't get that skirt with the butterflies just like a magazine cover." And there, too, was Ellen Ember, wearing a white book muslin and a rosy "nubia" that had been her mother's; and Ellen's face was uplifted, and of pale distinction under the bronze glory of her hair, but all that evening she smiled and sang and wondered, in utter absence of the spirit. ("Oh," poor Miss Liddy said, "I do so want Ellen to come herself before supper. She won't remember a thing she eats, an' she don't have much that's tasty an' good. It'll be just like she missed the whole thing, in spite of all the chore o' comin'.") And there were Mis' Doctor Helman in her new wine silk; Mis' Banker Mason in the black-and-white foulard designed to grace a festival or to respect a tomb; Mis' Sturgis, in a put-away dress that was a surprise to every one; Mis' Holcomb-that-was-Mame-Bliss, and Eppleby, and the "Other" Holcombs; Abigail Arnold, the Gekerjecks, Mis' Toplady and Timothy, even Mis' Mayor Uppers—no one was forgotten. And—save poor Ellen—every one was aglow with the sweet satisfaction of having sent abroad a brave array of pretty things, with stitches of rose and blue on flowered fabrics, with the flutter of ribbons, and the breath of sachets, and with many a gift of substance to those less generously endowed. To them all the delight of the season was in the gifts of their hands and in the night's merry-making, and in the joy of keeping holiday. Here, as Calliope had said, Christmas, begun in a stocking, was ending in a candle.

And yet it was Star of Bethlehem night, the night of Him who "didn't mention givin' *things* at all."

Fannie Hurst

(October 18, 1885-February 23, 1968)

"The Nth Commandment" was published in the 1914 Christmas issue of *The Saturday Evening Post* shortly after Fannie Hurst moved to New York to pursue her dream of becoming a writer. She worked as a department store clerk and a waitress by day, and by night she acted in bit-parts and haunted the streets and night court of Manhattan looking for stories. Within a few years, she had achieved great success: she became the most highly paid short story writer in the world. But she never abandoned the overworked, underpaid, sexually harassed working women among whom she had labored and whose stories she continued to tell.

This story was included in *Every Soul Hath Its Song* (1916), the second of her nine volumes of short stories. Hurst is best known today as the author of the novels made into the films *Back Street* and *Imitation of Life*.

The Nth Commandment

Fannie Hurst

The Christmas ballad of the stoker, even though writ from the fiery bowels of amidships and with a pen reeking with his own sweat, could find no holiday sale; nor the story of the waiter who serves the wine he dares only smell, and weary stands attendant into the joyous dawn. Such social sores—the drayman, back bent to the Christmas box whose mysteries he must never know; the salesgirl standing on her swollen feet on into the midnight hour—such sores may run and fester, but not to sicken public eyes.

For the Christmas spirit is the white flame of love burning in men's hearts and may not be defiled. Shop-windows, magazine covers, and post-cards proclaim good-will to all men; bedtime stories crooned when little heads are drowsy are of Peace on Earth; corporations whose draymen's backs are bent and whose salesgirls' feet are swollen plaster each outgoing parcel with a Good-Will-Toward-Men stamp, and remove the stools from behind the counters to give space to more of the glittering merchandise.

In the Mammoth Store the stools have long since been removed and the holiday hysteria of Peace on Earth rose to its Christ-

Reprinted by permission of Brandeis University and Washington University.

127

mas Eve climax, as a frenzied gale drives upward the sea into mountains of water, or scuds through black-hearted forests, bending them double in wild salaam.

Shoppers pushed through aisles so packed that the tide flowed back upon itself. A narrow-chested woman, caught in the whorl of such vortex, fainted back against the bundle-laden arms that pressed her on. Above the thin orchestra of musical toys, the tramp of feet like an army marching, voices raucous from straining to be heard, a clock over the grand central stairway boomed nine, and the crowd pulled at its strength for a last hour of bartering, tearing, pushing, haggling, sweating.

Behind the counters workers sobbed in their throats and shifted from one swollen foot to the other. A cash-girl, her eyeballs glazed like those of a wounded hare in the torture of the chase, found a pile of pasteboard boxes behind a door, and with the indifference of exhaustion dropped on to it asleep. The tide flowed on, and ever and again back upon itself. A Santa Claus in a red canton-flannel coat lost his white canton-flannel beard, nor troubled to recover it. A woman trembling with the ague of terror drew an imitation bisque doll off a counter and into the shallow recesses of her cape, and the cool hand of the law darted after her and closed over her wrist and imitation bisque evidence. A prayer, a moan, the crowd parting and closing again.

The mammoth Christmas tree beneath the grand central stairway loped ever so slightly of its own gorgeousness, and the gold star at its apex titillated to the tramp-tramp of the army. Across the novelty leather-goods counter Mr. Jimmie Fitzgibbons leaned the blue-shaven, predacious face that head waiters and underfed salesgirls know best over a hot bird and a cold bottle. Men's hands involuntarily close into tight fists when his well-pressed sleeve accidentally brushes their wives or sisters. Six-dollar-a-week salesgirls scrape their luscious rare birds to the bone, drink thin gold wine from thin, gold-edged glasses, and curse their God when the reckoning comes.

Behind the novelty leather-goods counter Mrs. Violet Smith, whose eyes were the woodland blue her name boasted, smiled back and leaned against the stock-shelves, her face upturned and like a tired flower.

"If the rush hadn't quit right this minute I—I couldn't have lasted it out till closing, honest I couldn't."

"Poor tired little filly!"

"Even them ten minutes I got leave to go up to old Ingram's office they made up for when I came back, and put another batch of them fifty-nine-cent leatherette purses out in the bin."

"Poor little filly! What you need is a little speed. I wanna blow you to-night, Doll. You went once and you can make it twice. Come on, Doll, it ain't every little girl I'd coax like this."

"I—Jimmie—I—"

"I wanna blow you to-night, Doll. A poor little blue-eyed queenie like you, all froze up with nothing but a sick husband for a Christmas tree—a poor little baby doll like you!"

"The kid, too, Jimmie, I—oughtn't!"

"Didn't you tell me yourself it sleeps through the night like a whippersnapper? Don't be a quitter, Doll, didn't you?"

"Yes, but—"

"A poor little baby doll like you! Why, there just ain't nothing too good for you. Some little time I showed you last Tuesday night—eh, Doll?"

"Yes—Jimmie!"

"Well, if you think that was some evening, you watch me to-night!"

"I—can't—go, Jimmie, him layin' there, and the kid and all!"

"Didn't I have to coax you last time just like to-night? And wasn't you glad when you looked out and seen how blasted cold and icy it was that you lemme blow you—wasn't you?"

"Yes, Jimmie, but—"

"Didn't I blow you to a bottle of bubble water to take home with you even after the big show was over, and wouldn't I have blown you to yellow instead of the red if you hadn't been a little cheap skate and wanted the red? Didn't I pin a two-dollar bunch of hothouse grapes on your hat right out of the fruit-bowl? Didn't I blow you for proper?"

"It was swell, Jimmie!"

"Well, I'm going to blow in my winnings on you to-night, Doll. It's Christmas Eve and—"

"Yes, it's Christmas Eve, Jimmie, and he—he had one of his bad hemorrhages last night, and the kid, she—she's too little to know she's getting cheated out of her Christmas, but, gee—a—a kid oughtta have something—a tree or something."

He leaned closer, hemmed in by the crowd. "It's *you* oughtta have something, Doll."

"I—I never oughtta gone with you last Tuesday night, Jimmie. When I got home, he—he was laying there like a rag."

"I like you, Doll. I'm going to blow in the stack of my winnings on you—that's how much I like you. There ain't nothing I wouldn't do for a little filly like you."

"Jimmie!"

"There ain't!"

"Aw!"

"You wouldn't be in the hole you are now, Doll, if you hadn't sneaked off two years ago and done it while I wasn't looking. Nearly two whole years you lemme lose track of you! That ain't a nice way to treat a fellow that likes you."

"We went boarding right away, Jimmie, and I only came back to the department two months ago, after he got so bad. 'Ain't I told you how things just kinda happened?"

"I liked you myself, Doll, but you fell for a pair of shoulders over in the gents' furnishing that wasn't wide from nothing but padding. I could have told you there was all cotton batting and no lungs there. I could have told you."

"Jimmie, ain't you ashamed! Jimmie!"

"Aw, I was just kidding. But you ain't real on that true-blue stuff, Doll. I can look into your eyes and see you're bustin' to lemme blow you. That's what you get, sweetness, when you don't ask your Uncle Fuller first. If you'd have asked me I could have told you he was weak in the chest when you married him. I could have told you that you'd be back here two years later selling leatherette vanity-cases and supportin' a—"

"You! Jimmie Fitzgibbons, you—"

"Gad, Doll, go to it! When you color up like that you look like a rose—a whole bouquet of them."

"You—you don't know nothing about him. He—he never knew he had a lung till a month after the kid came, and they moved the gents' furnishing over by the Broadway door where the draught caught him."

"Sure, he didn't, Doll; no harm meant. That's right, stand by him. I like to see it. Why, a little queen across the counter from you tole me you'd have married him if he'd had three bum lungs, that crazy you was!"

"Like fun! If me or him had dreamt he wasn't sound we—I wouldn't be in this mess, I—we—I wouldn't!"

Her little face was pale as a spray of jessamine against a dark background, and, try as she would to check them, tears sprang hot to her eyes, dew trembled on her lashes.

"Poor little filly!"

More tears rushed to her eyes, as if he had touched the well-springs of her self-compassion. "You gotta excuse me, Jimmie, I ain't cryin', only I'm dog tired from nursin' and drudgin', drudgin' and nursin'."

"Hard luck, little un!"

"Him layin' there and me tryin' to—to make things meet. You gotta excuse me, Jimmie, I'm done up."

"That's why I wanna blow you, sweetness. I can't bear to see a little filly like you runnin' with the odds dead agin her."

"You been swell to me, Jimmie."

"The sky's my limit, Doll."

"Maybe it wasn't right for me to go with you last Tuesday night, him layin' there, and the kid and all, but a girl's gotta have something, don't she, Jimmie? A girl that's got on her shoulders what I got has gotta have something—a laugh now and then!"

"That's the goods, Doll. A little filly like you has got to."

"Honest, the way I laughed when you stuck them hothouse grapes on my hat for trimming the other night, just like they didn't cost nothing—honest, the way I laughed gimme enough strength for a whole night's nursin'. Honest, I felt like in the old days before—before I was married."

"Gad! if you had treated me white in them days, Doll—if you hadn't pulled that saint stuff on me and treated me cold storage—there ain't nothing I wouldn't have done for you."

"I—I didn't mean nothing, Jimmie."

"I ain't sore, Doll. I like you and I like your style. I always did, even in the days when you turned me down, you great big beautiful doll, you!"

"Aw—you!"

"If you're the real little sport I think you are, you're going to lemme blow you to the liveliest Christmas a little queen like you ever seen. I didn't make that winnin' down in Atlanta for nothing. When I got the telegram I says to myself: 'Here goes! I'm goin' to make last Tuesday night look like a prayer-meeting, I am.' Eh, Doll?"

"I—I can't, Jimmie. I— 'S-s-s-s-h!'"

A tide flowed in about the counter, separating them, and she was suddenly the center of a human whorl, a battle of shoulders and elbows and voices pitched high with gluttony. Mr. Fitzgibbons skirted its edge, patient.

Outside a flake floated down out of the dark pocket of packed clouds, then another and yet another, like timid kisses blown down upon the clownish brow of Broadway. A motorman shielded his eyes from the right merry whirl and swore in his throat. A fruit-cheeked girl paused in the flare of a Mammoth Store show-window, looked up at her lover and the flaky star that lit and died on his mustache, and laughed with the musical glee of a bird. A beggar slid farther out from his doorway and pushed his hat into the flux of the sidewalk. More flakes, dancing upward like suds blown in merriment from the palm of a hand—light, lighter, mad, madder, weaving a blanket from God's own loom, from God's own fleece, whitening men's shoulders with the heavenly fabric.

Mrs. Violet Smith cast startled eyes upon the powdered shoulders and snow-clumped shoes passing down the aisleway, and her hand flew to her throat as if to choke its gasp.

"My! It ain't snowin', is it? It ain't snowin'?"

Mr. Jimmie Fitzgibbons wormed back to the counter. His voice was sunk to the golden mezzo of an amorous whisper.

"Snowin' is right, Doll! A real dyed-in-the-wool white Christmas for you and me!"

"Snowin'!"

"Don't you like snow, baby doll? Cheer up, I'm going to hire a taxicab by the hour. I'm—"

"Snowin'!"

She breathed inward, shivering, stricken, and her mouth, no older than a child's, trembled at the corners and would not be composed.

"He—he can't stand no snow-storm. That's why the doctor said if—if we could get him South before the first one, if we could get him South before the first one—South, where the sun shines and he could feel it clear through him, he— Oh, ain't I—ain't I in a mess!"

"Poor little filly!" He focused his small eyes upon her plump and throbbing throat. "Poor little filly, all winded!"

"I—oh, I—"

"There's the bell, Doll. Poor, tired little girlie, hurry and I'll buy you a taxicab. Hear it—there's the closing bell! Merry Christmas, Doll! Merry Christmas!"

A convulsion tore through the store, like the violent asthma of a thirty-thousand-ton ocean liner breathing the last breath of her voyage and slipping alongside her pier. On that first stroke of ten a girl behind the candy-counter collapsed frankly, rocking her left foot in her lap, pressing its blains, and blubbering through her lips salty with her own bitter tears. A child, qualified by legislation and his fourteen years to brace his soft-boned shoulder against the flank of life, bent his young spine double to the weight of two iron exit doors that swung outward and open. A gale of snow and whistling air danced in. The crowd turned about, faced, thinned, died.

Mrs. Violet Smith turned a rose-white face to the flurry. "Snowin'!"

"A real, made-to-order white Christmas for you and me, Doll. The kind you read about."

"It—it don't mean nothing to me, but—"

"Sure, it does; I'm goin' to blow you right, Doll. Half the money is yourn, anyways. You made that winning down in Atlanta

133

yesterday as much as me, girlie. If I hadn't named that filly after you she'd 'a' been left at the post."

"You—you never had the right to name one of your race-horses after me. There ain't a girl ever went out with you that you 'ain't named one after. You—you never had the right to!"

"I took it, kiddo, 'cause I like you! Gad! I like you! Nix, it ain't every little girl I'd name one of my stable after. 'Violet!'—some little pony that, odds ag'in her and walks off with the money."

"I—honest, I sometimes—I—just wish I was dead!"

"No, you don't, Doll. You know you just wanna go to-night, but you 'ain't got the nerve. I wanna show you a Christmas Eve that'll leave any Christmas Eve you ever spent at the post. Gad! look out there, will you? I'm going to taxicab you right through the fuzz of that there snow-storm if it costs every cent the filly won for us!"

Mrs. Smith leaned back against the shelves limp, as if the blood had run from her heart, weakening her, but her eyes the color of lake-water when summer's moment is bluest. Her lips, that were meant to curve, straightened in a line of decision.

"I'll go, Jimmie."

"That's the goods!"

"A girl's just gotta have something to hold herself together, don't she? It—it ain't like the kid and Harry was layin' awake for me—last Tuesday they was both asleep when I got home. They don't let each other get lonesome, and Harry—he— There ain't nothing much for me to do round home."

"Now you're talkin' the English language, Doll."

"I'll go, Jimmie."

He extended his cane at a sharper angle until it bent in upon itself, threatening to snap, and flung one gray-spatted ankle across the other.

"Sure, you're going! A poor little filly like you, sound-kneed, sound-winded, and full of speed, and nothin' but trouble for your Christmas stockin'. A poor little blue-eyed doll like you!"

"A girl's gotta have something! You knew me before I was married, Jimmie, and there never was a girl more full of life."

"Sure I knew you. But you was a little cold-storage queen and turned me down."

"He—Harry, he never asks me nothing when I come in, and the kid's asleep, anyways."

"Color up there a little, Doll. Where I'm going to take you there ain't nothing but live ones. I'm going to take you to a place where the color scheme of your greenbacks has got to be yellow. Color up there, Doll. You ain't going dead, are you?"

She stretched open her eyes to wide, laughing pools, plowed through the rear-counter débris of pasteboard boxes and tissue-paper, reached for her jacket and tan, boyish hat. A blowy, corn-colored curl caught like a tendril and curled round the brim.

"Going dead! Say, my middle name is Speed! It's like Harry used to tell me when we wasn't no farther along in the marriage game than his sneaking over here from the gents' furnishing three times a day to price bill-folders—he used to say that I was a live wire before Franklin flew his kite."

"Doll!"

"I ain't tired, Jimmie. Not countin' the year and a half I was home before Harry took sick, I been through the Christmas hell just six times. The seventh don't mean nothing in my life. I've seen 'em behind these very counters cursing Christmas with tears in their eyes and spending their merry holiday in bed trying to get some of the soreness out. It takes more than one Christmas to put me out of business."

"Here, lemme tuck that curl in for you, Doll."

"Quit!"

"Doll!"

"Quit, I say!"

"Color up there, girlie. Look live!"

She rubbed her palms briskly across her cheeks to generate a glow, and they warmed to color as peaches blush to the kiss of the sun.

"See!"

"Pink as cherries!"

"That's right, kid me along."

"Tried to dodge me to-night, didn't you, kitten?"

"I—I didn't think I ought to go to-night."

"It's a good thing my feelings ain't hurt easy."

"Honest, Jimmie, I didn't try to dodge you. I—I only thought, with the girls here gabbling so much about last Tuesday night and all, it wouldn't look right. And he had a spell last night again, and the doctor said we—we ought to get him South before the first snow— South, where the sun shines. But he's got as much chance of gettin' South as I have of climbing the South Pole!"

"A pretty little thing like you climbing the South Pole! I'd be there with field-glasses all-righty!"

"I—I went up and talked and begged and begged and talked to old Ingram up at the Aid Society to-day, but the old skinflint says they can't do nothing for an employee after he's been out of his department more'n eight weeks, and—and Harry's been out twelve. He says the Society can't do nothing no more, much less send him South. Just like a machine he talked. I could have killed him!"

"Poor little filly! I was that surprised when I seen you was back in the store again! There ain't been a classy queen behind the counter since you left."

"Aw, Jimmie, no wonder the girls say you got your race-horses beat for speed."

"That's me!"

Aisles thinned and the store relaxed into a bacchanalian chaos of trampled débris, merchandise strewn as if a flock of vultures had left their pickings—a battlefield strewn with gewgaws and the tinsel of Christmastide, and reeking with foolish sweat.

"Button up there, Doll, and come on; it's a swell night for Eskimos."

Mr. Fitzgibbons folded over his own double-breasted coat, fitted his flat-brimmed derby hat on his well-oiled hair, drew a pair of gray suède gloves over his fingers, and hooked his slender cane to his arm.

"Ready, Doll?"

"The girls, Jimmie—look at 'em rubbering and gabbling like ducks! It—it ain't like I could do any good at home, it ain't."

"I'd be the first to ship you there if you could. You know me, Doll!"

His words deadened her doubts like a soporific. She glanced about for the moment at the Dionysian spectacle of the Mammoth

Store ravished to chaos by the holiday delirium; at the weary stream of shoppers and workers bending into the storm as they reached the doors; at the swift cancan of snowflakes dancing whitely and swiftly without; at Mr. Jimmie Fitzgibbons standing attendant. Then she smiled.

"Come on, Jimmie!"

"Come on yourself, Doll!"

Snow beat in their faces like shot as they emerged into the merry night.

She shivered in her thin coat. "Gee! ain't it cold!"

"Not so you can notice it. Watch me, Doll!" He hailed a passing cab with a double flourish of cane and half lifted her in, his fingers closing tight over her arm. "Little Doll, now I got you! And we understand one another, don't we, Doll?"

"Yes, Jimmie."

She leaned back, quiescent, nor did his hold of her relax. A fairy etching of snow whitened the windows and wind-shield, and behind their security he leaned closer until she could feel the breath of his smile.

"Doll, we sure understand each other, don't we, sweetness? Eh? Answer me, sweetness, don't we? Eh? Eh?"

"Yes, Jimmie."

Over the city bells tolled of Christmas.

The gentle Hestia of Christmas Eve snug beside her hearth, with little stockings dangling like a badly matched row of executed soldiers, the fire sinking into embers to facilitate the epic descent from the chimney, the breathing of dreaming children trembling for their to-morrow—this gentle Hestia of a thousand, thousand Christmas Eves was not on the pay-roll of Maxwell's thousand-dol-lar-a-week cabaret.

A pandering management, with its finger ever on the thick wrist of its public, substituted for the little gray lady of tradition the glittering novelty of full-lipped bacchantes whose wreaths were grape, and mistletoe commingling with the grape.

An electric fountain shot upward its iridescent spray, now green, now orange, now violet, and rained down again upon its own bosom and into a gilt basin shaped like a grotto with the sea weeping round it. And out of its foam, wraithlike, rose a marble Aphrodite, white limbed, bathed in light.

On the topmost of a flight of marble steps a woman sang of love who had defiled it. At candle-shaded tables thick tongues wagged through thick aromas and over thick foods, and as the drama was born rhythmic out of the noisy dithyramb, so through these heavy discords rose the tink of Venetian goblets, thin and pure— the reedy music of grinning Pan blowing his pipes.

Rose-colored light lay like a blush of pleasure over a shining table spread beside the coping of the fount. A captain bowed with easy recognition and drew out two chairs. A statue-like waiter, born but to obey and, obeying, sweat, bowed less easy recognition and bent his spine to the backaching, heartbreaking angle of servitude. And through the gleaming maze of tables, light-footed as if her blood were foaming, Mrs. Violet Smith, tossing the curling ribbon of a jest over one shoulder. Following her Mr. Jimmie Fitzgibbons, smiling.

"Here, sit on this side of the table, Doll, so you can see the big show."

"Gee!"

"It's the best table in the room to see the staircase dancing."

"Gee!"

"Told you I was going to show you a classy time to-night, didn't I, Doll?"

"Yeh, but—but I ain't dressed for a splash like this, Jimmie, I—I ain't."

"Say, they know me round here, Doll. They know I'd fall for a pair of eyes like yourn, if you was doing time on a rock-pile and I had to bring you in stripes."

"I'm—a—sight!"

"If you wasn't such a little pepper-box I'd blow you to a feather or two."

"Ain't no pepper-box!"

"You used to be, Doll. Two years back there wasn't a girl behind the counter ever gimme the cold storage like you did. I liked your nerve, too, durned if I didn't!"

"I—I only thought you was guyin'."

"I 'ain't forgot, Doll, the time I asked you out to dinner one night when you was lookin' pretty blue round the gills, and you turned me down so hard the whole department gimme the laugh. It's a good thing I 'ain't got no hard feelings."

"Honest, Jimmie, I—"

"That was just before you stole the march on me with the Charley from the gents' furnishing. I ain't holding it against you, Doll, but you gotta be awful nice to me to make up for it, eh?"

A shower of rose-colored rain from the fountain threw its soft blush across her face.

"Aw, Jimmie, don't rub it in! Ain't I tryin' hard enough to—to square myself? I—I was crazy with the heat two years ago. I—aw, I— Now it's different. I— It's like you say, Jimmie, you 'ain't got no hard feelings." She swallowed a rising in her throat and took a sip of clear, cold water. A light film of tears swam in her eyes. "You 'ain't, have you, Jimmie?"

He leaned across the table and out of the hearing of the attendant waiter. "Not if we understand each other, Doll. You stick to me and you'll wear diamonds. Gad! I bet if I had two more fillies like Violet I'd run Diamond Pat Cassidy's string of favorites back to pasture, you little queenie, you!"

Her timid glance darted like the hither and thither of a wind-blown leaf. "I ain't much of a looker for a Broadway palace like you've brought me to, Jimmie. Look at 'em, all dolled up over there. Honest, Jimmie, I—I feel ashamed."

"Just you stick to me, peaches, and there ain't one at that table that's got on anything you can't have twice over. I know that gang—the pink queen and all. 'Longside of you they look like stacks o' bones tied up in a rag o' satin.

"Aw, Jimmie, look at 'em, so blond and all!"

"They're a broken-winded bunch. Look at them bottles on their table! We're going to have twice as many and only one color in our glasses, kiddo. Yellow, the same yellow as your hair, the kinda yellow that's mostly gold. That's the kind of bubble water we're going to buy, kiddo!"

"Jimmie, such a spender!"

"That's me!"

"It's sure like the girls say—the sky's your limit."

"Look, Doll, there's the swellest little dancer in this town—one swell little pal and a good sport. Watch her, kiddo—watch her do that staircase dance. Ain't she a lalapaloo!"

A buxom nymph of the grove, whose draperies floated from her like flesh-colored mist, spun to the wild passion of violins up the eight marble steps of the marble flight. A spotlight turned the entire range of the spectrum upon her. She was like a spinning tulip, her draperies folding her in a cup of sheerest petals, her limbs shining through.

"Classy, ain't she, Doll?"

"Well, I guess!"

"Wanna meet her? There ain't none of 'em that 'ain't sat at my table many a time."

"I like it better with just you, Jimmie."

"Sweetness, don't you look at me like that or you'll get me so mixed up I'll go out and buy the Metropolitan Tower for your Christmas present. Whatta you want for Christmas—eh, Doll?"

"Aw, Jimmie, I don't want nothing. I 'ain't got no right to take nothing from you!" She played with the rich, unpronounceable foods on her plate and took a swallow of golden liquid to wash down her fiery confusion. "I—ain't got no right."

"When I get to likin' a little girl there ain't nothing she ain't got a right to."

"Aw, Jimmie, when you talk like that I feel so—so—"

"So what, Doll?"

"So—so—"

"Gowann, Doll."

"Aw, I can't say it. You'll think I'm fresh."

But she regarded him with the nervous eyes of a gazelle and the red swam high up into her hair, and he drained his glass down to the bottom of its hollow stem and leaned his warming face closer.

"You treat me white, sweetness, and understand me right, and you won't be sorry for nothing you say. Drink, Doll, drink to you 'n' me—you 'n' me."

Their bubble-thin glasses met in a tink and a pledge and her ready laughter rose in duet with his. She caught the lilt of a popular song from the ten-piece orchestra and sang upward with the tirra-lirra of a lark, and the group at the adjoining table threw her a shout. Mr. Fitzgibbons beat a knife-and-fork tattoo on his plate and pinched her cheek lightly, gritting his teeth in a fine frenzy of delight.

"That's the way to make 'em sit up and take notice, Doll, that's the way I like 'em. Live! As live and frisky as colts!"

An attendant placed a souvenir of the occasion beside her plate—a white wool bear, upright and with bold bead eyes and a flare of pink bow beneath its chin.

"Oh-h-h!"

"See, Doll, a Teddy bear! By Gad! a Teddy bear with his arms stretched out to hug her! Gad! if I was that Teddy I'd hug the daylight out of her, too! Gad! wouldn't I!"

Mrs. Violet Smith wafted the bead-eyed toy a kiss, then slapped him sharply sidewise, toppling him in a heap, and her easy laughter mingled with her petulance.

"I wanna big grizzly, Jimmie; a great big brown grizzly bear with a grin. I wanna big brown grizzly."

"Ain't you got one, Doll? A little white one with a pink bow. Here, let's give him a drink!"

But the petulance grew upon her, nor would she be gainsaid. "I wanna big brown grizzly—a great big brown one with a grin."

"Aw, Doll, look at this little white one—a classy little white one. Look at his nose, cutie, made out of a button. Look, ain't that some nose! Look, ain't—"

"A big brown one that I can dance with, Jimmie. I wanna dance. Gee! who could dance with a little dinky devil like that! I wanna dance, Jimmie, honest I could dance with a great big brown one if he was big enough. I— Gee, I wanna dance. Jimmie, honest, I could dance with a great big brown one if he was big enough. I— Gee! I wanna dance, Jimmie! Gee, I wanna—"

He whacked the table and flashed the twinkle of a wink to the waiter. "Gad! Doll, if you look at me with them frisky eyes I—"

"I wanna bear, Jimmie, a great big brown—"

"Waiter!"

"A great big brown one, Jimmie, with a grin. Tell him a great big brown one!"

"Waiter, that ain't no kind of a souvenir to bring a lady—a cheap bunch o' wool like that. Bring her a great big brown one—"

"A great big brown one with a grin, tell him, Jimmie."

"We have no brown ones, sir; only the small white ones for the ladies."

"Get one, then! Get out and buy the biggest one they got on Broadway. Get out and get one then!"

"But, sir, the—"

"If the stores ain't open, bust 'em open! I ain't the best customer this joint has got not to get service when my lady friend wants to dance with a great big brown bear. If my lady friend can't get a great big brown bear—"

"With a grin, Jimmie."

"—with a grin, there are other places where she can get two great big brown bears if she wants 'em."

"I'll see, sir. I'll see what I can do."

Mr. Fitzgibbons brought a fist down upon the table so that the dishes rattled and the wine lopped out of the glasses. "Sure you'll see, and quick, too! A great big brown bear, d'you hear? My lady friend wants to dance, don't you, Doll? You wanna dance, and nothing but a great big brown bear won't do—eh, Doll?"

"With a grin, Jimmie!"

"With a grin, d'ye hear?" He whacked at her hand in delight and they laughed in right merry duet.

"Oh, Jimmie, you're killing!"

"The sky's my limit!"

She nibbled at a peach whose cheeks were pink as her own, and together from the great overflowing bowl of fruits they must trim her hat with its boyish brim. First, a heavy bunch of black hothouse grapes that she pinned deftly to the crown, a cluster of cherries, a purple plum, a tangerine stuck at a gay angle. They surveyed their foolish labor of caprice with little rills of laughter that rose and fell, and when she replaced her hat the cherries bobbed and kissed her cheek and the adjoining group leaned to her in the kinship of merriment.

"It's a sweller trimming than I gave it last Tuesday, Jimmie. Look how tight it's all pinned on. Look at the cherries! I'm going to blow 'em right off and then eat 'em—eat 'em! Pf-f-f-ft!"

She made as if to catch them with pursed lips, but they bobbed sidewise, and he regarded her with a swelling pride, then glanced about the room, pleased at the furor that followed her little antics.

"Gad, Doll, you're a winner! I can pick 'em every time! You ain't dolled up like the rest of 'em, but you're a winner!"

"Oh-oh-oh!"

"That's the ticket, waiter! I knew there wasn't nothing round here that tin wouldn't buy. I guess that ain't some great big brown grizzly with a grin for you, Doll!"

"Oh-oh-oh!"

"I guess they didn't rustle round when your Uncle Fuller began to get sore, and get a great big brown one for you! Gad! the biggest I ever seen—almost as big as you, Doll! That's the ticket! There ain't anything in this town tin can't buy!"

"Oh-oh-oh!" She lifted the huge toy off the silver tray held out to her and buried her shining face in the soft, silky wool. "Ain't he a beauty? Ain't he the softest, brownest beauty?"

"Now, peaches, now cherries, now you little fancy-fruit stand, there goes the music. Let's see that dance!"

"Aw, Jimmie, I—I was only kiddin'!"

"Kiddin' nothing! Come now, Doll, I blew me ten bucks if I blew me a cent for that bunch of wool. Come now, let's see that dance you been blowing about! Go as far as you like, Doll!"

"I—honest, I was only guyin', Jimmie."

"Don't be a quitter and make me sore, Doll! I wanna show 'em I pick the live ones every time. There's the music!"

"Aw, I—"

"Go as far as you like, Doll. Here, gimme your hat! Go to it, sister. If you land in the fountain by mistake I'll blow you to the swellest new duds on the Avenue."

"I don't know no dances no more, Jimmie. I—I can't dance with this big old thing anyways. Look, he's almost as big as me!"

"Go it alone, then, Doll; but get up and show 'em. Get up and show 'em that I don't pick nothing but the livest! Get up and show 'em, Doll; get up and show 'em!"

She set down her glass suddenly and pirouetted to her feet. "Here—I—go—Jimmie!"

"Go to it, Doll!"

She leaped forward in her narrow little skirt, laughing. Chairs scraped back and a round of applause went with her. Knives and forks beat tattoo on frail glasses; a tinsel ball flung from across the room fell at her feet. She stooped to it, waved it, and pinned it to her bosom. Her hair, rich as Australian gold, half escaped its chignon and lay across her shoulders. She danced light as the breeze up the marble stairway, and at its climax the spotlight focused on her, covering her with the sheen of mica; then just as lightly down the steps again, so rapidly that her hair was tossed outward in a fairy-like effect of spun gold.

"Go to it, Doll. I'm here to back you!"

"Dare me, Jimmie?"

"Dare what?"

"Dare me?"

"Yeh, I dare you to do anything your little heart desires. Gad! you— Gad! if she ain't!"

Like a bird in flight she danced to the gold coping, paused like an audacious Undine in a moment of thrilled silence, and then into the purple and gold, violet and red rain of the electric fountain, her arms outstretched in a radiant *tableau vivant,* water crowding in about her knees, spray dancing on her upturned face.

"Gad! the little daredevil! I didn't think she had it in her. Gad! the little devil!"

Clang! Clang! Tink! Tink! "Bravo, kiddo! Who-o-o-p!"

Shaking the spray out of her eyes, her hair, she emerged to a grand orchestral flare. The same obsequious hands that applauded her helped her from the gold coping. Waiters dared to smile behind their trays. Up to her knees her dark-cloth skirt clung dankly. Water glistened on her shoulders, spotted her blouse. Mr. Jimmie Fitzgibbons lay back in his chair, weak from merriment.

"Gad! I didn't think she had it in her! Gad! I didn't!"

"Bo-o-o-o!" She shook herself like a dainty spaniel, and he grasped the table to steady himself against his laughter.

"Gad! I didn't!"

"Fine weather for ducks!"

"Gad!"

"I'm a nice girl and they treat me like a sponge."

"Gad!"

"April weather we're havin', ain't it?"

"You ain't much wet, are you, Doll?"

"Bo-o-o-o!"

"Here, waiter, get the lady a coat or something. Gad! you're the hit of the place, Doll! Aw, you ain't cold, hon? Look, you ain't even wet through—what you shaking about?"

She drew inward little breaths of shivery glee. "I ain't wet! Say, whatta you think that fountain's spouting—gasoline? I—ain't—wet! Looka my hair curling up like it does in a rain-storm! Feel my skirt down here at the hem! Can you beat it? I ain't wet, he says!"

"Here, drink this, Doll, and warm up."

"No."

She threw a dozen brilliant glances into the crowd, tossed an invitational nod to the group adjoining, and clapped her hands for the iridescent Christmas ball that dangled over their table.

"Here, send 'er over—here, give you leave. I'm some little catcher myself."

It bounded to her light as air, and she caught it deftly, tossed it ceilingward until it bounced against an incandescent bulb, tossed it again, caught it lightly, nor troubled to heed the merry shouts for its return.

From across the room some one threw her a great trailing ribbon of gilt paper. She bound it about her neck like a ruff. A Christmas star with a fluted tissue-paper edge floated into her lap. She wore it like an earring, waggling it slyly so that her curls were set a-bobbing.

"Gimme my bear."

She hugged the woolly image to her as if she would get its warmth, her teeth clicking the while with chill.

"Take a little swallow or two to warm you up, Doll!"

"Gee! I took your dare, Jimmie—and—and—br-r-r-r!"

"A little swallow, Doll!"

"I took your dare, Jimmie, and I—I can feel my skirt shrinking up like it was rigging. I—I guess I'll have to go to work next week in a sheet."

"Didn't I tell you I was backing this toot, sister?"

"I didn't have no right to dive in there and spoil my duds, Jimmie. I—"

"Who had a better right?"

"Ain't it just like a nut like me? But I ain't had a live time for so long I—I lost my head. But I ain't got no right to spoil the only duds I got to my back. Looka this waist; the color's running. I ought to— I— Oh, like I wasn't in enough of a mess already without—without—acting the crazy nut!"

"Aw, Doll, cut the tragedy! Didn't I tell you I was going to blow you to anything your little heart desires?"

"But the only duds I got to my back, Jimmie! Oh, ain't I a nut when I get started, Jimmie! Ain't I a nut!"

She regarded him with tears in her eyes and the wraith of a smile on her lips. A little drop escaped and she dashed it away and her smile broke out into sunshine.

"Ain't I a nut, though!"

"You're a real, full-blooded little winner, that's what you are, and you can't say I ain't one, neither, Doll. Here's your damages. Now go doll yourself up like a Christmas tree!"

He tossed a yellowback bill lightly into her lap, and she made a great show of rejecting it, even pushing it toward him across the table and to the floor.

"I— Aw, what kind of a girl do you think I am? There, take your money. I—honest, I— What kind of a girl do you think I am?"

"Now, now, sister, don't we understand each other? Them's damages, kiddo. Wasn't it me dared you? Ain't it my fault you doused your duds?"

"Yes, but—"

"Aw, come now, Doll, don't pull any of that stuff on me! You and me understand each other—not?"

"Yes, but—"

"Take and forget it. You won it. That ain't even interest on the filly's winnings. Take it. I never started nothing in my life I couldn't see the finish to. Take it and forget it!" He crammed the bill into her reluctant fingers, closed them over it, and sealed her little fist with a grandiose pat. "Forget it, Doll!"

But her lids fluttered and her confusion rose as if to choke her. "I—honest, I— Aw, what kind of a girl do you think I am?"

"I told you I think you're the sweetest, livest little queen I know."

"Aw!"

"Come on, little live wire. Put on your swell, hothouse-trimmed hat. I'm going to take you to a place farther up the street where there are two staircases and a fountain twice as big for you to puddle your little footsies in. Waiter—here—check—get a cab! Here, little Doll, quit your shivering and shaking and lemme help you on—lemme help you."

She was suddenly pale, but tense-lipped like a woman who struggles on the edge of a swoon. "Jimmie, honest, I—I'm shaking with chills! Jimmie—I—I can't go in these duds, neither. I—I gotta go home now. He'll be wakin' and I—I gotta go home now. I'm all shaking." In spite of herself her lips quivered and an ague shot through her body. "I—I gotta go home now, Jimmie. Look at me shivering, all shivering!"

"Home now!" His eyes retreated behind a network of calculating wrinkles and she paled as she sat. "Home now? Say, Doll, I thought—"

"Honest, I wanna go to the other place, but I'm cold, Jimmie, and—wet through. I gotta keep well, Jimmie, and I—I oughtta go home."

"Pah!" he said, spluttering out the end of a bitten cigar. "If I'd 'a' known you was a puny Doll like that!"

"I ain't, Jimmie; I—"

"If I'd 'a' known you was that puny! It's like I been sayin', Doll, it ain't like you and me don't understand each other. I—"

"Sure we do, Jimmie. Honest, I— To-morrow night I—I can fix it so that—that the sky's my limit. I'll meet you at Hinkley's at eight, cross my heart on a wishbone, Jimmie."

"Cross it!"

"There!"

"To-night, Jimmie, I'm chilled—all in. Look at me in these duds, Jimmie. I'm cold. Oh, Jimmie, get me a cab quick, please; I'm co-old!"

She relaxed frankly into a chill that rumbled through her and jarred her knees together. A little rivulet of water oozed from her hair, zigzagged down her cheek and seeped into her blouse, but her blue-lipped smile persisted.

"Ain't I a nut, though! But wait till you see me dolled up to-morrow night, Jimmie! Eight at Hinkley's. I didn't have a hunch how cold—how cold that water was. Next time they gotta—heat it."

"Got to heat it is good, Doll! All I got to do is ask once, and my word's law round here. Here, take a swallow and warm up, hon. You don't need to go home if you warm up right."

But the glass tinked against her teeth.

"I—I can't!"

"Gowann, kiddo!"

"I'll take some home with me to warm me up when I get in bed, Jimmie. I— Not that kind, give it to me red like you did last Tuesday night, without the sparkles. That's the kind to warm me up. Order a bottle of red without the sparkles, Jimmie—without the sparkles. I—I can't stand no more bubbles to-night."

He helped her into her coat, and she leaned to him with a little movement of exhaustion that tightened his hold of her.

"Hurry a cab, waiter; the lady's sick!"

"Ain't I a nut, though!"

"Poor wet little Doll, I didn't think you was much more'n damp! You gotta make up for this to-morrow night, Doll. Eight sharp, Doll, and no funny business to-morrow night."

"Eight sharp!"

"Swell little sport you are, gettin' the chills! But we understand each other, don't we, Doll?"

"Sure, Jimmie!"

"Come on, hon. Shakin' like a leaf, ain't you? Wait till I get you out in the cab, I'll warm you up. You look just like a Christmas doll, all rigged up in that hat and that star and all—just like a Christmas doll."

"My grizzly, my brown grizzly! Gee, I nearly forgot my grizzly!"

And she packed the huge toy under her arm, along with the iridescent ball and the gewgaws of her plunder, and out into the cab, where an attendant tucked a bottle of the red warming wine between them.

"Ready, Doll?"

"Ready."

The silent storm had continued its silent work, weaving its blanket softer, deeper. The straggling pedestrians of early morning bent their heads into it and drove first paths through the immaculate mantle. The fronts of owl cars and cabs were coated with a sugary white rime. Broadway lay in a white lethargy that is her nearest approach to sleep.

Snow-plows were already abroad clearing tracks, dry snow-dust spinning from under them. At Longacre Square the flakes blew upward in spiral flurries, erratic, full of antics. The cab snorted, plunged, leaped forward. Mr. Fitzgibbons inclined toward the little huddle beside him.

"Sweetness, now I got you! You little sweetness you, now I got you, sweetness!"

"Jimmie! Quit! Quit! You—you old—you—you—"

The breath of a forgotten perfume and associations webby with age stir through the lethargy of years. Memories faded as flowers lift their heads. The frail scent of mignonette roused with the dust of letters half a century old, and eyes too dim and watery to show the glaze of tears turn backward fifty years upon the mignonette-bowered scene of love's young dream. A steel drawing-room car rolling through the clean and heavy stench of cow pasture, and a steady-eyed, white-haired capitalist, rolling on his rolling-stock, leans back against the upholstery and gazes with eyes tight closed upon a steady-eyed, brown-haired youngster herding in at eventide. The whiff of violets from a vender's tray, and a young man dreams above his ledger. The reek of a passing brewer's wagon, and white faces look after, suddenly famished.

When the familiar pungency of her boardinghouse flowed in and round Mrs. Violet Smith, she paused for a moment and could not push through the oppression. Then, with the associations of odor crowding in about her, she stripped herself of her gewgaws, as if here even the tarnished tinsel of pleasure could have no place, and tiptoed up the weary wind of three unlighted flights and through the staleness of unaired halls.

At the third landing a broom and a dirty tangled débris of scrub-cloths lay on the topmost stair, as if an aching slavey had not found the strength to remove them. They caught the heel of her shoe, pitching her forward so that she fell sharply against her own door. In the gloom she paused for a palpitating moment, her hands pressing her breast, listening; then deposited her laden hat, the little pile of tinsel and the woolen bear on the floor outside the door.

"Vi! Vi! That you, dear?"

She pulled at her strength and opened the door suddenly, blowing in like a gale. "It's me, darlin'."

She was suddenly radiant as morning, and a figure on the bed in the far corner of the dim-lit room raised to greet her with vague, white-sleeved arms outstretched. She flew to their haven.

"Darlin', darlin', how you feeling?"

"Vi, poor tired little girl!"

"Harry, how you feeling, darlin'? They worked the force all night—first time ever. How you feeling, darlin'—how?" And she burrowed kisses on the poor, white face, and then deep into the tiny crib and back again into the vague white arms. "Oh, my babies, both of you! How you feeling, darlin'? So worried I've been. And the kid! Oh, God, darlin', I—I been so busy rightin' stock and all—all night they kept the force. I got such news, darlin'. We should worry that it's snowing! Such news, darlin'! The kid, Harry—did Mrs. Quigley bring her milk on time? How you feeling, darlin'! You 'ain't coughed, have you?"

He kissed her damp hair and turned her face up like a flower, so that his deep-sunk eyes read into hers. "I ain't coughed once since noon, darlin'. We should worry if it snows is right! A doctor's line of talk can't knock me out. I can buck up without going South. I ain't coughed once since noon, Vi; I—"

A strangling paroxysm shook him in mockery of his words, and she crouched low beside the bed, her face etched in the agony of bearing each rack and pain with him.

"Oh, my darlin'! Oh—oh—"

"It's—all right now, Vi! It's all right! It's all right!"

"Oh, my darlin', yes, yes, it's all right now! All right now!"

She ran her hands over his face, as if to reassure herself of his very features, nor would she let him read into her streaming eyes.

"Lay quiet, Harry darlin'; it's all right! Oh, my darlin'!"

"'S-s-s-s-h, Vi dear! Sure it's all right. 'S-s-s-s-h! Don't cry, Vi!"

"I—I—oh—oh—"

"'S-s-s-s-h, darlin'! Don't!"

"I—oh, I can't help it; but I ain't cryin', Harry, I ain't!"

"All worn out and cold and wet, that's what's a-hurtin' you. All worn out and hysterical and all! Poor little Vi-dee!"

"I—I ain't."

"It's all over now, Vi. See, I'm all right! Everything's all right! Just my luck to have the first one since noon right when you get home. It's all over now, Vi. Everything's over, Christmas rush and all. Don't you worry about the snow, neither, darlin'. I knew it would scare you up, but it takes more than a doctor's line of talk to down-and-out me."

"I—I ain't worryin', darlin'."

"You're the one I been worryin' about, Vi. It's just like the kid was worried too—cried when Mrs. Quigley sung her to sleep."

"Oh, my baby! Oh, my baby!"

"Don't worry, dear. She don't even know it's Christmas—a little thing like her. And, anyways, look, Vi-dee, Mrs. Quigley brought her up that little stuffed lamb there. But she don't even know it's Christmas, dear; she don't even know. You poor, tired little kiddo!"

"I ain't tired."

"I been lying here all night, sweet, thinking and thinking—a little doll like you hustling and a big hulk like me lying here."

" 'S-s-s-s-h! Honest, Harry, it's fun being back in the store again till you get well—honest!"

"I never ought to let you done it in the beginning, darlin'. Remember that night, even when I was strong enough to move a ox team, I told you there was bum lungs 'way back somewhere in my family? I never ought to let you take a chance, Vi-dee—I never ought!"

" 'S-s-s-s-h! Didn't I say I'd marry you if you was playin' hookey from the graveyard? Wasn't that the answer I give you even when you was strong as a whole team?"

"I didn't have no right to you, baby—the swellest little peach in the store! I—I didn't have no right to you! Vi-dee, what's the matter? You look like you got the horrors—the horrors, hon! Vi-dee!"

"Oh, don't, Harry, don't. I—I can't stand it, hon. I—I'm tired, darlin', darlin', but don't look like that, darlin'. I—got news—I got news."

" 'S-s-s-s-h, baby, you're all hysterical from overwork and all tired out from worry. There ain't no need to worry, baby. Quigley'll say it can go over another week. She ain't dunning for board, she ain't, baby."

"I—oh—I—"

"Shaking all over, baby, just like you got the horrors! I bet you got scared when you see the snow coming and tackled Ingram to-day, and you're blue. What you got the horrors about, baby—Ingram?"

"No! No!"

"I told you not to ask the old skinflint. I told you they won't do nothing after twelve weeks. I ain't bluffed off by snow-storm, Vi. I don't need South no more'n you do, I don't, baby. I ain't a dead one by a long shot yet! Vi, for God's sake, why you got the horrors?"

She tried to find words and to smile at him through the hot rain of her tears, and the deep-rooted sobs that racked her subsided and she snuggled closer and burrowed into his pillow.

"I—I can't keep it no longer, darlin'. I ain't cryin', I—I 'ain't got the horrors. I'm laffin'. I—I seen him, Harry—Ingram—I seen him just before closin', and—and—oh, Harry, you won't believe it, he said—he—I— I'm laffin' for joy, Harry!"

"What? What, Vi? What?"

She fumbled into the bosom of her blouse and slid a small folded square of yellowback bill into his hand.

"What? What, Vi? What?"

"A cool hundred, darlin'. Ingram—the Aid Society, because it's Christmas, darlin'. They opened up—a cool hundred! We—we can light out to-morrow, darlin'. A cool hundred! Old Ingram, the old skinflint, he opened up like—like a oyster. South, all of us, to-morrow, darlin'; it ain't nothing for me to get a job South. When I seen it was snowin' I'd 'a' killed somebody to get it. I—I had to have it and we got it, darlin', we—we got it—a cool hundred!"

He lay back on the pillow, suddenly limp, the bill fluttering to the coverlet, and she slid her arm beneath his head.

"You could have knocked me down, too, darlin'. Easy, just like that he forked over. 'What's a Aid Society for?' he kept sayin'. 'What's a Aid Society for?' "

"Vi, I—"

"Don't cry, darlin', don't cry. I just can't stand it!"

"I—"

" 'S-s-s-s-h! Easy, just like that he gimme it, darlin'."

"And me lying here hatin' him for a skinflint and his store for a bloodsucker and the Aid Society for a fake!"

"Yes, yes, darlin'."

"I feel new already, Vi. I can feel the sun already shining through me. If he was here, I—I could just kiss his hand; that's how it feels for a fellow to get his nerve back. I got my chance now, Vi; there ain't nothing can keep me down. Just like he says—I'll be a new man out there. Look, hon, just talking about it! Feel how I got some strength back already. An hour ago I couldn't hold you like this."

"Oh, my darlin'!"

He sat up suddenly in bed and drew her into his arms and she laid her cheek against his, and in the silence, from the trundle crib beside them, the breathing of a child rose softly, fell softly.

"I—I blew us to a real Christmas, darlin', us and the kid. I—I couldn't help it. I couldn't bear to have her wake up without it, Harry, her and you—and me."

"A real Christmas, baby!"

"Red wine for you, darlin', like I brought you last Tuesday night and warmed you up so nice. The kind the doctor says is so grand for you, darlin'—red wine without bubbles like he says you gotta have."

"Red wine!"

"Yeh, and black grapes like I brought you last Tuesday, and like he says you oughtta have—black grapes and swell fruit that's good for you, darlin'."

"A real blow-out, Vi-dee."

"A bear for the kid, Harry!"

"Vi!"

"Yeh, a real brown grizz, with the grin and all, like she cried for in the window that Sunday—a real big brown one with the grin and all."

"That cost a real bunch of money, sweet!"

"Yeh, I blew me like sixty for it, hon, but she cried for it that Sunday and she had to have a Christmas, didn't she, darlin', even if she is too little. It—it would 'a' broke my heart to have her wake up to-morrow without one."

He regarded her through the glaze of tears. "My little kiddo!"

" 'S-s-s-s-h!"

"It just don't seem fair for you to have to—"

" 'S-s-s-s-h! Everything's fair, darlin', in love and war. All the rules for the game of living ain't written down—the Eleventh Commandment and the Twelfth Commandment and the Ninth Commandment."

"My little kiddo!"

"To-morrow, Harry, to-morrow, Harry, we're going! South, darlin', where he says the sun is going to warm you through and through. To-morrow, darlin'!"

"The next day, sweetness. You're all worn out and to-morrow's Christmas, and—"

But the shivering took hold of her again, and when she pressed her hand over his mouth he could feel it trembling.

"To-morrow, darlin', to-morrow before eight. Every day counts. Promise me, darlin'. I—I just can't live if you don't. To-morrow before eight. Promise me, darlin'! Oh, promise me, darlin'!"

"Poor, tired little kiddo, to-morrow before eight, then, to-morrow before eight we go."

Her head relaxed.

"You're tired out, darlin'. Get to bed, baby. We got a big day to-morrow. We got a big day to-morrow, darlin'! Get to bed, Vi-dee."

"I wanna spread out her Christmas first, Harry. I want her to see it when she wakes up. I couldn't stand her not seein' it."

She scurried to the hall and back again, and at the foot of the bed she spread her gaudy wares: An iridescent rubber ball glowing with six colors; a ribbon of gilt paper festooned to the crib; a gleaming Christmas star that dangled and gave out radiance; a huge brown bear standing upright, and with bead eyes and a grin.

Edna Ferber

(August 15, 1885-April 16, 1968)

Originally published in the December 16, 1939 issue of *Collier's Magazine,* "No Room at the Inn" was issued as a gift book in 1941. It was included in the 1947 collection of selected Ferber stories entitled *One Basket.*

Ferber's introduction to the story in that collection is still moving:

> Here is pure plagiarism. My source is the Eternal Best Seller. I happened to read in *The New York Times* the brief and poignant news paragraph quoted at the top of this story. The persecution, torture, and death of six million European Jews had actually brought little or no protest from a Christian world whose religion was based on the teachings of a Jew.
>
> I took the story and characters involved in the birth of the infant Jesus and modernized these to fit the German Nazi pattern. So Joe, Mary, Lisabeth, and Zach are rather well known to you—I hope. It is to be regretted that this story, written in 1939, is not what we call dated even today in 1946.

No Room at the Inn

Edna Ferber

"NOBODY" IS BORN IN NO MAN'S LAND

Prague, Oct. 25 (U.P.)—*A baby born in the no man's land south of Brno, where 200 Jewish refugees have been living in a ditch between Germany and Czechoslovakia for two weeks, was named Niemand (Nobody) today.*

She had made every stitch herself. Literally, every stitch, and the sewing was so fairylike that the eye scarcely could see it. Everything was new, too. She had been almost unreasonable about that, considering Joe's meager and uncertain wage and the frightening time that had come upon the world. Cousin Elisabeth had offered to give her some of the clothing that her baby had outgrown, but Mary had refused, politely, to accept these.

"That is dear and good of you, 'Lisbeth," Mary had said. "I know it seems ungrateful, maybe, and even silly not to take them.

It's hard to tell you how I feel. I want everything of his to be new. I want to make everything myself. Every little bit myself."

Cousin Elisabeth was more than twice as old as Mary. She understood everything. It was a great comfort to have Elisabeth so near, with her wisdom and her warm sympathy. "No, I don't think it's silly at all. I know just how you feel. I felt the same way when my John was coming." She laughed then, teasingly: "How does it happen you're so sure it's going to be a boy? You keep saying 'he' all the time."

Mary had gone calmly on with her sewing, one infinitesimal stitch after the other, her face serene. "I know. I know." She glanced up at her older cousin, fondly. "I only hope he'll be half as smart and good as your little John."

Elisabeth's eyes went to the crib where the infant lay asleep. "Well, if I say so myself, John certainly is smart for his age. But then"—hastily, for fear that she should seem too proud—"but, then, Zach and I are both kind of middle-aged. And they say the first child of middle-aged parents is likely to be unusually smart."

The eighteen-year-old Mary beamed at this. "Joe's middle-aged!" she boasted happily. Then she blushed the deep, flaming crimson of youth and innocence; for Joe's astonishment at the first news of the child's coming had been as great as her own. It was like a miracle wrought by some outside force.

Cousin Elisabeth had really made the match between the young girl and the man well on in years. People had thought it strange; but this Mary, for all her youth, had a wisdom and sedateness beyond her years, and an unexpected humor, too, quiet and strangely dry, such as one usually finds associated with long observation and experience. Joe was husband, father, brother to the girl. It was wonderful. They were well mated. And now, when life in this strange world had become so frightening, so brutal, so terrible, it was more than ever wonderful to have his strength and goodness and judgment as a shield and staff. She knew of younger men, hotheaded, who had been taken away in the night and never again heard from. Joe went quietly about his business. But each morning as he left her he said, "Stay at home until I come back this evening.

Or, if you must do your marketing, take Elisabeth with you. I'll stop by and tell her to call for you. Don't go into the streets alone."

"I'll be all right," she said. "Nobody would hurt me." For here pregnant women were given special attention. The government wanted children for future armies.

"Not our children," Joe said bitterly.

So they lived quietly, quietly they obeyed the laws; they went nowhere. Two lower-middle-class people. Dreadful, unspeakable things were happening; but such things did not happen to her and to her husband and to her unborn child. Everything would right itself. It must.

Her days were full. There were the two rooms to keep clean, the marketing, the cooking, the sewing. The marketing was a tiring task, for one had to run from shop to shop to get a bit of butter, an egg for Joe, a piece of meat however coarse and tough. Sometimes when she came back to the little flat in the narrow street and climbed the three flights of stairs, the beads of sweat stood on her lip and forehead and her breath came painfully, for all her youth. Still, it was glorious to be able at night to show Joe a pan of coffeecake, or a meat ball, or even a pat of pretty good butter. On Friday she always tried her hardest to get a fowl, however skinny, or a bit of lamb because Friday was the eve of the Sabbath. She rarely could manage it; but that made all the sweeter her triumph when she did come home, panting up the stairs, with her scrap of booty.

Mary kept her sewing in a wicker basket neatly covered over with a clean white cloth. The little pile grew and grew. Joe did not know that she had regularly gone without a midday meal in order to save even that penny or two for the boy's furnishings. Sometimes Joe would take the sewing from her busy hands and hold it up, an absurd fragment of cloth, a miniature garment that looked the smaller in contrast with his great, work-worn hand. He would laugh as he held it, dangling. It seemed so improbable that anything alive and sentient should be small enough to fit into this scrap of cloth. Then, in the midst of his laugh, he would grow serious. He would stare at her and she at him and they would listen, hushed, as for a dreaded and expected sound on the stairs.

Floors to scrub, pots and pans to scour, clothes to wash, food to cook, garments to sew. It was her life, it was for Joe, it was enough and brimming over. Hers was an enormous pride in keeping things in order, the pride of possession inherited from peasant ancestors. Self-respect.

The men swarmed up the stairway so swiftly that Mary and Joe had scarcely heard their heavy boots on the first landing before they were kicking at the door and banging it with their fists. Joe sprang to his feet and she stood up, one hand at her breast and in that hand a pink knitted hood, no bigger than a fist, that she was knitting. Then they were in the room; they filled the little clean room with their clamor and their oaths and their great brown-clad bodies. They hardly looked at Joe and Mary, they ransacked the cupboards, they pulled out the linen and the dishes, they trampled these. One of the men snatched the pink cap from her hand and held it up and then put in on his own big, round head, capering with a finger in his mouth.

"Stop that!" said one in charge. "We've no time for such foolishness." And snatched off the pink hood, and blew his nose into it, and threw it in a corner.

In the cupboard they came upon the little cakes. She had saved drippings, she had skimmed such bits of rare fat as came their way, she had used these to fashion shortening for four little cakes, each with a dab of dried plum on top. Joe had eaten two for his supper and there had been two left for his breakfast. She had said she did not want any. Cakes made her too fat. It was bad for the boy.

"Look!" yelled the man who had found these. "Cakes! These swine have cakes to eat, so many that they can leave them uneaten in the cakebox." He broke one between his fingers, sniffed it like a dog, then bolted it greedily.

"Enough of this!" yelled the man in authority. "Stop fooling and come on! You want to stay in this pigsty all night! There's a hundred more. Come on. Out!"

Then they saw Mary, big as she was, and they made a joke of this, and one of them poked her a little with his finger, and still Joe did nothing; he was like a man standing asleep with his eyes wide open. Then they shoved them both from the room. As they went,

Mary made a gesture toward the basket in the corner—the basket that had been covered so neatly with the clean white cloth. Her hand was outstretched; her eyes were terrible. The little stitches so small that even she had scarcely been able to see them, once she had pricked them into the cloth.

The man who had stuffed the cakes into his mouth was now hurriedly wiping his soiled boots with a bit of soft white, kneeling by the overturned basket as he did so. He was very industrious and concentrated about it, as they were taught to be thorough about everything. His tongue was out a little way between his strong yellow teeth and he rubbed away industriously. Then, at an impatient oath from the leader, he threw the piece of cloth into a corner with the rest of the muddied, trampled garments and hurried after so that he was there to help load them into the truck with the others huddled close.

Out of the truck and on the train they bumped along for hours—or it may have been days. Mary had no sense of time. Joe pillowed her head on his breast and she even slept a little, like a drugged thing, her long lashes meeting the black smudges under her eyes. There was no proper space for them all; they huddled on the floor and in the passages. Soon the scene was one of indescribable filth. Children cried, sometimes women screamed hysterically, oftenest they sat, men and women, staring into space. The train puffed briskly along with the businesslike efficiency characteristic of the country.

It was interesting to see these decent middle-class people reduced to dreadful squalor, to a sordidness unthought of in their lives. From time to time the women tried to straighten their clothing, to wash their bodies, but the cup of water here and there was needed for refreshment. Amidst these stenches and sounds, amidst the horror and degradation, Joe and Mary sat, part of the scene, yet apart from it. She had wakened curiously refreshed. It was as though a dream she had dreamed again and again, only to awake in horror, had really come to pass, and so, seeing it come true, she was better able to bear it, knowing the worst of it. Awake, she now laid his head in its turn on her breast and through exhaustion he slept, his eyes closed flutteringly but his face and hands clenched even in sleep. Joe had aged before her eyes, overnight. A strong and robust man, of sturdy frame, he had withered; there were queer hollows in his temples and blue veins throbbed there in welts she had never before seen.

Big though she was with her burden, she tried to help women younger and older than she. She was, in fact, strangely full of strength and energy, as often is the case with pregnant women.

The train stopped, and they looked out, and there was nothing. It started again, and they came to the border of the next country. Men in uniform swarmed amongst them, stepping over them and even on them as if they were vermin. Then they talked together and alighted from the train, and the train backed until it came again to the open fields where there was nothing. Barren land, and no sign of habitation. It was nowhere. It was nothing. It was neither their country nor the adjoining country. It was no man's land.

They could not enter here, they could not turn back there. Out they went, shoved and pushed, between heaven and hell, into purgatory. Lost souls.

They stumbled out into the twilight. It was October, it was today. Nonsense, such things do not happen, this is a civilized world, they told themselves. Not like this, to wander until they dropped and died.

They walked forward together, the two hundred of them, dazedly but with absurd purposefulness, too, as if they were going somewhere. They children stumbled and cried and stumbled again. Shed, barn, shelter there was none. There was nothing.

And then that which Mary had expected began to take place. Her pains began, wave on wave. Her eyes grew enormous and her face grew very little and thin and old. Presently she could no longer walk with the rest. They came upon a little flock of sheep grazing in a spot left still green in the autumn, and near by were two shepherds and a tiny donkey hardly bigger than a dog.

Joe went to the shepherds, desperate. "My wife is ill. She is terribly ill. Let me take your donkey. There must be some place near by—an inn. Some place."

One of the shepherds, less oafish than the other, and older, said, "There's an inn, but they won't take her."

"Here," said Joe, and held out a few poor coins that had been in his pocket. "Let her ride just a little way."

The fellow took the coins. "All right. A little way. I'm going home. It's suppertime. She can ride a little way."

So they hoisted her to the donkey's back and she crouched there, but presently it was her time, and she slipped off and they helped her to the ditch by the side of the road.

She was a little silly by now, what with agony and horror. "Get all the nice clean things, Joe. The linen things, they're in the box in the cupboard. And call Elisabeth. Put the kettle on to boil. No, not my best nightgown, that comes later, when everything is over and I am tidy again. Men don't know."

Her earth rocked and roared and faces were blurred and distorted and she was rent and tortured and she heard someone making strange noises like an animal in pain, and then there came merciful blackness.

When she awoke there were women bending over her, and they had built a fire from bits of wood and dried grass, and in some miraculous way there was warm water and strips of cloth and she felt and then saw the child by her side in the ditch and he was swaddled in decent wrappings. She was beyond the effort of questioning, but at the look in her eyes the woman bending over her said, "It's a boy. A fine boy." And she held him up. He waved his tiny arms and his hair was bright in the reflection of the fire behind him. But they crowded too close around her, and Joseph waved them away with one arm and slipped his other under her head and she looked up at him and even managed to smile.

As the crowd parted there was the sound of an automobile that came to a grinding halt. They were officials, you could see that easily enough, with their uniforms and their boots and their proud way of walking.

"Hr-r-rmph!" they said. "Here, all of you. Now then, what's all this! We had a hell of a time finding you, we never would have got here if we hadn't seen the light in the sky from your fire. Now, then, answer to roll call; we've got the names of all of you, so speak up or you'll wish you had."

They called the roll of the two hundred and each answered,

some timidly, some scornfully, some weeping, some cringing, some courageously.

"Mary!" they called. "Mary."

She opened her eyes. "Mary," she said, in little more than a whisper.

"That must be the one," they said amongst themselves, the three. "That's the one had the kid just born." They came forward then and saw the woman Mary and the newborn babe in the ditch. "Yep, that's it. Born in a ditch to one of these damned Jews."

"Well, let's put it on the roll call. Might as well get it in now, before it grows up and tries to sneak out. What d'you call it? Heh, Mary?" He prodded her a little, not too roughly, with the toe of his boot.

She opened her eyes again and smiled a little as she looked up at him and then at the boy in her arms. She smiled while her eyes were clouded with agony.

"Niemand," she whispered.

"What's that? Speak up. Can't hear you."

She concentrated all her energies, she formed her lips to make sound again, and licked them because they were quite dry, and said once more, "Niemand . . . Nobody."

One man wrote it down, but the first man stared as though he resented being joked with, a man of his position. But at the look in her eyes he decided that she had not been joking. He stared and stared at the boy, the firelight shining on his tiny face, making a sort of halo of his hair.

"Niemand, eh? That the best you can do for him! . . . Jesus! . . . Well, cheer up, he's a fine-looking boy. He might grow up to be quite a kid, at that."

Frances Gray Patton
(b. March 19, 1906)

"First Principles," first published not in a Christmas issue but in the January 8, 1949 issue of *The New Yorker* as an *after*-Christmas story, poses questions about the transition from holiday to everyday. How does everyday life get started again? Will we be advantaged or disadvantaged once back in the diurnal world by whatever has happened to us during the Christmas recess? The story also raises, in a muted and gentle way, some of the financial problems that threaten so many of today's families.

This complex mother-daughter story was included both in Patton's first volume of stories, *The Finer Things of Life,* in 1951 and then again in her 1969 volume of selected stories, *Twenty-eight Stories.*

Patton, the daughter of writers and the mother of daughters, is best known for her 1954 novel, *Good Morning, Miss Dove,* adapted from a short story in answer to readers' urging and made into a film in 1955.

First Principles

Frances Gray Patton

No family had ever had a nicer Christmas, Emily Wade thought
happily as she drove the children to school for the first time after
the holidays, and, of course, it had been largely Laura's doing. She
glanced at Laura, a slim, dark-haired girl of fourteen, sitting beside
her, and felt warm with that most comfortable of parental emotions,
gratitude to one's own child. The weather suited Emily's mood, for
it was one of those anomalous mornings that happen sometimes in
the very teeth of a Baltimore winter and persuade the human imagination that everything is likely to turn out better than it could have
been expected to. The air was soft with the vapors of melting snow,
and almost fragrant, as if some delicate flower, like a freesia, were
blooming near at hand; the pale-blue sky was full of loose clouds,
and sun and shadow chased each other on the wet surface of the

Reprinted by permission of Dodd, Mead & Company, Inc. from *The Finer Things in
Life* by Frances Gray Patton. Copyright 1949, 1951 by Frances Gray Patton. Copyright renewed.
This story was first published in *The New Yorker*.

Reprinted by permission of Russell & Volkening, Inc. Copyright © 1949 by Frances
Gray Patton.

streets. "It's like spring, isn't it?" she said to Laura. "And tomorrow we'll probably have a raging sleet storm."

"King Claudius weather," said Laura, looking prettily shy as she made the literary allusion. "It can smile and smile and still be a villain."

"Exactly," Emily agreed. She wasn't sure for a moment who King Claudius was, and then she saw a copy of "Hamlet" among Laura's books. She thought her heart would burst with pride (imagine a child saying that!), and she thought how wise she and Henry had been when they'd decided to make every possible sacrifice for the sake of Laura's education.

On the back seat, the two boys, aged six and eight, were playing with the silver-metal airplanes they had found in the toes of their Christmas stockings. "B-rr-rrrrr—mmm-mmmmmmmm," their voices went. "Zoo-ooommmm—zzzz-oot!" Emily drew up to the curb in front of the public school. "You'd better keep those planes in your pockets during class," she advised them, "or the teacher'll take them away from you."

The boys didn't reply. They hugged her around the neck, knocking her hat somewhat askew, and flung themselves out of the car. As they did, the younger one tripped and dropped his silver plane in the gutter. "Oh!" he cried. He stooped and picked it up gingerly. It was a grimy object now, filmed with slush and black grease. His babyish face was stricken with sorrow as he winked hard to hold his tears back.

"Bring it here, Tommy," Laura said kindly. "I'll fix it for you." She took a piece of Kleenex from her purse and wiped the plane carefully, rubbing it back to its pristine brilliance. How charming the girl looked, thought Emily, and how womanly, with that half-whimsical expression of sympathy lighting her face. "Here you are, Tommikins," said Laura. "And here's the dirty paper. Put it in the trash can, now. Don't throw it down just anywhere."

"Thanks," Tommy said breathlessly. He ran off to join a crowd of his contemporaries, dropping the Kleenex on the concrete path and waving his plane in a great downward curve like a power dive. "Zooo-oo-oom!" he cried. "Mnnm-nm-nm-mmmmmm!"

Laura laughed. "If the American boy doesn't watch out, he's going to forget how to use words," she said. "He'll have to communicate by motor noises."

"Yes," Emily said, laughing appreciatively as she started the car. "I wonder how it would feel to be proposed to by a B-29 or a Diesel engine."

"Or an atomic bomb!" suggested Laura.

Her mother shuddered. "I think I'd turn that offer down right quick."

"Kind sir, I am sensible of the honor you do me, *but, . . .*" murmured Laura. "Which reminds me," she continued, "I'd better brush up on my physics. They say old Superman goes pop-quiz-happy after vacations." She opened a red textbook and began to read it with a frown of concentration and a look of having shut a door upon the visible world.

Laura, who was in first-year high, had gone to the same public school that her brothers now attended, but this year she was a pupil at Green Valley Academy, a small country day school on the outskirts of the city. It was a very good school and a very expensive one, and most of the Wades' friends thought they were being rather fancy in sending Laura there. They knew Laura was smart, of course, but some of the other Baltimore private schools for girls were excellent and had lower tuitions, and even the public high schools were all right. They maintained a strict scholastic standard, and lots of nice kids, whose fathers, incidentally, had twice as big an income as Henry Wade, went to them. Besides, you weren't doing a girl a favor when you encouraged her to develop tastes she couldn't afford to gratify. You either spoiled her or made her bitter. These arguments were cogent, Emily Wade admitted, but they simply didn't apply to Laura's case. Nothing was too good for that child. She was too mature to be thrown off balance by envy, and she had a grace of mind and character that demanded something special in the matter of education. Moreover, it was Emily's theory that children learned love as well as discipline by family example; if you did all you could for them, keeping their best interests in mind, they wouldn't let you down in a crisis. And events had certainly proved her theory.

Emily had been enchanted with Green Valley Academy since the day she had gone there to discuss the possibility of enrolling Laura. Everything about it was right: the main hall, which suggested a quiet Georgian manor house; the stable; the playing fields; the studio, where girls in faded-blue smocks messed earnestly with clay and charcoal and tubes of bright paint; the music building, with its delightful mixture of sounds floating from the windows (the piano scales, the sad, squeaking violins, and the fresh, light voices of a chorus singing, "Unfold! Unfold! Unfold! Ye portals everlasting!"); the girls themselves, so courteous and so modestly self-confident; and Miss St. John, the headmistress.

Miss St. John was a woman of fifty or thereabouts, with a strong, scholarly brow and firm lines of good humor around her mouth. Drinking tea with her, Emily had felt so much at ease that she had been able to speak without embarrassment about money. "The only thing that bothers me," she had said, "is the difference in circumstances between Laura and the other girls. You see, we aren't people of means and—"

"I understand your position," Miss St. John had interrupted, "but I think you need have no qualms about Green Valley. It's true that most of our girls come from well-to-do—I might even say rich—families, but they won't do Laura any harm unless she's a fool herself, which she doesn't seem to be. You see—well, I hope I'm not snobbish, but, frankly, we discourage the *nouveau riche.* Our girls, for all their money, are as well bred as you or I." She laughed. "Of course, we do give a few scholarships to daughters of Hopkins professors. We find them a wholesome influence, because, though faculty children are notoriously rough-mannered, they leaven the intellectual lump. No, I think Laura can keep her own standards here."

How true that had been, thought Emily, driving slowly because she had a quarter hour to spare and she might as well give Laura time to study. Her mind went back to that black moment, a month before, when she'd met Henry for lunch and he'd told her that the bottom had dropped out of their finances.

She had been planning to do most of her gift-shopping in one swoop that afternoon. It was more fun that way, she had always thought—to wait until the stores were decorated and the streets crowded, and you felt Christmas in your bones and let yourself go with a bang. She had planned to go to Hutzler's after lunch and buy the party dress she knew Laura coveted, and then she would meet Laura at the Walters' gallery and they would poke about the shops together, choosing quaint remembrances for cousins and splendid, enormous toys for the little boys. But when Henry had entered the small German restaurant where she was waiting, she'd known at once, by the set of his shoulders, that something was wrong.

Something really was wrong. He was out of a job. The branch sales office he'd been managing had been absorbed by a larger firm, and its whole staff was out in the cold without so much as a month's salary to tide them over. He was pretty sure he could get another and a better position; there was a firm that had been making overtures to him, and only a sense of loyalty to his old firm had made him ignore them up to this point. But the man he'd have to see was in Florida and wouldn't be back until the first of the year. Then, too, he'd just had a letter from his brother in Ohio; it seemed that the whole family out there was shot to hell. His brother, who was a schoolteacher, was broke, his stomach ulcers were troubling him, one of his children had to have a serious operation, and his wife was about to have twins. He needed five hundred dollars.

"I should think he would!" Emily had said, swallowing air. "We'll have to send it to him." She'd laughed giddily. "He's got so much trouble it's plumb ridiculous!"

"I guess if we let him have it, we can still eat," Henry had said, brooding gloomily. "But it knocks Christmas into a cocked hat. I hate to borrow on my insurance."

"Oh, no!" Emily had exclaimed. "We'll manage. We can cut our list to the bone and concentrate on the kids. You know how they are—all they want is the illusion of abundance and cheerful confusion."

"That goes for the young ones," Henry had said, "but what does Laura want?"

"The only thing she's mentioned is a ballerina dress she saw at Hutzler's. She's been invited to some parties by her friends at school. I haven't priced the dress yet."

"Well . . . Couldn't you charge that?" Henry had asked.

"No," she'd said. "I'm charged to the hilt already, and I don't want to risk being refused. As a matter of fact, I'd planned to pay my bill today." Just then, a waiter had come to take her order. "Pigs' knuckles and sauerkraut," she'd said, instead of the lobster she'd planned on. She had sat silent for a moment, looking at Henry's discouraged face. "The only thing to do, dear," she'd said at last, "is to return to first principles."

"What do you mean by that?"

"Well, Christmas has been commercialized out of its real meaning. The gifts people give have become a sort of advertising display, like the prizes in a Hush contest. What we ought to do is give to people we love—give memorable things according to our ability. If you could give your child a horse, say, that would be fine. But if you can't, give her a little locket or a book of verse."

Henry had looked hopeful but skeptical.

"I'll tell you what we'll do," she had continued. "We'll go to the farm for the holidays."

"And sell it afterward," Henry had said.

"Maybe we'll have to," she'd agreed, "but we'll have a good time there first. We won't have to do any entertaining—the liquor bills alone are always staggering at Christmas. We'll have our turkey and our tree and take long walks and sing carols and forget the world."

"Did you ever have a Christmas like that?" Henry had asked.

"Lord, no!" she'd answered. "In the Deep South, we used to celebrate with firecrackers. We'd start the little ones popping before daylight. Then we'd go to church, and the minister would tell us how disrespectful it was to commemorate the Nativity with noise and violence, and we'd all feel ashamed. But we'd go home and shoot off the blockbusters before dinner. Then the eggnog would start flowing. But I've read about the quiet kind in books."

"So have I," Henry had said dubiously. "Well, you're the captain. But try to break it gently to Laura."

"Laura'll be all right," Emily had said with a smile.

In the restaurant, it had sounded easy as an idyll, but once she was alone again, she hadn't felt so sanguine. She'd gone to Hutzler's and examined the white-and-gold dress; it was perfectly lovely, just right for Laura, and priced at a hundred and twenty-five dollars. She had looked at some less expensive dresses, but they'd all seemed bunchy or nondescript, and wandering through various shops, fingering rhinestone necklaces, fur gloves, and rayon housecoats, she'd felt more and more miserable. Out on the street, the throngs of jolly people had irritated her and made her want to cry. She had paused for a minute by Hochschild Kohn's window to stare at the laughing Santa Claus. He was a great, inflated figure about ten feet high with terrible, manic blue eyes, and his continuous laughter seemed to Emily to be the most frightening sound in the world. It ran the whole gamut of mirth, from a sly chuckle through a deep, coarse belly laugh and the cackle of a hysterical woman to a strange, soblike sound of abandon and despair. It was the way a depressed mental invalid might laugh if some disordered shaft of lucidity had suddenly pierced his darkened mind. But when she had met Laura at the gallery and, standing beneath a tranquil Corot landscape, had explained the situation to her, she'd been blessedly relieved.

"Poor Daddy!" the girl had cried, and then, being reassured as to his future prospects, had clasped her hands. "But how marvellous to go to the farm, Mother! It'll be just like a picture on a Christmas card. I adore it there, and I don't care a thing about presents or parties!" She had raised herself on the tips of her toes, as if she were about to dance.

"We'll get some pretty things for your school friends, of course," Emily had said.

But Laura had explained that Miss St. John had asked them not to exchange gifts this year. She wanted them to give something instead to a fund for European relief. Emily had said she thought that was fine, but she'd been somewhat uneasy as she asked, "How much are you supposed to contribute?"

"Oh, Miss St. John said she couldn't tell us that," Laura had explained. "She asked us not even to tell each other. She said it was a private matter for us to decide separately, after we'd talked to our parents."

And that, Emily had thought, was another star in the head-mistress's crown.

Several days before Christmas, they'd gone down to their little farm in Virginia. It was just a half-dozen acres that Henry had bought for taxes during the depression and had hung on to, because it made him feel good to own a piece of land. On it, there was a four-room cottage, furnished with iron beds and hickory chairs and tables, and heated by open fireplaces. There was a big, wood-burning iron range in the kitchen, and you had to get water from a pump in the yard. They'd all had a wonderful time, really. They had cut a tree and climbed for mistletoe in their own woods. They had eaten and slept, and read by the light of oil lamps. The children had been more than satisfied with their presents; there had been balls, Erector sets, a number of storybooks, and a lot of junk from the five-and-ten for the boys, and for Laura, a Breughel print Emily had found cheap in a second-hand art shop and a small amethyst brooch that had belonged to Henry's mother. It was Laura's obvious pleasure that had brightened everything. Whether she was chopping wood, or romping with her brothers, or basting the turkey, or talking politics very sensibly with her father, she'd seemed to radiate a contagious warmth of happiness. On New Year's Eve, they had given her a weak highball, the first she'd ever had, and she had gone to sleep sitting on the floor with her rosy cheek against Henry's knee. "By God, I believe she's the best girl in the world," he had said softly.

"She probably is," Emily had agreed.

"If I don't hand her the earth someday, on a silver platter," Henry had declared, "may I be damned from here to eternity!"

Emily slowed the car to a full stop near the gates of the Academy. "Here we are," she said. "I'm going to miss you today."

Laura closed her book. "I'll miss you, too," she said. "It's been a beautiful holiday." She made no move to leave the car. Instead, she looked hesitantly at a group of girls who stood chatting on the steps of the school. What nice girls they seemed, reflected Emily, hearing their merry, modulated laughter and observing their simple, practical clothes, which were exactly like Laura's—the sweaters, the flannel skirts, the vivid-colored, hooded coats, hanging open now because of the warm weather. "What shall I say, Mother?" Laura asked in a small, childish voice.

"What shall you say?" Emily echoed, puzzled. A sleek black Packard drew to the curb just ahead of them. A girl hopped out and leaped across a puddle on the sidewalk. A puffy Negro chauffeur leaned out of his window. "You come back here directly and put on your overshoes, Peggy," he said in the governessy tone with which old servants of the rich address the young. Peggy looked cross, but she did as she was told.

"There's Peggy Sylvester," said Laura. "Her family took her to Bermuda for Christmas."

Peggy, in shiny black rubbers, started again toward the school, leaving the rear door of the Packard wide open. As she turned her head to make sure the chauffeur was properly annoyed by her negligence, she saw the Wades' car. Her face glowed and she started toward it, but she drew back. She was too well instructed to interrupt a tête-à-tête between mother and daughter. "Hi, there!" she called to Laura. "Happy New Year, Mrs. Wade," she added demurely.

"What shall I tell the girls?" said Laura. "About Christmas?"

"Why," Emily said in amazement, "why, tell them what a nice time we had. Tell them . . ." She paused, and looked at Laura. The child's face was white with the pallor of quiet panic. Her eyes were wide and dark. Emily thought, with a sensation of visceral pain, of a face seen in a small, wavy mirror long ago. She had a strange feeling of being acutely aware of Laura's thoughts, of being actually under Laura's skin. Tell them about cutting the tree, she was going to say. Tell them about your grandmother's pin, and about the boot of Icarus in the Breughel print, sticking up out of the water while the farmers go on complacently about their tasks. But she didn't say it. She lit a cigarette and looked again at the knot of girls on the steps. Peggy was one of them now. She was gesticulating, boasting about something. Their voices rose in squeals of incredulous envy. Their clothes, Emily noticed, weren't really quite like Laura's. There was a slight difference in the hang of the skirts, in the soft, jewel colors of the sweaters. Laura had asked her a sensible question. This was no time for an inspirational sermon. In the distance, the copper weathercock glittered above the steep slate roof of the stable. She turned to Laura.

"I think you'd better lie, darling," she said.

"What?" whispered Laura.

"There's supposed to be a time for everything, you know," Emily said gently, "and this is the time to lie like a lady. I think you got a horse. Would you like that?"

"Wouldn't I!" exclaimed Laura. "But—"

"You had to leave him at the farm," said Emily.

Laura was flushed. Her eyes were shining. "But next summer . . ." she faltered. "Somebody might want to drive down and see."

"Horses aren't immortal," Emily said airily. "Don't they get spavined or something, or catch hoof-and-mouth disease?"

"I hope not," cried Laura in a grieving tone. "Not *my* horse!" She laughed. "A bay mare," she said dreamily, "with a white star on her forehead. Named Princess Elizabeth. Ah! I'm feeding her lumps of sugar right now!" She caught Emily's hand. "I *love* the picture and the pin!"

"Of course you do, Laura," said Emily. "Now run!"

She watched Laura hurry up the path, but she didn't stay to watch her triumph. She felt vaguely that it would be something not quite decent for a mother to witness. She drove about aimlessly for a while, admiring the handsome suburban houses and expecting to feel her conscience grow heavy. But, to her surprise, she only felt increasingly lighthearted. She went at last to the Lexington Market and bought a baking fish and a big bunch of white freesias. The cool blossoms, with powdered gold in their flute-shaped throats, perfumed the car all the way home. They made her think of the ballerina dress, and of all the pure, proud, filmy beauty of the world that belonged, by right, to Laura.

Dorothy Canfield Fisher

(February 17, 1879–November 9, 1958)

Dorothy Canfield Fisher appears to have lived a life most of us would love to live—but few who write about writers' lives would choose to write about. She was the child of devoted, socially responsible, imaginative parents who supported her intellectual and artistic ambitions. She married a man with whom she was happy, in whose company she was able to be productive (she published forty books between 1907 and 1958), and who shared her commitments to education, peace, feeding the hungry, healing the hurt, and ending prejudice. It was she who introduced Americans to Maria Montessori's theories and practice.

"As Ye Sow—," originally in the *Rotarian,* December 1950, is one of the few stories Canfield Fisher wrote after the tragedy of her son's death in the Philippines at the end of World War II. It is included in her 1968 collection, *Harvest of Stories.*

As Ye Sow—

Dorothy Canfield Fisher

Casually, not that she was especially interested, just to say something, she asked as she handed out the four o'clock pieces of bread
and peanut butter, "Well, what Christmas songs are you learning in
your room this year?"

There was a moment's pause. Then the three little boys, her
own and the usual two of his playmates, told her soberly, first one
speaking, then another, "We're not going to be let to sing." "Teacher
don't want us in the Christmas entertainment." Their round, eight-
year-old faces were grave.

"Well—!" said the mother. "For goodness' sakes, why not?"

Looking down at his feet, her own small David answered sadly,
"Teacher says we can't sing good enough."

"Well enough," corrected his mother mechanically.

"Well enough," he repeated as mechanically.

One of the others said in a low tone, "She says we can't carry a
tune. She's only going to let kids sing in the entertainment that can
carry a tune."

David, still hanging his head humbly, murmured, "She says we'd spoil the piece our class is going to sing."

Inwardly the mother broke into a mother's rage at a teacher. "So that's what she says, does she? What's she *for,* anyhow, if not to teach children what they don't know. The idea! As if she'd say she would teach arithmetic only to those who are good at it already."

The downcast children stood silent. She yearned over their shame at falling behind the standards of their group. "Teachers are callous, that's what they are, insensitively callous. She is deliberately planting an inferiority feeling in them. It's a shame to keep them from going up on the platform and standing in the footlights. Not to let them have their share of being applauded! It's cruel."

She drew in a deep breath, and put the loaf of bread away. Then she said quietly, "Well, lots of kids your age can't carry a tune. Not till they've learned. How'd you like to practice your song with me? I could play the air on the piano afternoons, after school. You'd get the hang of it that way."

They brightened, they bit off great chunks of their snacks, and said, thickly, that would be swell. They did not say they would be grateful to her, or regretted being a bother to her, busy as she always was. She did not expect them to. In fact it would have startled her if they had. She was the mother of four.

So while the after-school bread-and-butter was being eaten, washed down with gulps of milk, while the November-muddy rubbers were taken off, the mother pushed to the back of the stove the interrupted rice pudding, washed her hands at the sink, looked into the dining room where her youngest, Janey, was waking her dolls up from naps taken in the dining room chairs, and took off her apron. Together the four went into the living room to the piano.

"What song is it your room is to sing?"

"It came upon the midnight—" said the three little boys, speaking at once.

"That's a nice one," she commented, reaching for the battered songbook on top of the piano. "This is the way it goes." She played the air, and sang the first two lines. "That'll be enough to start on," she told them. "*Now—*" she gave them the signal to start.

They started. She had given them food for body and heart. Refreshed, heartened, with unquestioning confidence in a grown-up's ability to achieve whatever she planned, they opened their mouths happily and sang out.

It came upon the midnight clear,
That glorious song of old.

They had evidently learned the words by heart from hearing them.

At the end of that phrase she stopped abruptly, and for an instant bowed her head over the keys. Her feeling about Teacher made a rightabout turn. There was a pause.

But she was a mother, not a teacher. She lifted her head, turned a smiling face on the three bellowing children. "I tell you what," she said. "The way, really, to learn a tune, is just one note after another. The reason why a teacher can't get *every*body in her room up to singing in tune, is because she'd have to teach each person separately—unless they happen to be naturally good at singing. That would take too much time. A teacher has such a lot of children to see to."

They did not listen closely to this. They were not particularly interested in having justice done to Teacher, since they had not shared the mother's brief excursion into indignation. But they tolerated her with silent courtesy. They were used to parents, teachers, and other adults, and had learned how to take with patience and self-control their constantly recurring prosy explanations of things that did not matter.

"Listen," said the mother, "I'll strike just the two first notes on the piano—'It came—'" She struck the notes, she sang them clearly. Full of good will the little boys sang with her. She stopped. Breathed hard.

"Not quite," she said, with a false smile, "pret-t-ty good. Close to it. But not quite, yet. I think we'd better take it *one* note at a time. Bill, *you* try it."

They had been in and out of her house all their lives, they knew her very well, none of them had reached the age of self-consciousness. Without hesitation, Bill sang, "I-i-it—" loudly.

The mother, as if fascinated, kept her eyes fixed on his still open mouth. Finally, "Try again," she said. "But first, *listen.*" Oracularly she told them, "Half of carrying a tune is listening first."

She played the note again. And again. And again. Then, rather faintly, she said, "Peter, you sing it now."

At the note emitted by Peter, she let out her breath, as if she had been under water and just come up. "Fine!" she said. "Now we're getting somewhere! David, your turn." David was her own. "Just that one note. No, not *quite.* A little higher. Not quite so high." She was in a panic. What could she do? "Wait," she told David. "Try just breathing it out, not loud at all. Maybe you can get it better."

The boys had come in a little after four. It was five when the telephone rang—Bill's mother asking her to send Bill home because his Aunt Emma was there. The mother turned from the telephone to say, "Don't you boys want to go along with Bill a ways, and play around for awhile outdoors? I've got to get supper ready." Cheerful, relieved to see a door opening before them that had been slammed shut in their faces, yet very tired of that one note, they put on their muddy rubbers and thudded out.

That evening when she told her husband about it, after the children had gone to bed, she ended her story with a vehement "You never heard anything like it in your life, Harry. Never. It was appalling! You can't *imagine* what it was!"

"Oh, yes I can too," he said over his temporarily lowered newspaper. "I've heard plenty of tone-deaf kids hollering. I know what they sound like. There *are* people, you know, who really *can't* carry a tune. You probably never could teach them. Why don't you give it up?"

Seeing, perhaps, in her face, the mulish mother-stubbornness, he said, with a little exasperation, "What's the use of trying to do what you *can't* do?"

That was reasonable, after all, thought the mother. Yes, that was the sensible thing. She would be sensible, for once, and give it up. With everything she had to do, she would just be reasonable and sensible about this.

So the next morning, when she was downtown doing her marketing, she turned in at the public library and asked for books about teaching music to children. Rather young children, about eight years old, she explained.

The librarian, enchanted with someone who did not ask for a light, easy-reading novel, brought her two books, which she took away with her.

At lunch she told her husband (there were just the two of them with little Janey; the older children had their lunch at school), "Musical experts say there really is no such thing as a tone-deaf person. If anybody seems so, it is only because he has not had a chance to be carefully enough trained."

Her husband looked at her quickly. "Oh, all right," he said, "all *right!* Have it your own way." But he leaned to pat her hand. "You're swell," he told her. "I don't see how you ever keep it up as you do. Gosh, it's one o'clock already."

During the weeks between then and the Christmas entertainment, she saw no more than he how she could ever keep it up. The little boys had no difficulty in keeping it up. They had nothing else to do at four o'clock. They were in the indestructible age, between the frailness of infancy and the taut nervous tensions of adolescence. Wherever she led they followed her cheerfully. In that period of incessant pushing against barriers which did not give way, she was the one whose flag hung limp.

From assiduous reading of those two books on teaching music she learned that there were other approaches than a frontal attack on the tune they wanted to sing. She tried out ear-experiments with them, of which she would never have dreamed without her library books. She discovered to her dismay that sure enough, just as the authors of the books said, the little boys were musically so far below scratch that, without seeing which piano keys she struck, they had no idea whether a note was higher or lower than the one before it. She adapted and invented musical "games" to train their ears. The boys, standing in a row, their backs to the piano, listening to hear whether the second note was "uphill or downhill" from the first note, thought it as good a game as any other, rather funnier than most because so new to them. They laughed raucously over each other's mistakes, kidded and joshed each other, ran a contest to see who came out best, while the mother, aproned for cooking, her eye on the clock, got up and down for hurried forays into the kitchen where she was trying to get supper.

David's older brother and sister had naturally good ears for music. That was one reason why the mother had not dreamed that David had none. When the two older children came in from school, they listened incredulously, laughed scoffingly, and went off to skate or to rehearse a play. Little Janey, absorbed in her family of dolls, paid no attention to these male creatures of an age so far from hers that they were as negligible as grownups. The mother worked alone, in a vacuum, with nobody's sympathy to help her. Toilsomely, she pushed her heavy stone uphill, only to see it, as soon as she took away her hand, begin to roll rapidly back.

Not quite a vacuum. Not even in a vacuum. Occasionally the others made a comment, "Gee, Mom, those kids are fierce. *You* can't do anything with them." "Say, Helen, an insurance man is coming to the house this afternoon. For heaven's sake keep those boys from screeching while he is here. A person can't hear himself think."

So, she thought, with silent resentment, her task was not only to give up her own work, to invent and adapt methods of instruction in an hour she could not spare, but also to avoid bothering the rest. After all, the home was for the whole family. They had the right to have it the background of what *they* wanted to do, needed to do. Only not she. Not the mother. Of course.

She faltered. Many times. She saw the ironing heaped high, or Janey was in bed with a cold, and as four o'clock drew near, she said to herself, "Now today I'll just tell the boys that I can *not* go on with this. We're not getting anywhere, anyhow."

So when they came storming in, hungry and cheerful and full of unquestioning certainty that she would not close that door she had half-opened for them, she laid everything aside and went to the piano.

As a matter of fact, they *were* getting somewhere. She had been so beaten down that she was slow to notice the success of the exercises ingeniously devised by the authors of those books. Even with their backs to the piano, the boys could now tell, infallibly, whether a second note was above or below the first one. Sure. They even thought it distinctly queer that they had not been able to, at first. "Never paid any attention to it, before," was their own accurate surmise as to the reason.

They paid attention now, their interest aroused by their first success, by the incessant practicing of the others in their classroom, by the Christmas-entertainment thrill which filled the schoolhouse with suspense. Although they were allowed no part in it, they also paid close attention to the drill given the others, and sitting in their seats, exiled from the happy throng of singers, they watched how to march along the aisle of the Assembly Hall, decorously, not too fast, not too slow, and when the great moment came for climbing to the platform how not to knock their toes against the steps. They fully expected to climb those steps to the platform with the others, come the evening of the entertainment.

It was now not on the clock that the mother kept her eye during those daily sessions at the piano, it was on the calendar. She nervously intensified her drill, but she remembered carefully not to yell at them when they went wrong, not to screw her face into the grimace which she felt, not to clap her hands over her ears and scream, "Oh, horrible! *Why* can't you get it right!" She reminded herself that if they knew how to get it right, they would of course sing it that way. She knew (she had been a mother for sixteen years) that she must keep them cheerful and hopeful, or the tenuous thread of their interest and attention would snap. She smiled. She did not allow herself even once to assume the blighting look of patience.

Just in time, along about the second week of December, a gleam shone in their musical darkness. They could all sound—if they remembered to sing softly and to "listen to themselves"—a note, any note, within their range, she struck on the piano. Little Peter turned out, to his surprise and hers, to have a sweet clear soprano. The others were—well, all right, good enough.

They started again, very cautiously, to sing that tune, to begin with "It ca-ame—" having drawn a deep breath, and letting it out carefully. It was right. They were singing true.

She clapped her hands like a girl. They did not share her overjoyed surprise. That was where they had been going all the time. They had got there, that was all. What was there to be surprised about?

From now on it went fast; the practicing of the air, their repeating it for the first skeptical, and then thoroughly astonished Teacher, their triumphant report at home, "She says we can sing it good enough. She says we can sing with the others. We practiced going up on the platform this afternoon."

Then the Christmas entertainment. The tramping of class after class up the aisle to the moment of footlighted glory; the big eighth graders' Christmas pantomime, the first graders' wavering performance of a Christmas dance as fairies—or were they snowflakes? Or perhaps angels? It was not clear. They were tremendously applauded, whatever they were. The swelling hearts of their parents burst into wild hand-clapping as the first grade began to file down the steps from the platform. Little Janey, sitting on her mother's lap, beat her hands together too, excited by the thought that next year she would be draped in white cheesecloth, would wear a tinsel crown and wave a star-tipped wand.

Then it was the turn of the third grade, the eight- and nine-year-olds, the boys clumping up the aisle, the girls switching their short skirts proudly. The careful tiptoeing up the steps to the platform, remembering not to knock their toes on the stair-treads, the two lines of round faces bland and blank in their touching ignorance of—oh, of everything! thought David's mother, clutching her handbag tensely.

The crash from the piano giving them the tone, all the mouths open,

It came upo-on the midnight clear,
That glorious song of old.

The thin pregnant woman sitting in front of the mother leaned to the shabbily-dressed man next to her, with a long breath of relief. "They do real *good,* don't they?" she whispered proudly.

They did do real good. Teacher's long drill and hers had been successful. It was not howling, it was singing. It had cost the heart's blood, thought the mother, of two women, but it was singing. It would never again be howling, not from those children.

It was even singing with expression—some. There were swelling crescendos, and at the lines

The world in solemn stillness lay
To hear the angels sing

the child-voices were hushed in a diminuendo. She ached at the thought of the effort that had gone into teaching that hushed tone, of the patience and self-control and endlessly repeated persistence in molding into something shapely the boys' puppylike inability to think of anything but aimless play. It had taken hours out of her life, crammed as it was far beyond what was possible with work that must be done. Done for other people. Not for her. Not for the mother.

This had been one of the things that must be done. And she had done it. There he stood, her little David, a fully accredited part of his corner of society, as good as anybody, the threat of the inferiority-feeling averted for this time, ready to face the future with enough self-confidence to cope with what would come next. The door had been slammed in his face. She had pushed it open, and he had gone through.

The hymn ended. The burst of parental applause began clamorously. Little Janey, carried away by the festival excitement, clapped with all her might—"learning the customs of *her* corner of society" thought her mother, smiling tenderly at the petal-soft noiselessness of the tiny hands.

The third grade filed down the steps from the platform and began to march to their seats. For a moment, the mother forgot that she was no longer a girl who expected recognition when she had done something creditable. David's class clumped down the aisle. Surely, she thought, David would turn his head to where she sat and thank her with a look. Just this once.

He did turn his head as he filed by. He looked full at his family, at his father, his mother, his kid sister, his big brother and sister from the high school. He gave them a formal, small nod to show that he knew they were there, to acknowledge publicly that they were his family. He even smiled, a very little, stiffly, fleetingly. But his look was not for her. It was just as much for those of his family who had been bored and impatient spectators of her struggle to help him, as for her who had given part of her life to roll that stone uphill, a part of her life she never could get back.

She shifted Janey's weight a little on her knees. Of course. Did mothers ever expect to be thanked? They were to accept what they received, without bitterness, without resentment. After all, that was what mothers worked for—not for thanks, but to do their job. The sharp chisel of life, driven home by experience, flaked off expertly another flint-hard chip from her blithe, selfish girlhood. It fell away from the woman she was growing to be, and dropped soundlessly into the abyss of time.

After all, she thought, hearing vaguely the seventh graders now on the platform (none of her four was in the seventh grade)—after all, David was only eight. At that age they were, in personality, completely cocoons, as in their babyhood they had been physical cocoons. The time had not come yet for the inner spirit to stir, to waken, to give a sign that it lived.

It certainly did not stir in young David that winter. There was no sign that it lived. The snowy weeks came and went. He rose, ravenously hungry, ate an enormous breakfast with the family, and raced off to school with his own third graders. The usual three stormed back after school, flinging around a cloud of overshoes, caps, mittens, windbreakers. For their own good, for the sake of their wives-to-be, for the sake of the homes which would be dependent on them, they must be called back with the hard-won, equable reasonableness of the mother, and reminded to pick up and put away. David's special two friends came to his house at four to eat her cookies, or went to each other's houses to eat other cookies. They giggled, laughed raucously, kidded and joshed each other, pushed each other around. They made snow-forts in their front yards, they skated with awkward energy on the place where the brook overflowed the meadow, took their sleds out to Hingham Hill for coasting, made plans for a shack in the woods next summer.

In the evening, if the homework had been finished in time, they were allowed to visit each other for an hour, to make things with Meccano, things which were a source of enormous pride to the eight-year-olds, things which the next morning fell over at the lightest touch of the mother's broom.

At that age, thought the mother, their souls, if any, were certainly no more than seeds, deep inside their hard, muscular, little-boy flesh. How do souls develop, she wondered occasionally, as she washed dishes, made beds, selected carrots at the market, answered the telephone. How do souls develop out of those rough-and-ready little males? If they do develop?

David and Peter, living close to each other, shared the evening play-hour more often than the third boy who lived across the tracks. They were allowed to go back and forth by themselves, even though the midwinter blackness had fallen by seven o'clock. Peter lived on the street above theirs, up the hill. There was a short cut down across a vacant lot, which was in sight of one or the other house, all the way. It was safe enough, even for youngsters, even at night. The little boys loved that downhill short cut. Its steep slope invited their feet to fury. Never using the path, they raced down in a spray of snow kicked up by their flying overshoes, arriving at the house, their cheeks flaming, flinging themselves like cannon balls against the kitchen door, tasting a little the heady physical fascination of speed, on which, later, as ski-runners, they would become wildly drunken.

"Sh! *David!* Not so *loud!*" his mother often said, springing up from her mending at the crash of the banged-open door. "Father's trying to do some accounts," or "Sister has company in the living room."

Incessant acrobatic feat—to keep five people of different ages and personalities, all living under the same roof, from stepping on each other's feet. Talk about keeping five balls in the air at the same time! That was nothing compared to keeping five people satisfied to live with each other, to provide each one with approximately what he needed and wanted without taking away something needed by one of the others. (Arithmetically considered, there were of course six people living under that roof. But she did not count. She was the mother. She took what she got, what was left. . . .)

That winter, as the orbits of the older children lay more outside the house, she found herself acquiring a new psychological skill that was almost eerie. She could be in places where she was not, at all. She had an astral body which could go anywhere. Anywhere, that is, where one of her five was. She was with her honeysweet big daughter in the living room, playing games with high school friends (was there butter enough, she suddenly asked herself, for the popcorn the young people would inevitably want, later?). She was upstairs where her husband sat, leaning over the desk, frowning in attentiveness at a page of figures—that desk light was not strong enough. Better put the floodlight up there tomorrow. She was in the sunporch of the neighbor's house, where her little son was bolting Meccano strips together with his square, strong, not-very-clean hands—his soul, if any, dormant far within his sturdy body. She floated above the scrimmage in the high school gym, where her first-born played basketball with ferocity, pouring out through that channel the rage of maleness constantly gathering in his big frame which grew that year with such fantastic rapidity that he seemed taller at breakfast than he had been when he went to bed. She sent her astral body upstairs to where her little daughter, her baby, her darling, slept with one doll in her arms, and three others on the pillow beside her. That blanket was not warm enough for Janey. When she went to bed, she would put on another one.

She was all of them. First one, then another. When was she herself? When did *her* soul have time to stretch its wings?

One evening this question tried to push itself into her mind, but was swept aside by her suddenly knowing, as definitely as if she had heard a clock strike or the doorbell ring, that the time had passed for David's return from his evening play-hour with Peter. She looked at her watch. But she did not need to. A sixth sense told her heart, as with a blow, that he should before this have come pelting down the hill, plowing the deep snow aside in clouds, hurling himself against the kitchen door. He was late. Her astral self, annihilating time and space, fled out to look for him. He must have left the other house some time ago. Peter's mother always sent him home promptly.

She laid down the stocking she was darning, stepped into the dark kitchen, and put her face close to the window to look out. It was a cloudless cold night. Every detail of the back yard world was visible, almost transparent, in the pale radiance that fell from the stars. Not a breath of wind. She could see everything: the garbage pail at the woodshed door, the trampled snow of the driveway, the clothes she had washed that morning and left on the line, the deep unbroken snow beyond the yard, the path leading up the hill.

Then she saw David. He was standing halfway down, as still as the frozen night around him.

But David never stood still.

Knee-deep in the snow he stood, looking all around him. She saw him slowly turn his head to one side, to the other. He lifted his face towards the sky. It was almost frightening to see *David* stand so still. What could he be looking at? What was there he could be seeing? Or hearing? For as she watched him, the notion crossed her mind that he seemed to be listening. But there was nothing to hear. Nothing.

She did not know what was happening to her little son. Nor what to do. So she did nothing. She stood as still as he, her face at the window, lost in wonder.

She saw him, finally, stir and start slowly, slowly down the path. But David never moved slowly. Had he perhaps had a quarrel with Peter? Had Peter's mother been unkind to him?

It could do no harm now to go to meet him, she thought, and by that time, she could not, anxious as she was, not go to meet him. She opened the kitchen door and stepped out into the dark, under the stars.

He saw her, he came quickly to her, he put his arms around her waist. With every fiber of her body which had borne his, she felt a difference in him.

She did not know what to say, so she said nothing.

191

It was her son who spoke. "It's so still," he said quietly in a hushed voice, a voice she had never heard before. "It's so still!"

He pressed his cheek against her breast as he tipped his head back to look up. "All those stars," he murmured dreamily, "they shine so. But they don't make a sound. They—they're *nice,* aren't they?"

He stood a little away from her to look up into her face. "Do you remember—in the song—'the world in solemn stillness lay'?" he asked her, but he knew she remembered.

The starlight showed him clear, his honest, little-boy eyes wide, fixed trustingly on his mother's. He was deeply moved. But calm. This had come to him while he was still so young that he could be calmed by his mother's being with him. He had not known that he had an inner sanctuary. Now he stood in it, awe-struck at his first sight of beauty. And opened the door to his mother.

As naturally as he breathed, he put into his mother's hands the pure rounded pearl of a shared joy. "I thought I heard them singing—sort of," he told her.

Alice Childress
(b. October 12, 1920)

"Merry Christmas, Marge!" is one of sixty-two conversations between Mildred, a black domestic day worker, and her friend Marge—whose voice we never hear but are invited to imagine. These conversations, originally published in *Freedom,* a newspaper edited by Paul Robeson, then in the *Baltimore Afro-American,* were collected and published in 1956 as *Like One of the Family: Conversations from a Domestic's Life.* Long unavailable, it was reprinted in 1986.

Childress, an accomplished and versatile playwright, novelist, screen writer, and essayist, is the author of the 1973 novel *A Hero Ain't Nothin' but a Sandwich,* the script of the 1978 film based on it, and the powerful historical novel, *A Short Walk* (1979). More than a dozen of her plays have been produced on stage and television.

When the peace and social justice Mildred describes comes about, I hope we will all be there to share an eggnog toast—TOGETHER!

Merry Christmas, Marge!

Alice Childress

Merry Christmas, Marge! Girl, I just want to sit down and catch my breath for a minute. . . . I had a half a day off and went Christmas shopping. Them department stores is just like a madhouse. They had a record playin' real loud all over Crumbleys. . . . "Peace On Earth." Well sir! I looked 'round at all them scufflin' folks and I begun to wonder. . . . What is peace?

You know Marge, I hear so much talk about peace. I see it written on walls and I hear about it on the radio, and at Christmas time you can't cut 'round the corner without hearin' it blarin' out of every store front. . . . Peace . . . Peace . . . Peace.

Marge, what is peace? . . . Well, you're partly right, it do mean not havin' any wars . . . but I been doin' some deep thinkin' since I left Crumbleys and I been askin' myself. . . . How would things have to be in order for *me* to be at peace with the world? . . . Why thank you, dear. . . . I will take an egg nog. Nobody can make it like you do. . . . That's some good. I tell you.

And it begun to come to my mind. . . . If I had no cause to hate "white folks" that would be good and if I could like most of 'em . . . *that* would be peace. . . . Don't laugh, Marge, 'cause I'm talkin' some deep stuff now!

If I could stand in the street and walk in any direction that my toes was pointin' and go in one of them pretty apartment houses and say, "Give me an apartment please?" and the man would turn and say, "Why, it would be a pleasure, mam. We'll notify you 'bout the first vacancy." . . . That would be peace.

Do you hear me? If I could stride up to any employment agency without havin' the folk at the desk stutterin' and stammerin' . . . *That,* my friend, would be peace also. If I could ride a subway or a bus and not see any signs pleadin' with folks to be "tolerant" . . . "regardless" of what I am . . . I know that would be peace 'cause then there would be no need for them signs.

If you and me could have a cool glass of lemonade or a hot cup of coffee anywhere . . . and I mean *anywhere* . . . wouldn't that be peace? If all these little children 'round here had their mamas takin' care of them instead of other folks' children . . . that would be peace, too. . . . Hold on, Marge! Go easy on that egg nog . . . it goes to my head so fast. . . .

Oh yes, if nobody wanted to kill nobody else and I could pick up a newspaper and not read 'bout my folks gettin' the short end of every stick . . . that would mean more peace.

If all mamas and daddies was sittin' back safe and secure in the knowledge that they'd have toys and goodies for their children . . . that would bring on a little more peace. If eggs and butter would stop flirtin' 'round the dollar line, I would also consider that a peaceful sign. . . . Oh, darlin' let's don't talk 'bout the meat!

Yes girl! You are perfectly right. . . . If our menfolk would *make* over us a little more, THAT would be peaceful too.

When all them things are fixed up the way I want 'em I'm gonna spend one peaceful Christmas . . . and do you know what I'd do? . . . Look Marge . . . I told you now, don't give me too much of that egg nog. . . . My dear, I'd catch me a plane for Alageorgia somewhere and visit all my old friends and we'd go 'round from door to door hollerin' "Christmas Gift!" Then we'd go down to

Main Street and ride front, middle and rear on the street-car and the "whitefolk" would wave and cry out, "Merry Christmas, neighbors!" . . . Oh hush now! . . . They would do this because they'd understand *peace.*

And we'd all go in the same church and afterwards we'd all go in the same movie and see Lena Horne actin' and singin' all the way through a picture. . . . I'd have to visit a school so that I could see a black teacher teachin' white kids . . . an' when I see this . . . I'll sing out . . . Peace it's *truly* wonderful!

Then I'd go and watch the black Governor and the white Mayor unveiling a bronze statue of Frederick Douglass and John Brown shakin' hands. . . .

When I was ready to leave, I'd catch me a pullman back to New York. . . . Now that's what you'd call "sleepin' in heavenly peace." When I got home the bells and the horns would be ringin' and tootin' "Happy New Year!" . . . and there wouldn't be no mothers mournin' for their soldier sons . . . Children would be prancin' 'round and ridin' Christmas sleds through the sparklin' snow . . . and the words "lynch," "murder" and "kill" would be crossed out of every dictionary . . . and nobody would write peace on no walls . . . 'cause it would *be* peace . . . and our hearts would be free!

What? . . . No, I ain't crazy, either! All that is gonna happen . . . just as sure as God made little apples! I promise you that! . . . and do you know who's gonna be here to see it? *Me* girl . . . yes, your friend Mildred! Let's you and me have another egg nog on that. . . . Here's to it. MERRY XMAS Marge! PEACE!

Pearl S. Buck

(June 26, 1892–March 6, 1973)

Pearl Buck loved Christmas. She wrote Christmas stories and essays year after year and edited two collections of her own Christmas writings. The holiday gave her an opportunity to write about the subjects closest to her heart: peace and reconciliation between and among people and nations.

The publishing history of "A Certain Star"—a plea for the development of peaceful uses of atomic energy, a reaffirmation of faith in a divine being, and a very human tale of a family's attempt to become whole again—is remarkable. When it was first published in the December 22, 1957 issue of *American Weekly,* a popular mass market magazine, twelve hundred little books were printed by the publisher and distributed privately to governors, mayors, congressmen, and selected important businessmen. Within months it had been translated and published in seven languages in ten countries.

Although some aspects of the story seem naive to contemporary readers, its message continues to be moving and important.

A Certain Star

Pearl S. Buck

He woke at dawn this Christmas morning. For a brief instant he could not remember where he was. Then the warmth of childhood memory crept into his drowsy mind. He was here at the farm, in his old home, the broken rafters of his old room above his head. It was yesterday, only yesterday, that he had insisted upon this homecoming and against the subdued but massive revolt of his family he had carried it through.

"Oh, Dad," his daughter Anne had wailed. "Go to the farm now? On Christmas Eve? But we've planned—"

She had protested with such sparkling anger that he had turned on her with like anger.

"It's been years since I asked anything of you!"

His son spoke. "I have a date, Dad."

"You'll break your date, Hal," he had said firmly.

He had turned then from his two mute and furious children to Helen, his wife.

"Christmas has departed from this house," he told her.

She had smiled patiently. "I'm used to your large announcements, darling. And things are about as they have been, since the war ended. Everything's changed. It's inevitable."

"The foundations don't change," he had insisted. "We must get back to being a family. I'll have the car ready in an hour."

He was aware of the command in his voice. He had grown used to command during the war, and no less in these years of continuing atomic research. He was accustomed to obedience in his great laboratory of scientists and he did not stay to hear more protest in his house. And knowing his punctual ways, they had assembled in an hour, and in total silence, for the long drive to the farm.

Well, they had obeyed him, at least. They were here together, miles away from late dancing and much drinking and the time-wasting frivolities that he detested. And it was Christmas. During this day surely he would win them back again. For he had lost them somehow during these years which had been absorbed in his work.

His name, his fame, Arnold Williams, nuclear scientist, one of the top three in the world, had overwhelmed them—and, to some extent, him. Scientists of every country turned to him for advice and argument and, compelled by the rapid growth of knowledge, he had dedicated his whole being to his researches.

This was his duty, of course, during the war, when his experiments had belonged to his government, but the line between duty and the pleasurable excitement of successful work was not so clear after the war ended.

While he pursued his separate way, his children had grown up, and Helen was certainly older than she should be. The old joy between them was gone. Yesterday, in his own home within easy distance of his laboratory at the university, he had suddenly realized that whatever was going on, in spite of last-minute shopping and an artificial, modernized tree, it was not Christmas. . . .

He remembered Anne, his daughter, so pretty, so feverish, not at all gay, flying to the telephone, always to be disappointed. It was never the right voice. . . . So whose was the voice for which she listened? Oh, Anne, beloved child, it was for her sake above all that he wanted to be alone today with his family. . . .

And what of the star? On Christmas mornings, when he was a boy lying here in this bed, there had been a certain star, high over the barn. He saw it always when he rose, earlier than usual, so that he could get the milking done before they opened the doors to the parlor where the Christmas tree stood. The Christmas Star! He threw back the covers and leaped out of bed—nonsense, probably, for the star might not be there now.

As he fumbled in the closet for his old clothes, it occurred to him that in a way this star was responsible for the direction of his life. It had led him to the heavens.

"What do you want for Christmas, boy?" His father had asked the question the year he was fourteen.

"I want a telescope," he had said.

His father had stared at him, his small blue eyes sharp and inquisitive above his ragged beard.

"What for?"

"To look at stars with."

His father had grunted, without sympathy it seemed, but on Christmas morning there was a mail-order telescope under the tree. It was the only gift he wanted. Impatient for the night, he had been compelled to wait until darkness fell. Then lifting his telescope to his eye, he peered at the star. What disappointment! It was larger, more glowing, but as far off as ever.

The next day, in sheer experiment, he had looked at the sun, and to his astonishment he saw spots upon it, and this had led to the buying of a book, an introduction to the sky, and so had begun his interest in cosmic rays.

He was dressed now in ski pants, sheepskin coat and fur boots. He slammed the door as he left the room, then winced, for Helen was still asleep, he hoped. If he had waked her, she would be patient with him, as indeed she had always been ever since his dark prowlings (begun long ago because his famous hunches came by night as well as by day) made it necessary for him to sleep alone. He could bear no interruption when he was seized by a theory and knew no peace until he had pursued it.

"When you marry me," he told Helen the day they were engaged, "you don't marry a man. You marry a sort of—of monster."

She had only laughed. Then one day during the war, when they were living in a barracks at Los Alamos, she had looked at him thoughtfully.

"What does that look mean?" he had inquired.

"Perhaps you *are* a sort of monster," she had said.

He had laughed, but the words came back to him now as he stepped outside the kitchen door into the darkness. The cold was solid enough to cut, the colder because the house was warm. He had put in an oil burner years ago when the children were small, but when he was a boy there was only the huge wood range in the kitchen. It was still there, for memory's sake. . . .

The snow creaked under his boots as he walked toward the barn. The sky was clear, the stars luminous and twinkling through the icy air. He looked up, searching the heavens. Ah, his star was plain! There it hung over the ridgepole of the barn, not so large as he had imagined, but unmistakably the same.

The years had painted it bigger and more golden than it was now, or perhaps his boy's imagination had seen it so. Yet there it shone, steady and true, as he had remembered it.

His feet found the familiar groove in the path under the snow and as he stood in the windless air the old wonder came flooding back again, the wonder of the universe. He had known it years ago, distilled through the single star. He had lost it in the hurry and excitement of his youth, in the years when he had been working for a living by day in the laboratory of a great industry. In his own small laboratory, by night, he had explored the secrets of the explosive rays of the sun, and using his meager holidays he had made pilgrimages to Einstein in Germany and Rutherford in England.

Skeptic and daring, he had wandered far from this humble place upon which he now stood to gaze again at a star on Christmas morning. He had been a proud and argumentative man, until the day when he had found terror and a new humility in the nucleus of an atom, laid bare before him in a hidden place in the desert. Infinite energy, encased in a shape so small that eyes could not see it!

Yes, this star upon which he now gazed had guided his life. What next? Where would the path lie from this Christmas morning?

He shivered suddenly and remembered that he was standing halfway to his knees in snow. It had fallen during the night, the soft stuff clinging to every branch and twig, and the air from the lake was icy. He turned reluctantly and followed his own tracks back to the house and into the kitchen.

The light was on when he opened the door and Helen, wrapped in her red flannel bathrobe, was standing at the gas stove, making coffee.

"Merry Christmas," he said and kissed her cheek. "Did I wake you?"

"You're as cold as a snowman," she said, rubbing that cheek. "And you didn't wake me. I couldn't sleep."

"Christmas in your bones?"

She shook her head. "I don't sleep as well as I used to." She set two cups on the table and poured the coffee. "You want breakfast now?"

"No, but I'll have coffee."

They sat down. She sipped her coffee slowly, but he took a hot gulp.

"That's good—I was cold all the way through."

"What were you doing outside at this hour?" she asked.

"What would you say if I told you I went out to see a star?" he replied.

"It's been a long time since you were interested in stars," she said.

He glanced at her. She looked too tired, this slender wife of his. "Maybe we shouldn't have come here to the farm. Maybe it's too much for you. Don't you feel well, Helen?"

"I'm all right," she said. "Just getting old, I suppose."

"Nonsense! You're worried about something."

She got up to make more coffee. "I heard Anne crying in the night."

He stared at her in consternation. "Why should Anne cry?"

"They don't say anything," she told him. "You know they never say anything nowadays. One doesn't know what goes on in anybody."

She threw him a strange, sad look which he did not comprehend.

"Anne seemed perfectly willing to come here yestetday," he reminded her. "She was more willing than Hal was—he had a dance or something."

"They both had parties." She stirred her coffee thoughtfully. "It isn't like Anne to give up so easily—not if she wants something."

"That's true."

Anne never gave up easily when she wanted something very much. So yesterday obviously there wasn't anything she wanted very much.

"I hope she wants the bracelet I've bought her for Christmas," he grumbled. "It cost enough."

"I don't know what they want any more. Everybody's changed somehow." She sighed and began sipping her coffee again, holding her cup in both hands as though they were cold.

He examined her face, still so pretty in spite of its pallor. It had been a long time since he had seen her in the morning before she made up her face. He was an early worker, and she slept late.

"Are you all right?" he asked again.

"Tired," she said. "My time of life, maybe."

"Woman's retreat," he declared. He got up and kissed her cheek. "Remember how you used to climb Mont Blanc with me when we were measuring cosmic rays? That wasn't so long ago."

She smiled faintly and did not reply. He tousled her hair to tease her and she caught his hand and slapped it gently. "I'll bet that your Christmas presents aren't wrapped."

"You're wrong! I had them wrapped at Tiffany's," he said.

She looked shocked. "Did you get everything there?"

"Everything," he said, "and when I said I wanted them gift-wrapped, the clerk said stiffly that the usual Tiffany wrapping *is* a gift wrapping."

That made her laugh and he felt victorious.

"And now," he said. "I am going upstairs to the attic to bring down my precious parcels for the tree."

"Why on earth did you take them to the attic?" she inquired. "The children won't snoop—you forget they're grown up."

"Habit. Before I knew it last night I was in the attic, putting my small expensive packages in the corner where we hid Anne's doll house and Hal's bicycle. . . . How many years has it been since we spent Christmas here?"

"Not since you fell in love with the nucleus of an atom," she said. There was a glint of old mischief in her blue eyes. "I wish I knew the enchantment in a nucleus!"

"Ah, there's enchantment!" he retorted. He left her then and climbed the stairs to the attic and found his gifts in the brown paper bag in which he had thrust them for safekeeping yesterday. Halfway down the stairs again to the second floor he heard Anne's voice in the upper hall as she talked to someone—a man, of course.

"What's the use of my coming into town tonight? . . . Yes, I could come with Hal—he's got a date—but what's the use? It would be midnight before you could get away from your family and we'd have fifteen minutes—well, half an hour then—and you uneasy all the time. What good is that?"

He heard the passion and the pain and, his heart suddenly aching, he saw her there at the telephone. She was still in her pink flannel nightgown, her yellow hair curling about her head, a mere child in spite of her twenty years. No man had the right to hurt this child he had begotten! How could he persuade her to tell his name so that he could defend her from the fellow?

"Anne," he said.

She hung up instantly. Then she turned and looked up at him with huge, startled blue eyes.

"It's early for you to be up on Christmas morning, isn't it?" he asked.

"I couldn't sleep," she said. "It's terribly cold here by the lake."

"It's just as well you're up," he said. "We have the tree to cut, Hal and I, and we'll trim it and get dinner together the way we used to do. I'll bring in some branches for you to decorate the house with—maybe some ground pine, eh?"

He deposited the brown paper bag on the stairs and came toward her.

"Feeling sentimental, aren't you, Santa Claus?" Anne crossed the hall to meet him and standing tiptoe, she kissed his cheek. "You're a sweet old thing," she said suddenly.

"Thank you," he said. "I haven't heard even that for a long time."

"I haven't said anything to you for a long time," she agreed. "You've been away somewhere these ten years, haven't you?"

She was tracing the outline of his eyebrow with a delicate forefinger.

"It's you," he said, capturing the forefinger. "You've grown up without asking me. I get only glimpses of the daughter I used to have."

All the same, he was thinking, if he hadn't insisted on being here today there would not have been even this interchange. She'd have been asleep in her bed, exhausted by dancing and carryings-on. She leaned her head against his chest unexpectedly.

"I wish I were little again," she whispered. "I wish I had never grown up!"

He pressed her soft hair. "Why, Anne—why, Anne—"

"Silly, isn't it!" She lifted her head and shook the tears from eyes that smiled up at him too brightly. Then running to her room she shut the door against him.

"Merry Christmas," he called after her, but she did not answer.

He opened Hal's door then. There, sprawled across the bed, lay his dear and only son—eighteen, a six-footer, handsome, brilliant—and a total stranger.

He tiptoed across the floor and looked down at his sleeping child. A man, this child—a child, this man. Tall, thin with youth, big bones, fresh skin and dark hair too long, here was his son, holding within the new shape of manhood a thousand memories of boyhood.

Hal it used to be who could not wait to get to the lake in summer, to swim, to fish, to sail. Twice he was nearly drowned in the deep, still waters, the first time swimming beyond his strength, the second time by a blow on the head against a rock when he dived. Twice he was saved, both times by his father. Three times, then, this son had been given to him alive, the first time fresh from his mother's womb.

Now he was a stranger who drove wildly into the night, who danced crazy dances with persons unknown, who came home, sometimes drunk, to break the hearts of parents. How could his son be saved? For inside that noble skull there was a brain worth saving. His own old professor at Harvard had written him about Hal. "If you can pull him through this pretentious youthfulness, this cult of 'beat,' you'll have a man."

Suddenly Hal opened his eyes and looked at him.

"What do you want, Dad?"

"Merry Christmas," he said.

Hal yawned. "Is it time to get up?"

"We have the tree to cut after breakfast."

Hal turned and burrowed into his pillow. "Okay—okay—"

He stood an instant longer, stifling his sudden impatience. Christmas, and the boy wanted to sleep! He remembered other mornings when Hal came into his room at dawn, shouting for the day to begin. And he had cut short his own sleep and had got out of bed so that his son could be happy.

He turned abruptly and left the room, closing the door just short of a bang. Patience! He was exhausted with being patient. Hal had no self-discipline. Why did men have children?

He went into his own room and stood by the window. The snow was falling again in a flurry from a sky overcast with gray clouds. The star was gone.

The day was clear again when he and Hal went tramping through the snow after breakfast. His spirits rose in spite of himself. Filled with warm and nourishing food, encouraged by the sight of a pretty flush on Helen's cheeks, though it might be no more than the heat of the old wood range which he had insisted upon lighting in honor of the day, and softened by Anne's sporadic tenderness, he inclined his heart anew to this tall and silent youth who was his son.

"When I was a kid," he said, "we always had a white Christmas. We took it for granted. And I believe that you and Anne always took snow for granted, too, in the years when we came here for your Christmas holidays. Snow isn't so important in the city."

Behind him he heard Hal's crunching tread, but there was no answer to his small talk. He glanced over his shoulder, breathing out his frosty breath, and saw Hal's blank face. The boy was not listening. Then he caught his father's sharp glance.

"Did you say something, Dad?"

"Nothing important," he said shortly.

They tramped on. Why talk to a son who heard nothing? And he had a great deal to say to a son, a very great deal.

He longed to share with Hal something of his own life, the excitement of being a scientist in the atomic age when a scientist had suddenly become the most important man in the world.

In the past, isolated in his laboratory, working alone, often experimenting haphazardly, and usually in vain, a scientist had been scarcely human, a magician, or a crank. Now, with the knowledge of the energy that was in the core of the universe, that infinitely small core, he was respected—and feared. . . . Did Hal dream of such things? There was no way of knowing, no communication between father and son.

He paused to examine the spruce woods in which they stood. The trees had grown too tall. They would have to look for young growth beyond.

"How far are you going?" Hal asked.

"We must find a tree of reasonable size," he said. "We'll go to the edge of the forest."

"We could cut the top out of any tree," Hal said.

He shook his head. "I'm too good a woodsman for that. My father's ghost would rise. Kill a whole tree for its top?"

"It's getting late," Hal urged.

"What's your hurry?"

Hal stopped in the snow. "Dad, I want to get back to town by eight o'clock tonight."

He turned and faced his son. "One thing I asked of my family this Christmas—the one gift I really want—that we spend the day together here. And the day includes the evening. It will be six o'clock before we get dinner over. Then we'll have the tree."

He saw a strange look in Hal's eyes, a muted rebellion. If the boy felt that way, why didn't he fling out his anger? Once when he himself was eighteen, he had fought his father first with words, and then with fists. It had concerned a day, too, a summer's day when he had wanted to go to the state fair, and his father had forbidden it.

"Hay's fit to cut," his father had said roughly. "Nobody's goin' nowheres."

"I'm going," he had said.

"Try it!" his father had shouted.

They had glared at each other. Suddenly his father had bellowed at him, "If you feel like you look, we'll fight it out—see who's the better man—"

They had fought, wrestling like bulls, young and old, and he had downed his father. He had watched his father get to his feet, pride and shame tearing his heart in two.

"All right," his father had said sullenly. "I'll make hay alone."

"I'm not going," he said and the two of them had worked side by side throughout the long hot hours until sunset. . . . Yes, that boy—himself—had been someone he could understand. Why didn't Hal defy him?

"You're the boss," Hal said. "Guess you'll always be the boss now."

He stared at his son's bitter face. "What the hell do you mean by that?"

"Just what I said. You're the boss. You've been the big boss ever since the war, haven't you? Atomic killer!"

He stared at the dark young giant, who glowered at him. Then rage ran over his body like fire and he hit his son on the jaw, a clean right-hander that amazed him. In the same instant he recognized pride in the blow—a low male pride that shocked him. His hand dropped.

"Hal!" he stammered. "Hal, I didn't mean—I don't know what got into me. But you called me an evil name. Still, I shouldn't have done it."

Hal pulled his handkerchief out of his pocket and mopped his face.

"Is it bleeding?" he asked casually.

"Yes, a little. It's a bad bruise. . . . What made you call me that name, boy?"

"It's what you are, aren't you? A sort of master killer—"

"No!"

Hal inspected the handkerchief spattered with blood. He rolled it up and put it back in his pocket.

"Okay. . . . Let's cut the Christmas tree."

"Hal, I can't just let this pass."

"I said okay—okay."

"Okay, then!"

He was furious again and he stalked grimly ahead of his son for fifty paces. Then he stopped before a graceful young spruce.

"Here's our tree," he said.

"I'll cut it," Hal said.

He swung the ax three times against the trunk, each time missing the groove. Then he threw down the ax.

"I'm dizzy, Dad."

"Let me look at your face." He cupped his hand under his son's chin and examined the blackening bruise. "I'll ask you to forgive me for such an act on Christmas Day," he said abruptly.

"It's all right," Hal said. "I called you a name."

"Which I don't deserve," he maintained. "But rest yourself—I'll chop down the tree."

He struck four clean blows and the tree fell away with a long groan. He lifted the stump end and Hal took the top. In silence they carried it down their tracks and across the meadow to the front porch of the house.

"I'll brush the snow off," Hal said.

"Let's go into the house and get warm first."

He led the way into the kitchen. The room was warm and fragrant with sage and roasting turkey.

"Hi there, you two," Helen called cheerfully. She was basting the bird in the oven, her face rosy and her hair a tumble of silvery curls.

"There's no oven like this one," she went on. "I wonder that we were ever willing to give up wood ranges."

"Wait until you have an atomic oven," he retorted. "A couple of minutes and your turkey is done. We sit down to the table and you press a button. We exchange a little small talk, pass the time of day, and the bird will be ready to carve."

Nobody answered. He was pulling off his boots and did not notice the silence. At the kitchen table Anne was polishing the old farmhouse silver.

"Any telephone calls?" Hal asked.

"None," Anne said. She looked up and gave a cry. "What's the matter with your face?"

"Your face," Helen echoed. She closed the oven door. "Why, it's awful!"

"I hit him," Arnold said harshly. He got up and drew a glass of water and drank it.

"I called Dad a name," Hal said.

Helen sat down on the kitchen stool. "Oh dear, oh dear—what is the matter with us—"

"A Christmas gift!" Anne said, and laughing hysterically, she buried her face in her hands.

"Anne!" he shouted "Stop it! Stop laughing. Stop it, I tell you—"

He seized her shoulders and shook her. She lifted her face to him, broken with laughter or weeping, he did not know which.

"Are you going to hit me, too, Dad? Is that the sort of man you are now?"

He stepped back. "What do you mean?" he demanded. He looked from one face to another. "What do any of you mean?"

It was Anne who answered. She was the fierce one, the little fierce one who flew at him and bit him one day when she was seven. In all justice, he had been compelled to spank her for unparalleled naughtiness because she had drawn pictures of lambs and daisies over his sheets of equations. The scars of her little teeth were on his thumb still.

"We don't know you," Anne said distinctly. "You're changed. You've become a stranger to us."

He contemplated these three whom he loved. For a moment

he felt helpless and driven to escape. He thought of flight—anywhere to get away from them. Why had he ever left the comfort of his laboratory? Yet he could not escape them, wherever he was. He loved them, each of them differently and all too well. Wherever he went he carried them with him because he loved them. . . . And now he must face them as he had faced the other terrifying decisions of a scientist's life.

Should he pursue this knowledge to the uttermost, too, as he had pursued the quest of the energy locked in the nucleus of the atom? There had been times when he longed to escape that ultimate knowledge, yet he had been stern with himself. There could be no escape for the scientist.

Even while he knew that a secret energy could and might destroy the world, he had pursued the knowledge of it as his duty. It could, rightly used, bring life instead of death.

In a strange way love was like that, a power for evil or for good. Everything depended upon the human being. . . . So why were these three strangers to him now when he loved them so much? On this Christmas morning, he was conscious only of love. What could he say to make them understand?

He sat down at the kitchen table and looked from one face to another. They were watching him and he made himself gentle before them.

"Anne," he said at last, choosing her face among the three. "You're as honest as the Christmas star. I appreciate it. You say I'm a stranger to you, my family . . . and all the time I've been thinking that *you* were the strangers—you and Hal, and even you, Helen. I've felt lost here. But I've felt lost for a long time—in my own house."

Anne was embarrassed. He saw it. He must take it more slowly. "You've been busy, Dad—" she said.

"I've been busy, of course," he agreed. "Too much away from you all, too busy about what I thought was my duty—my job. But I can't live without you, my—my dears, whatever I am."

He yearned for understanding but, searching their faces, he saw them still wary. . . . They didn't know him as he was now. Other memories crowded their minds. He could guess what they were thinking: That he'd make love to them, try to win them back again, prove that he was still the gay and tender father, the passionate lover and husband.

But he wouldn't plead. He spoke to Anne again.

"Go on being honest. . . . Why do you feel I am a stranger?"

Her lovely little face seemed to be shut tight against him. "People ask me how it feels to have a father who—who made the atomic bomb. They ask me what you're making now. And I say I don't know. Because I don't. You never tell us anything."

Hal broke in. "Don't blame Dad for the bomb. Whatever he had to do about that, I guess he had to do it. Besides, it's all over—long ago."

In the big, warm kitchen the delicious smells of pine branch and roasting turkey combined. Outside the day had changed. The sky was darkening again and snow was beginning to fall in the windless air, great soft flakes. To the outer eye it was a Christmas scene as traditional as the turkey in the oven, the spruce tree waiting on the front porch.

He remembered it the same on every Christmas of his childhood, and yet today there was something in this house that had never been here before. A fear had unfolded itself, a human fear of a future—hideous but possible—because of what he and his fellow scientists had done.

And if the fear were here, was it not in every other house, in every other heart, a secret unspoken, a shadow unexplained? He who had discovered a miracle had failed to share it with these he loved. They knew only the fear.

He lifted his head. "Let me try," he said. "Let me try to explain myself. I think I understand why you are afraid of me."

Anne could not bear this. "Dad, not afraid of you, exactly. But nobody feels safe any more. That's why we rush around—we don't want to think about it. None of us do. . . . So we just keep rushing around, not thinking."

His wife took pity. "I know you can't help it, Arnold. . . . "

"I have a fear, too," he said at last. "The fear you have is a fear I share."

They were listening to him as they had not listened before. He was saying something new.

"Are you afraid of yourself?" Anne asked.

"No," he said strongly. "I know myself. Yes, I am changed, but not as you think. No one can discover the things I've discovered and not be changed. I am a humble man as I was never humble before. I believe in God. . . ."

He spoke the words simply, aware of their significance. He had never spoken the Name before. Agnostic and skeptic, he had taken pride in disbelief.

"Not the God of my fathers, perhaps," he went on, trying to be plain and not sentimental, "but yes, I believe in the eternal Creator, maker of heaven and earth. How can I not believe? I have met creation at work in the center of the atom—invisible, but full of purpose, immeasurable in power and energy. . . . I believe where I cannot see."

They were so still that they seemed not to breathe. It occurred to him now that he had never spoken to them of his serious thoughts. The days of their years together had skimmed by upon the surface of life. He had been too shy, perhaps, to uncover the hidden realities. And they had starved for reality.

They were relaxing, listening, Anne on the floor, her hands clasped about her drawn-up knees, Hal leaning against the door, hands in his pockets, and Helen sitting at the table, her head bent. She was listening, he knew, but skeptically, perhaps? Perhaps they were all skeptical.

He faltered. He tried to laugh. "Sounds big, doesn't it? Maybe I'm fooling myself . . ." He let the words trail off.

"I must baste the turkey again," Helen said suddenly.

He suspected, from the look on her too sensitive face, that the moment was more than she could bear. They waited while she opened the iron door of the oven. They watched while she dipped the fat juice with a big spoon and poured it over the huge bird. In these ways, he thought, were the vast, the small, mingled in their lives today. Christmas star and atomic fears.

She drew a glass of cold water, drank it and sat down again at the table.

"Go on, Dad," Anne said.

"I don't know how to go on now," he said abruptly. "It's true I've been away for years. Even though I sleep and eat at home a good deal of the time—I'm somewhere else. Maybe I can't get back. Maybe we'll never really meet again, you three and I.

"It's lonely, being a scientist—a lonely life. We don't make contact except with one another in our own world. That's why we keep going to conferences and meetings, I suppose—trying to find people who speak our language—with whom we can communicate through equations. . . . You've got to meet me halfway, you three!"

"Suppose we can't," Anne said in a low voice.

"Then I suppose I'll have to go my way alone," he said somberly.

Helen got up and went to the window and stood there watching the drifting snow. "We're all in the atomic age together," she said. "You got there first, that's all."

"That's very perceptive of you, darling," he said gratefully.

The telephone rang. Hal went into the hall to answer it and they waited.

"I don't know whether I'm coming," they heard him say. "I won't know for a while yet. . . . I'll be late if I do come."

He came back into the room. He threw himself down on the shaggy rug before the kitchen range, crossed his hands under his head and stared at the ceiling.

"Go on, Pop," he said.

"I can't go on," he said to his son. "You'll have to take me on faith. You can believe in me whatever I do, or you can't believe in me. All I can say is that I have seen a vision as truly as those men of old who followed the star—the wise men. They believed that a child would bring in a new and better age . . . and so do I."

"Plenty of people were afraid of that new age, too," Helen said.

"Right again," he said, and again was grateful.

She had been peering out the window and now she went to the bread box and found a crust and crumbled it. Then she opened the window and put the crumbs on the outside sill.

"I see a belated wood thrush," she said.

"Herod tried to kill the child, remember?" This was Anne, remembering the old story.

He turned to her. "He wanted to stop the new age. But nobody can do that—nobody and nothing. There's no going back to what we were—Herod couldn't kill the child . . . and we can't destroy the creative nucleus of the atom. It's eternal. It's there. We have to learn how to use it—for good and only for good."

He got to his feet restlessly and began pacing the floor, from the window to the south to the window to the north while the snow drove white against the panes. The big old kitchen stretched the width of the solid house. And he mused aloud . . .

"I wish it could have begun differently—in peace instead of in war. I wish I could have lighted cities and made houses warm and perfected a fuel for wonderful machines that aren't even invented yet. . . . But it couldn't begin that way, it seems. First of all we had to stop a subhuman man from destroying the world."

He paused and faced them.

"You understand? Hitler would have destroyed us! He was after the bomb, too. We were only months ahead."

"But Germany had surrendered," Anne said.

"Japan hadn't," he retorted. "And there were subhumans there who wanted to keep on fighting. It's the subhumans we have to watch."

He was pacing the floor again. "The only thing I fear in life is the subhuman. I trust the energy in the atom—you can know it and learn to use it—it's predictable. And I trust a good man as I trust God. But the subhuman—no! He's the enemy—the only one we have. And he may live next door as well as across the sea. He might be alive in one of us—even in me!"

He stopped in front of Anne and jabbed his long forefinger at her. "That's why you're afraid of me!"

His hand dropped. "Good God, child—you *should* be afraid of me! I was afraid of myself this morning." He turned to Hal. "Son, why did I hit you?"

"Forget it," Hal said under his breath. "I was mad at you, too."

"I can't forget," his father said. "There's something subhuman in me, too."

He was talking aloud to himself, putting his soul into words this Christmas morning. But they listened. Even though it was too much for them, they knew what he was talking about. Helen held out her hand to him and he grasped it. Anne laid her forehead against her hunched knees and he saw her body tremble. Was she weeping? He did not know.

Hal leaped up from the floor and clapped him on the back. "Enough talk! I guess we understand each other a little, anyway. . . . We'd better get the tree up, Dad. I'll drag it into the living room through the front door."

"I'll find the Christmas tree trimmings," Helen said.

She stopped on her way and kissed his cheek. But Anne sat crouched on the floor, her head bent. He glanced at her and went to the window and looked out. The snow had ceased to fall and between the wintry gray of the sky he saw lines of blue again. A variable sort of day, he thought, and it was not half over. Getting up early, even to see a star, was beginning to tell on him. And all this commotion in his family—who knew how deep it went? He had lost too much time to retrieve in one day.

And then Anne lifted her head and began to talk. "I've wanted for weeks to tell you . . . I'm terribly unhappy."

He felt his heart leap. Then he had not utterly failed!

"Tell me why you're unhappy, Anne."

"I've fallen in love."

He drew up the hassock and sat down within reach if she put out her hand to him.

"But that's wonderful," he said gently.

"It's not," she said. "I love someone who doesn't love me."

"Not possible," he declared. "I don't believe there's a man on earth who can't love you. Even if he's blind and can't see the way you look."

She laughed brokenly and scrambled to her feet. She came to him and leaned her cheek on top of his head so that he could not see her face.

"He doesn't love me enough," she said. "Not enough to give up anything for me—only enough to kiss me—and so on."

"And so on . . ." he repeated. "That's not enough, I agree."

"No," she said. "Because I love him too much. So it's got to be everything or nothing—Dad, he's married. So it's nothing."

"That's bleak," he agreed gravely. "That's very bleak."

She broke at his tenderness. "Oh, Dad, the world's empty!"

He pulled her to his knees, a child again as she used to be and a child still. She buried her face against his shoulder and began to weep soundlessly, as a broken heart must weep. No, she was not a child. A child sobs aloud. . . .

He held her, waiting. He could not throw out the usual snips and bits of comfort. You are only twenty—there are other men, young and handsome. This will pass, my child, this will pass. He would speak only the truth.

She lifted her distraught face. "Shall I ever get over this, Dad?"

"Never," he said. "One never gets over these big things. They stay in you. Other things will come—other loves. You'll live in them, too. You'll live in everything. We must—there's no escape from living."

Her head dropped to his shoulder again but she was not weeping now. He felt the heart in agony but her mind was working, her will assembling itself. She sat up and smoothed her hair.

"What would have happened to me if you hadn't made us come here for Christmas?" she asked.

"Tell me," he said.

"I planned to run away—with him—for a weekend. And this morning I couldn't. I heard you get up and go outside. I went to the window and watched you tramp through the snow and stand there by the barn a long time."

"I had to see the star again," he said.

"The star?"

He told her then of what the Christmas star had meant to the child he had once been, here in this old house, and how yesterday in the city he had longed intolerably to come back, to get his bearings once more by the star.

She slipped from his knees, no more the child. "That's what I need—to get my bearings.

"Sense of proportion," he said. "What's important and what isn't."

She walked to the window as he spoke and now she, too, stood looking out upon the snowy scene.

"Don't tell anyone about me, Dad—"

He was shocked. "How can you think I would?"

"I thought you might say something to Mother."

"You haven't?"

"No. She has enough to worry her."

"Something I don't know?"

"She thinks nobody knows. The doctor told me."

He went cold. "I should have been told at once, Anne."

"She didn't want *you* told, especially, and none of us until after Christmas. That's why the doctor told me. 'Somebody ought to know,' he said."

"She doesn't want me told," he repeated, stupefied. "But the doctor ought not to have listened to her!"

"She wouldn't even let him give her the tests until after Christmas. That's why he told me—in case she didn't feel well meanwhile."

He groaned. "All these doors shut between us!"

She came back to him and put out her hand and he clasped it for comfort. "You've opened one door today, Dad. And one open door helps the rest of us. Now we can communicate."

"But will you?"

"I will—I promise."

She smiled at him, a wise and sad smile. Some of the brightness of youth was already gone from her face.

"You'll be all right," he said. "Not at once, but step by step, a day at a time."

"Yes . . ."

She paused and sniffed. "Dad—the turkey!"

She flew to the oven and he grinned and went away. Out in the hall he called, "Helen, where are you?"

From afar off, from behind a closed door, her voice answered indistinctly.

"She's upstairs," Hal said from the living room.

The tree was up and fastened in its stand and he was pounding a last nail. "She went up to get the tree decorations and she hasn't come down. Maybe she can't find the star for the top. She couldn't remember where she put it."

He did not wait for Hal to finish. Up the stairs he leaped and to her door. It was locked. He tried the handle again.

"Let me in, Helen!"

"Just a minute, dear."

Her voice came faintly through the panels, but in less than a minute she turned the key and opened the door. She did look faint. Her eyes were enormous in her white face.

"Darling, what is the matter?" he cried.

He took her in his arms and she clung to him without answer.

"Why did you come up here all by yourself and lock the door?" he demanded.

"I don't want to tell you," she whispered after a time. "I don't want to spoil our Christmas."

"It's a day for telling," he said. "It's a day for trust."

"I'm not well," she faltered. "Something is wrong with me."

He looked down at the beloved face, pressed against his chest. The eyes were closed.

"Why didn't you tell me?"

"I couldn't—you were so far away."

"You went to the doctor by yourself?"

"Yes." The word was a sigh.

"What did he say?"

"The tests aren't complete."

"Am I far away now?"

"No."

"Never again?"

"Never."

"I'm going with you to the doctor tomorrow—and I'm staying with you."

She lifted a face suddenly bright. "Oh, Arnold, will you?"

"And maybe nothing is wrong," he said, "nothing that can't be mended."

"I can believe it possible—now."

She looked up at him, in her eyes a trust renewed. He bent his head and kissed her with a passion deeper than he had known in years. They were close again.

Downstairs Hal was telephoning.

"Hi, kid! Say, I can't get there tonight. . . . No, not even late, . . . I'm just not coming, see? . . . We're having our tree and everything."

The receiver slammed and he yelled up the stairs. "Dad— Mom—you two up there! Are you bringing the Christmas stuff down? And don't forget the star!"

They drew apart and smiled. It was impossible not to hope on this Christmas day. That indeed was the whole meaning of the star.

Grace Paley

(b. December 11, 1922)

"The Loudest Voice" was included in *The Little Disturbances of Man,* the collection of Paley's stories first published in 1959. Never before published as an occasional story, this story can give readers already familiar with it renewed pleasure in this juxtaposition to other Christmas stories, for that is what it is.

Paley's story portrays an almost complete catalog of the responses to Christmas of those for whom it is *not* their holiday. The immigrant Jewish adults of Shirley Abromovitch's world struggle in different ways to come to terms with the uninvited and apparently unavoidable invasion of their community by the foreign celebration. But for Shirley, the child with the loudest voice, this holiday means nothing at all—or everything—depending on how you interpret the delight of an outgoing, curious, ambitious, talented child who has the opportunity to be a star.

The Loudest Voice

Grace Paley

There is a certain place where dumb-waiters boom, doors slam, dishes crash; every window is a mother's mouth bidding the street shut up, go skate somewhere else, come home. My voice is the loudest.

There, my own mother is still as full of breathing as me and the grocer stands up to speak to her. "Mrs. Abramowitz," he says, "people should not be afraid of their children."

"Ah, Mr. Bialik," my mother replies, "if you say to her or her father 'Ssh,' they say, 'In the grave it will be quiet.'"

"From Coney Island to the cemetery," says my papa. "It's the same subway; it's the same fare."

I am right next to the pickle barrel. My pinky is making tiny whirlpools in the brine. I stop a moment to announce: "Campbell's Tomato Soup. Campbell's Vegetable Beef Soup. Cambell's S-c-otch Broth . . ."

"Be quiet," the grocer says, "the labels are coming off."

"Please, Shirley, be a little quiet," my mother begs me.

In that place the whole street groans: Be quiet! Be quiet! but steals from the happy chorus of my inside self not a tittle or a jot.

There, too, but just around the corner, is a red brick building that has been old for many years. Every morning the children stand before it in double lines which must be straight. They are not insulted. They are waiting anyway.

I am usually among them. I am, in fact, the first, since I begin with "A."

One cold morning the monitor tapped me on the shoulder. "Go to Room 409, Shirley Abramowitz," he said. I did as I was told. I went in a hurry up a down staircase to Room 409, which contained sixth-graders. I had to wait at the desk without wiggling until Mr. Hilton, their teacher, had time to speak.

After five minutes he said, "Shirley?"

"What?" I whispered.

He said, "My! My! Shirley Abramowitz! They told me you had a particularly loud, clear voice and read with lots of expression. Could that be true?"

"Oh yes," I whispered.

"In that case, don't be silly; I might very well be your teacher someday. Speak up, speak up."

"Yes," I shouted.

"More like it," he said. "Now, Shirley, can you put a ribbon in your hair or a bobby pin? It's too messy."

"Yes!" I bawled.

"Now, now, calm down." He turned to the class. "Children, not a sound. Open at page 39. Read till 52. When you finish, start again." He looked me over once more. "Now, Shirley, you know, I suppose, that Christmas is coming. We are preparing a beautiful play. Most of the parts have been given out. But I still need a child with a strong voice, lots of stamina. Do you know what stamina is? You do? Smart kid. You know, I heard you read 'The Lord is my shepherd' in Assembly yesterday. I was very impressed. Wonderful delivery. Mrs. Jordan, your teacher, speaks highly of you. Now listen to me, Shirley Abramowitz, if you want to take the part and be in the play, repeat after me, 'I swear to work harder than I ever did before.'"

I looked to heaven and said at once, "Oh, I swear." I kissed my pinky and looked at God.

"That is an actor's life, my dear," he explained. "Like a soldier's, never tardy or disobedient to his general, the director. Everything," he said, "absolutely everything will depend on you."

That afternoon, all over the building, children scraped and scrubbed the turkeys and the sheaves of corn off the schoolroom windows. Goodbye Thanksgiving. The next morning a monitor brought red paper and green paper from the office. We made new shapes and hung them on the walls and glued them to the doors.

The teachers became happier and happier. Their heads were ringing like the bells of childhood. My best friend Evie was prone to evil, but she did not get a single demerit for whispering. We learned "Holy Night" without an error. "How wonderful!" said Miss Glacé, the student teacher. "To think that some of you don't even speak the language!" We learned "Deck the Halls" and "Hark! The Herald Angels" . . . They weren't ashamed and we weren't embarrassed.

Oh, but when my mother heard about it all, she said to my father: "Misha, you don't know what's going on there. Cramer is the head of the Tickets Committee."

"Who?" asked my father. "Cramer? Oh yes, an active woman."

"Active? Active has to have a reason. Listen," she said sadly, "I'm surprised to see my neighbors making tra-la-la for Christmas."

My father couldn't think of what to say to that. Then he decided: "You're in America! Clara, you wanted to come here. In Palestine the Arabs would be eating you alive. Europe you had pogroms. Argentina is full of Indians. Here you got Christmas. . . . Some joke, ha?"

"Very funny, Misha. What is becoming of you? If we came to a new country a long time ago to run away from tyrants, and instead we fall into a creeping pogrom, that our children learn a lot of lies, so what's the joke? Ach, Misha, your idealism is going away."

"So is your sense of humor."

"That I never had, but idealism you had a lot of."

"I'm the same Misha Abramovitch, I didn't change an iota. Ask anyone."

"Only ask me," says my mama, may she rest in peace. "I got the answer."

Meanwhile the neighbors had to think of what to say too.

Marty's father said: "You know, he has a very important part, my boy."

"Mine also," said Mr. Sauerfeld.

"Not my boy!" said Mrs. Klieg. "I said to him no. The answer is no. When I say no! I mean no!"

The rabbi's wife said, "It's disgusting!" But no one listened to her. Under the narrow sky of God's great wisdom she wore a strawberry-blond wig.

Every day was noisy and full of experience. I was Right-hand Man. Mr. Hilton said: "How could I get along without you, Shirley?"

He said: "Your mother and father ought to get down on their knees every night and thank God for giving them a child like you."

He also said: "You're absolutely a pleasure to work with, my dear, dear child."

Sometimes he said: "For God's sakes, what did I do with the script? Shirley! Shirley! Find it."

Then I answered quietly: "Here it is, Mr. Hilton."

Once in a while, when he was very tired, he would cry out: "Shirley, I'm just tired of screaming at those kids. Will you tell Ira Pushkov not to come in till Lester points to that star the second time?"

Then I roared: "Ira Pushkov, what's the matter with you? Dope! Mr. Hilton told you five times already, don't come in till Lester points to that star the second time."

"Ach, Clara," my father asked, "what does she do there till six o'clock she can't even put the plates on the table?"

"Christmas," said my mother coldly.

"Ho! Ho!" my father said. "Christmas. What's the harm? After all, history teaches everyone. We learn from reading this is a holiday from pagan times also, candles, lights, even Chanukah. So we learn it's not altogether Christian. So if they think it's a private holiday, they're only ignorant, not patriotic. What belongs to history, belongs to all men. You want to go back to the Middle Ages? Is it better to shave your head with a secondhand razor? Does it hurt Shirley to learn to speak up? It does not. So maybe someday she won't live between the kitchen and the shop. She's not a fool."

"Here," said my father kindly, "have some lemon, it'll sweeten your disposition."

They debated a little in Yiddish, then fell in a puddle of Russian and Polish. What I understood next was my father, who said, "Still and all, it was certainly a beautiful affair, you have to admit, introducing us to the beliefs of a different culture."

"Well, yes," said Mrs. Kornbluh. "The only thing . . . you know Charlie Turner—that cute boy in Celia's class—a couple others? They got very small parts or no part at all. In very bad taste, it seemed to me. After all, it's their religion."

"Ach," explained my mother, "what could Mr. Hilton do? They got very small voices; after all, why should they holler? The English language they know from the beginning by heart. They're blond like angels. You think it's so important they should get in the play? Christmas . . . the whole piece of goods . . . they own it."

I listened and listened until I couldn't listen any more. Too sleepy, I climbed out of bed and kneeled. I made a little church of my hands and said, "Hear, O Israel . . . " Then I called out in Yiddish, "Please, good night, good night. Ssh." My father said, "Ssh yourself," and slammed the kitchen door.

I was happy. I fell asleep at once. I had prayed for everybody: my talking family, cousins far away, passersby, and all the lonesome Christians. I expected to be heard. My voice was certainly the loudest.

Wilma Shore

(b. October 12, 1913)

"May Your Days Be Merry and Bright" by Wilma Shore first appeared in *The Saturday Evening Post* of December 21, 1963 and was included in her 1965 collection of stories, *Women Should Be Allowed*.

As in Alice Childress's story, Shore's reader is not being addressed directly. However, unlike that other story, where we are given clues about the person being addressed and her responses, Shore's unresponding manicurist is left entirely to our imaginations. The reader, forced to identify with a listener about whom she or he knows *nothing* beyond the gender, feels off balance.

And because we are off balance, we understand how off balance the storyteller feels.

It's a very painful story.

But it's also a hopeful story.

When the narrator and Mrs. Hecksher share their moment of truth, we know it is possible for them to begin to create a community in their new situation, to transform their place of exile into a sharing community where people live *together*.

May Your Days Be Merry and Bright

Wilma Shore

Make them just a little shorter.

I wasn't even going to bother with my nails. So then at the last minute when my plans changed my regular girl couldn't take me. The girl in my hotel. "Oh, I feel terrible, Mrs. Siddell," she said. "But you know how it is, day before Christmas."

I said, "Never mind, I'll get a *good* manicure for a change." She laughed. She knew I was kidding. But some older people, they go so sour. We have a few lulus in the hotel. There's one woman in particular, what a story, you wouldn't believe me if I told you. But why think about unpleasant things this time of year?

This woman, I knew I didn't care for her the minute I laid eyes on her in the elevator. A big, heavy woman, bony, like a cow. On top of which, this mutation mink. September I moved in, and when I began riding up and down with this silver mutation it was blinding. We were both on the top floor, this woman and me. It costs more, but Sidney always carried enough insurance, so when he . . .

Oh, that's plenty short. Anyhow, I didn't meet her for a while. I didn't meet anybody the first couple of weeks, while Janet was with me. My daughter Janet. We were always very close, more like friends. Some mothers, when the husband passes on they're alone, but Janet came every day, rain or shine, and Julian called every night. My son-in-law, but I couldn't love him any more if he was my own.

Hecksher I knew. That's how I came to the hotel, because Hecksher was there. Mrs. Hecksher, my best friend. From high school, nearly forty years. And it's a lovely hotel, the bus stops at the corner, and you have hairdresser, florist, restaurant, everything you need. A fine restaurant, but dear. I have a little electric plate in the room, in the morning I make a cup of coffee. The management don't mind.

So then after Janet stopped coming I asked Hecksher who was the big mutation mink? Hecksher says, "Mrs. Gleason. Her son is a Wall Street broker. She's not very popular, but she only came last month. A very lovely person, really." Hecksher has a good word for everyone.

"She looks like a cow," I said. "A very lovely cow." Hecksher laughed, she had to wipe her eyes. Hecksher always enjoyed a good laugh. I remember sometimes the teachers had to send her out of the room.

That's fine, I don't like them too pointed. The reason Janet stopped coming was that I told her, I said, "You can't keep running down here, you have a husband and child." And she said yes, but she didn't want me to be lonely. I said, "Lonely? With Hecksher right downstairs?" She really worries about me, Janet.

Most mothers, whatever the children do, it's not eough. They keep asking for more, the children keep making excuses. They know it's excuses, but they can't stop asking. Not me. Like I told this woman, some woman at the hotel, I didn't know her from Adam, I was only there two weeks, but she says, "Where's your daughter? Not here today?"

You could have knocked me down. The woman didn't even know me. But I just said, "I told her, don't come. Or she would have. She's very attentive. I consider myself lucky." Which I did. Do. But it isn't luck, it's how I handle it. My mother, if we didn't come every day, pandemonium. We used to try and spread the burden. I made up my mind I would never be a burden.

So then . . . But I'll tell you a funny thing, a month later I knew when anybody's daughter came. When they called on the phone, even. The news spreads.

Well, anyhow, this Gleason, I said to Hecksher, "She's like Camembert, doesn't improve with age." That was an old joke of Sidney's. My husband. No, but seriously, some people, the longer you know them, the more you see you were right to hate them in the first place.

You know what it was? In the hotel it's like a big race between the ladies, whose children do the most for them. And Gleason kept winning. Her marvelous son Gerald. Anything anybody's boy did, Gerald did it twice. Honestly, I said to Hecksher, "I'm glad she doesn't bring him around, this miracle. It's enough just hearing about him."

"She's scared," said Hecksher. "Some other mother might grab him."

"He might find out he's the only son in the city invites his mother every single Sunday and speaks to her fifteen minutes every night." I was kidding. I didn't care who won the race. Personally, I was in the grandstand. So if this one's boy takes her to the theater, or that one's daughter brings the children for lunch, well and good. Janet's boy is too young to take to a restaurant.

But that's all they have, these old ladies. It's an empty life. You watch them try and fill it up. Take Mrs. Roote; runs that one room like a mansion, Monday wash, Tuesday iron, Wednesday polish silver . . . Mrs. Tormey: foot trouble. Greene follows the sales; office furniture, garden hose; what she can't use herself she phones around till she finds someone that can. Between Gleason talking to her son Gerald and Greene giving out the marketing reports, nobody can get into the downstairs phone booth. It's seven cents less than from the room.

It wasn't so much Gleason winning, it was the way she kept rubbing it in. The mutation from her son Gerald, the transistor radio from her son Gerald, the diamond from her son Gerald, eight carats. Gerald, the Wall Street broker. My son-in-law Julian is in advertising. A wonderful business.

It wasn't that she visited Gerald in Larchmont every Sunday. It was the way she went sashaying through the lobby like Queen Marie of Roumania. You understand, Sunday is the big day, everybody is on lobby duty. The ones that are going to their children, to make sure you know. Or if their children are coming to them, to show them off, to everyone, even Harry the elevator boy; my son, my daughter, my daughter, my son. The others . . . You went to summer camp? You remember visiting day? The ones whose parents can't come, how they hang around anyhow?

Then after the chosen elite leave, the remainders console each other. Sunday dinner, a game. Sometimes we take in a show. I don't mean I'm a remainder, but if Janet didn't happen to invite me. In advertising they work Sundays, seeing clients, and anyhow I'm not one of the ones that have a rule, you have to ask Mama for Sunday. Even the ones that left the kids with the maid all day when they were little; and now all of a sudden the kids are supposed to turn around and shower them with every kindness, just because they got old. They should have thought of that sooner. I always took care of Janet myself. Such a darling little thing.

So that's Gleason. Not popular? They could have scalped her. Her and her mutation both. Hecksher was the only one that stuck up for her. So why did she turn around and go after Hecksher?

You may not believe me if I say, persecution. But I saw it. Listen to this: one Sunday Hecksher is on top of the world, her boy Steve brought her a box of caramels. She passed it around in the lobby. Good caramels.

Fine. So what happens two days later? In marches Gleason with a box. . . . A box? A steamer trunk, should have come with a wheelbarrow. Imported chocolates. Passes it around to everyone, desk clerk, bellboys, didn't even use up the top layer.

Hecksher . . . You have to hand it to Hecksher, she's a sport. "Delicious!" she says. "And such a big box!"

Gleason has this skimpy little smile, like on a studio portrait. "*Too* big. I tell Gerald he'll die a poor man. He always says, poor but happy."

Well, if you could have seen Hecksher's face. I know Steve from a baby and I love him like my own, but he is tight, a car as big as a hearse and a nine-room house in Great Neck, but for Hecksher a ten-cent card on Mother's Day, a room on the fourth floor, a little portable television. Why portable? She's not going anywhere.

Afterward I said, "Hecksher, the old cow has it in for you."

She only laughed. That's Hecksher. "Fish feathers," she says. "My son gives me caramels, I'm proud; her son gives her chocolates, she's proud. What can you make out of it?"

"I'm not making anything," I says. "She is."

Hecksher just says, "Fish feathers." Everything is fish feathers with her.

But that night she didn't get one good laugh out of Jack Benny. It was all about Benny being stingy. And then later she started in, how Steve is expanding the business, putting back the profits, everything had to go into the business. I said sure, sure.

Then one day Steve called, I was right there in the room, and suddenly I hear Hecksher: "Mrs. Gleason's son takes her to the Tavern on the Green." That's something I never did; if Janet doesn't call for a week I never told her Mrs. So and So's daughter calls every day. I mean while Sidney was alive I always had plenty to think about, running a house, and my own friends. Now not so much. People can still like you, but if you're a couple they invite you quicker than a single woman. But why pressure Janet? She has her hands full. Those other women, their daughters have full-time help.

And when I say, if Janet doesn't call for a week, I'm only giving an example. Not a week goes by without a call, and mostly every two, three days.

Well, I never heard Hecksher talk like that before. Never. It didn't even work, he took her downstairs in the hotel, as usual. And left at half past seven. Where he usually stays till nine, nine-thirty.

So of course next day when Gleason puts out her bulletin it seems Gerald is taking her to 21, and she says to Hecksher, "You know the place?"

All Hecksher could say was, "From the outside." You could have lied, I could have lied, but not Hecksher.

But you couldn't keep her away from Gleason. I tried. It was almost Thanksgiving, and we had so many spot announcements about the lavish feast Gerald was planning in Larchmont, the capon and the imported French wines and English puddings, you could get heartburn from walking through the lobby. "Who cares?" I said. But Hecksher was like a moth to the flame, had to have her daily kick in the pants.

Then she saw this ad for smoked turkey. Whoever heard of smoked turkey for Thanksgiving? But it costs more than capon, so that's enough for Hecksher, she begins mulling. Steve and Harriet should get one, it's supposed to be so wonderful, it would be something for the kids to remember. I tell you, this time I gave it to her good. "You leave that boy alone!" I said. "Which do you want, a nice Thanksgiving or a big announcement in the lobby? Make a choice!"

So she shut up. And I thought it would be okay, but Thanksgiving night I got back too late to check, I sat for Janet because they had to go to some client's house. After dinner, I mean. Everybody sits, even with a full-time maid the kids get sick, or the parents want to go to Miami.

Next morning Hecksher's in bed. Neuralgia, is the story, but when I went down to her room I got it out of her, she and Steve had a fight. "About the smoked turkey?" She just shakes her head, yes. Couldn't keep her mouth closed, after all the work I put in.

And it must have been a beaut, there was no calls all week, and the week after. And Gleason. Ambushed us in the lobby every day. "What do you hear from your boy? What's new with Steve?" But you think Hecksher would duck? Not Hecksher. Not Mrs. Fish Feathers.

What made it worst was, by now the tree is in the lobby, the wreath is in the elevator, the whole hotel is training for the Christmas handicap, greatest race of the year. We're starting to get the line-up, who's going for the day, the evening, Christmas Eve. The ones that didn't hear yet, pins and needles. I heard from Janet the first week in December. I got Janet an alligator bag, for Julian a pinseal wallet with his initials, a beautiful animal for the baby, this high off the ground.

And still not a peep out of Mr. Steve Hecksher. Not till the twelfth. She rang me right away. "I'm not excited. Why should I be excited? I knew he'd call." But by the time I put on my hat and went downstairs, it was all through the hotel. The chambermaid stopped me in the hall, and Harry the elevator boy says, "Isn't it nice about Mrs. Hecksher?" They're all crazy about Hecksher. She's a real sport.

She's sitting right opposite the elevator, and the minute Gleason steps out, up she jumps. She wasn't excited. In a pig's ear. "I'm going to Christmas for Great Neck," she says. "I mean, for Great Neck to Christmas. Anyhow," she says, "I'm going Christmas Eve and sleep over and be there all day Christmas and help trim the tree and bake the Stollen." Hecksher used to be a wonderful baker.

Gleason just stands and smiles. Strokes her mutation. I got cold. I thought, what has she got up her sleeve?

It was the Bahamas. "Gerald absolutely insists on going away."

Tormey got excited. "They're taking a cruise and leave you home alone at Christmas?" Tormey is always counting her eggs before.

"Oh, no," says Gleason. "The whole idea is for me to go, he wants to get me out of the cold but he knows I would never desert them over the holidays."

You should have seen them. Their lips were blue, like from staying too long in the lake. "Well," says Greene, "It'll be a big help, having you there with the children if they want to go dancing or something."

"They're taking the governess," says Gleason. "Gerald wants me to have a good rest." Grand slam.

I could have killed her, the big cow. Not for myself, for them. It's nothing in my young life, when they start in comparing I just sit and listen. Sometimes I have to smile. I mean, Janet and me, we were always more like friends.

Later I told Hecksher, "She must need a rest, carrying around that heavy mutation and those eight carats."

Hecksher didn't crack a smile. Hecksher knows she won't live to the day Steve takes her on a boat, except maybe to Staten Island.

The day Gleason left I was walking down Broadway. It was a terrible day, that kind of damp cold that goes right through to your bones. I'll tell you the truth, the only reason I was out in such weather was on account of Gleason, I just didn't feel like being in the lobby for the launching party. And anyhow that was the day Janet called to say she had to change the plans.

Sure, I was disappointed. Anyone would be. But like I told her, I said, "Janet darling, a person's boss comes first. You should be overjoyed, three days in the country! And that he singled Julian out of the whole office, at Christmas, think what that means!" She felt terrible, I could tell, but I said, "Janet darling, they serve a marvelous meal downstairs, more and better than you'll get at Mr. What's-his-name; I'll eat with my friends, we'll go to the Music Hall and we'll have a grand time." So I took the presents up last Sunday and they gave me mine.

Anyhow, there I am on Broadway, and when I got down around Eighty-second I passed this florist's window. White poinsettias. Beautiful! And I thought, Janet would love it, I can get it now and take it up Christmas morning. So then I remembered I wasn't going Christmas morning.

Well, anyhow, after a minute I look up, and who do I see inside the florist but Gleason. I jumped away. After all, I walked all the way to Eighty-second to miss her. I thought, what's she doing way down here, when we have the florist in the hotel? And then I thought, I got the time mixed up, she already left and she was on her way down to the boat and she decided to stop off for a corsage for the daughter-in-law. You know how you can figure out a thing like that, that you don't even care?

But if she already left, at least I could go home. I crossed over to the bus stop, but I had to wait so long, and then when the bus came it went right by without stopping. Sometimes a little thing like that, you feel like crying.

But the next bus stopped and I went home. I thought, I'll take two aspirin and get in bed with the heating pad. But when I walk in the lobby Hecksher grabs me. "Siddell!" she says. "Where were you? You missed it, she just left this minute! You should have seen the orchid from Gerald! So big, she had to go out the door sideways!"

I just stood there looking at her. "What is it?" she says.

"What's up, Siddell?"

I put her in the elevator and took her up to my room and made her sit down before I told her. I thought it would bowl her over.

Not Hecksher. You know what she said? "Poor old thing."

"Poor old thing!" I said. "Poor old *thing?* A woman that persecuted you for four months? With her marvelous Gerald, the Wall Street broker, that we never laid eyes on? With all the presents, that she bought herself? Not just the orchid, everything! The diamond, the chocolates, the cruise! To make you miserable! A whole campaign, a whole career, to make you eat your heart out! And you sit there and say, 'Poor old thing'?"

"Well, but don't you see, Siddell," she says, "If Gerald didn't take her, then she's all alone there on the boat. All alone for Christmas."

"Who cares?" I said. "After what she did to you? The visits every Sunday, the calls every night? In the lobby, so you could see? On the pay phone, not to save seven cents but so no one could listen in, and hear her talking to herself! A phony! The woman is a phony!"

She looked down at the floor. "Listen, Siddell," she says. "Everybody is a phony, one way or another."

"Who?" I said. "Who? Tell me! Say the name!"

At the floor. Wouldn't meet my eyes. "All of us," she says. "I. You."

Hecksher. From high school. I swear I don't know what got into her. Later she said she was upset, didn't know what she was saying. It takes a big person like Hecksher to make that kind of an apology. Just the same, I was sick for three days. Flu. Went to bed and didn't eat, didn't answer the phone. Sometimes with flu you don't care if you live or die.

Anyhow, we made it up. She said she was just upset. "I'm not calm like you," she said. "You're a calm, sensible person. Look how you took it when Janet changed the plans for Christmas! No wonder you and Janet get on so well. You're a lucky woman, Siddell."

But it's more than luck. It's how you handle it. I don't know why it's so hard for them to grasp. Even Hecksher. Spoiled her whole Christmas. I'm sure that must be why her plans are changed, because of some trouble with Steve, some foolish thing she said or did. I don't know what, exactly. Generally I can get it out of her but this time she just clammed up. But otherwise why would she be coming back to the hotel first thing Christmas morning?

Won't even be there for Christmas dinner, imagine. We'll eat together. For myself I'm glad, not to be all by myself in the dining room. But I'm sorry for her, she was really counting on being in Great Neck the whole twenty-four hours.

Isn't it a funny thing, they can't learn? But you take Janet and me, we're more like friends.

Ntozake Shange
(b. October 18, 1948)

Ntozake Shange, author of the beloved and much-produced chor-
eopoem, *For Colored Girls Who Have Considered Suicide / When
the Rainbow Is Enuf,* first published "Christmas with Sassafrass,
Cypress & Indigo" in the Christmas 1982 issue of *Essence.* It was
incorporated into her 1982 novel, *Sassafrass, Cypress & Indigo.*

The similarities between Meg, Jo, Beth, Amy, and Marmee
March in "A March Christmas" and Sassafrass, Indigo, Cypress, and
Hilda Effania in this story are many. The two loving families—a
mother, her daughters, and a missing and missed husband and
father—struggle to make ends meet, share creative fun, and cherish
family traditions. Both mothers labor heroically and lovingly as
administrators and financial managers of their households, nur-
turers of their daughters' creativity, and historians of all of their
lives. Playfulness, concern for the emerging characters of the
daughters, and the exchange of gifts of love guarantee our delight in
these two American families.

Christmas for Sassafrass, Cypress & Indigo

Ntozake Shange

Hilda Effania couldn't wait till Christmas. The Christ Child was born. Hallelujah. Hallelujah. The girls were home. The house was humming. Hilda Effania just a singing, cooking up a storm. Up before dawn. Santa's elves barely up the chimney. She chuckled. This was gonna be some mornin'. Yes, indeed. There was nothing too good for her girls. Matter of fact, what folks never dreamt of would only just about do. That's right, all her babies home for Christmas Day. Hilda Effania cooking up a storm. Little Jesus Child lyin' in his Manger. Praise the Lord for all these gifts. Hilda Effania justa singin':

> Poor little Jesus Child, Born in a Manger
> Sweet little Jesus Child
> & they didn't know who you were.

Breakfast with Hilda Effania & Her Girls on Christmas Morning

Hilda's Turkey Hash

1 pound diced cooked turkey meat (white & dark)
2 medium onions, diced
1 red sweet pepper, diced
1 full boiled potato, diced

1 tablespoon cornstarch
3 tablespoons butter
Salt to taste, pepper too
(A dash of corn liquor, optional)

In a heavy skillet, put your butter. Sauté your onions & red pepper. Add your turkey, once your onions are transparent. When the turkey's sizzling, add your potato. Stir. If consistency is not to your liking, add the cornstarch to thicken, the corn liquor to thin. Test to see how much salt & pepper you want. & don't forget your cayenne.

Catfish / The Way Albert Liked It

½ cup flour
½ cup cornmeal
Salt
Pepper
½ cup buttermilk

3 beaten eggs
Oil for cooking
Lemons
6 fresh catfish

Sift flour and cornmeal. Season with your salt & pepper. Mix the beaten eggs well with the buttermilk. Dip your fish in the egg & milk. Then roll your fish in the cornmeal-flour mix. Get your oil spitting hot in a heavy skillet. Fry your fish, not too long, on both sides. Your lemon wedges are for your table.

Trio Marmalade

1 tangerine
1 papaya
1 lemon

Sugar
Cold Water

Delicately grate rinds of fruits. Make sure you have slender pieces of rind. Chop up your pulp, leaving the middle section of each fruit. Put the middles of the fruits and the seeds somewhere else in a cotton wrap. Add three times the amount of pulp & rind. That's the measure for your water. Keep this sitting overnight. Get up the next day & boil this for a half hour. Drop your wrapped seed bag in there. Boil that, too. & mix in an exact equal of your seed bag with your sugar (white or brown). Leave it be for several hours. Come back. Get it boiling again. Don't stop stirring. You can test it & test it, but you'll know when it jells. Put on your table or in jars you seal while it's hot.

Now you have these with your hominy grits. (I know you know how to make hominy grits.) Fried eggs, sunny-side up. Ham-sliced bacon, butter rolls & Aunt Haydee's Red Pimiento Jam. I'd tell you that receipt, but Aunt Haydee never told nobody how it is you make that. I keep a jar in the pantry for special occasions. I get one come harvest.

Mama's breakfast simmering way downstairs drew the girls out of their sleep. Indigo ran to the kitchen. Sassafrass turned back over on her stomach to sleep a while longer, there was no House Mother ringing a cowbell. Heaven. Cypress brushed her hair, began her daily *pliés* & leg stretches. Hilda Effania sat at her kitchen table, drinking strong coffee with Magnolia Milk, wondering what the girls would think of her tree.

"Merry Christmas, Mama." Indigo gleamed. "May I please have some coffee with you? Nobody else is up yet. Then we can go see the tree, can't we, when they're all up. Should I go get 'em?" Indigo was making herself this coffee as quickly as she could, before Hilda Effania said "no." But Hilda was so happy Indigo could probably have had a shot of bourbon with her coffee.

"Only half a cup, Indigo. Just today." Hilda watched Indigo moving more like Cypress. Head erect, back stretched tall, with some of Sassafrass' easy coyness.

"So you had a wonderful time last night at your first party?"

"Oh, yes, Mama." Indigo paused. "But you know what?" Indigo sat down by her mother with her milk tinged with coffee. She stirred her morning treat, serious as possible. She looked her mother in the eyes. "Mama, I don't think boys are as much fun as everybody says."

245

"What do you mean, darling?"

"Well, they dance. & I guess eventually you marry 'em. But I like my fiddle so much more. I even like my dolls better than boys. They're fun, but they can't talk about important things."

Hilda Effania giggled. Indigo was making her own path at her own pace. There'd be not one more boy-crazy, obsessed-with-romance child in her house. This last one made more sense out of the world than either of the other two. Alfred would have liked that. He liked independence.

"Good morning, Mama. Merry Christmas." Sassafrass was still tying her bathrobe as she kissed her mother.

"Merry Christmas, Indigo. I see Santa left you a cup of coffee."

"This is not my first cup of coffee. I had some on my birthday, too."

"Oh, pardon me. I didn't realize you were so grown. I've been away, you know?" Sassafrass was never very pleasant in the morning. Christmas was no exception. Indigo & her mother exchanged funny faces. Sassafrass wasn't goin' to spoil this day.

"Good morning. Good morning. Good morning, everyone." Cypress flew through the kitchen: *coupé jeté en tournant.*

"Merry Christmas, Cypress," the family shouted in unison.

"Oh, Mama, you musta been up half the night cooking what all I'm smelling." Cypress started lifting pot tops, pulling the oven door open.

"Cypress, you know I can't stand for nobody to be looking in my food till I serve it. Now, come on away from my stove."

Cypress turned to her mama, smiling. "Mama, let's go look at the tree."

"I haven't finished my coffee," Sassafrass yawned.

"You can bring it with you. That's what I'm gonna do," Indigo said with sweet authority.

The tree glistened by the front window of the parlor. Hilda Effania had covered it, of course, with cloth & straw. Satin ribbons of scarlet, lime, fuchsia, bright yellow, danced on the fat limbs of the pine. Tiny straw angels of dried palm swung from the upper branches. Apples shining, next to candy canes & gingerbread men, brought shouts of joy & memory from the girls, who recognized their own handiwork. The black satin stars with appliqués of the Christ Child Cypress had made when she was ten. Sassafrass fingered the lyres she fashioned for the children singing praises of the little Jesus: little burlap children with lyres she'd been making since she could thread a needle, among the miniatures of Indigo's dolls. Hilda Effania had done something else special for this Christmas, though. In silk frames of varied pastels were the baby pictures of her girls & one of her wedding day: Hilda Effania & Alfred, November 30, 1946.

Commotion. Rustling papers. Glee & Surprise. Indigo got a very tiny laced brassiere from Cypress. Sassafrass had given her a tiny pair of earrings, dangling golden violins. Indigo had made for both her sisters dolls in their very own likenesses. Both five feet tall, with hips & bras. Indigo had dressed the dolls in the old clothes Cypress & Sassafrass had left at home.

"Look in their panties," Indigo blurted. Cypress felt down in her doll's panties. Sassafrass pulled her doll's drawers. They both found velvet sanitary napkins with their names embroidered cross the heart of silk.

"Oh, Indigo. You're kidding. You're not menstruating, are you?"

"Indigo, you got your period?"

"Yes, she did." Hilda Effania joined, trying to change the subject. She'd known Indigo was making dolls, but not that the dolls had their period.

"Well, what else did you all get?" Hilda asked provocatively.

Cypress pulled out an oddly shaped package wrapped entirely in gold sequins. "Mama, this is for you." The next box was embroidered continuously with Sassafrass' name. "Here, guess whose?" Cypress held Indigo's shoulders. Indigo had on her new bra over her nightgown. Waiting for her mother & sister to open their gifts, Cypress did *tendues*. "Hold still, Indigo. If you move, my alignment goes off."

"Oh, Cypress, this is just lovely." Hilda Effania didn't know what else to say. Cypress had given her a black silk negligée with a very revealing bed jacket. "I certainly have to think when I could wear this & you all won't be home to see it."

"Aw, Mama. Try it on," Cypress pleaded.

"Yeah, Mama. Put that on. It looks so nasty." Indigo squinched up her face, giggled.

"Oh, Cypress, these are so beautiful. I can hardly believe it." Sassafrass held the embroidered box open. In the box lined with beige raw silk were seven cherry-wood hand-carved crochet needles of different gauges.

"Bet not one white girl up to the Callahan School has ever in her white life laid eyes on needles like that!" Cypress hugged her sister, flexed her foot. "Indigo, you got to put that bra on under your clothes, not on top of 'em! Mama, would you look at this little girl?"

Hilda Effania had disappeared. "I'm trying on this scandalous thing, Cypress. You all look for your notes at the foot of the tree." She shouted from her bedroom, thinking she looked pretty good for a widow with three most grown girls.

Hilda Effania always left notes for the girls explaining where their Christmas from Santa was. This practice began the first year Sassafrass had doubted that a fat white man came down her chimney to bring her anything. Hilda solved that problem by leaving notes from Santa Claus for all the children. That way they had to go search the house, high & low, for their gifts. Santa surely had to have been there. Once school chums & reality interfered with this myth, Hilda continued the practice of leaving her presents hidden away. She liked the idea that each child experienced her gift in privacy. The special relationship she nurtured with each was protected from rivalries, jokes & Christmas confusions. Hilda Effania loved thinking that she'd managed to give her daughters a moment of their own.

> *My Oldest Darling, Sassafrass,*
> *In the back of the pantry is*
> *something from Santa. In a red box*
> *by the attic window is something your*
> *father would want you to have. Out*
> *by the shed in a bucket covered with*
> *straw is a gift from your Mama.*
> *Love to you,*
> *Mama*

Darling Cypress,
Underneath my hat boxes in the
2nd floor closet is your present from
Santa. Look behind the tomatoes I
canned last year for what I got you
in your Papa's name. My own choice
for you is under your bed.
XOXOX,
Mama

Sweet Little Indigo,
This is going to be very simple.
Santa left you something outside your
violin. I left you a gift by the outdoor
stove on the right hand side. Put your
coat on before you go out there. And
the special something I got you from
your Daddy is way up in the china
cabinet. Please, be careful.
I love you so much,
Mama

In the back of the pantry between the flour & rice, Sassafrass found a necklace of porcelain roses. Up in the attic across from Indigo's mound of resting dolls, there was a red box all right, with a woven blanket of mohair, turquoise & silver. Yes, her father would have wanted her to have a warm place to sleep. Running out to the shed, Sassafrass knocked over the bucket filled with straw. There on the ground lay eight skeins of her mother's finest spun cotton, dyed so many colors. Sassafrass sat out in the air feeling her yarns.

Cypress wanted her mother's present first. Underneath her bed, she felt tarlatan. A tutu. Leave it to Mama. Once she gathered the whole thing out where she could see it, Cypress started to cry. A tutu *juponnage,* reaching to her ankles, rose & lavender. The waist was a wide sash with the most delicate needlework she'd ever seen. Tiny toe shoes in white & pink graced brown ankles tied with ribbons. Unbelievable. Cypress stayed in her room dancing in her tutu till lunchtime. Then she found *The Souls of Black Folks* by DuBois near the tomatoes from her Papa's spirit. She was the only one who'd insisted on calling him Papa, instead of Daddy or Father. He didn't mind. So she guessed he wouldn't mind now. "Thank you so much, Mama & Papa." Cypress slowly went to the 2nd floor closet where she found Santa'd left her a pair of opal earrings. To thank her mother Cypress did a complete *port de bras,* in the Cecchetti manner, by her mother's vanity. The mirrors inspired her.

Indigo had been very concerned that anything was near her fiddle that she hadn't put there. Looking at her violin, she knew immediately what her gift from Santa was. A brand-new case. No second-hand battered thing from Uncle John. Indigo approached her instrument slowly. The case was out of crocodile skin, lined with white velvet. Plus, Hilda Effania had bought new rosin, new strings. Even cushioned the fiddle with cleaned raw wool. Indigo carried her new case with her fiddle outside to the stove where she found a music stand holding *A Practical Method for Violin* by Nicolas Laoureux. "Oh, my. She's right about that. Mama would be real mad if I never learned to read music." Indigo looked through the pages, understanding nothing. Whenever she was dealing with something she didn't understand, she made it her business to learn. With great difficulty, she carried her fiddle, music stand & music book into the house. Up behind the wine glasses that Hilda Effania rarely used, but dusted regularly, was a garnet bracelet from the memory of her father. Indigo figured the bracelet weighed so little, she would definitely be able to wear it every time she played her fiddle. Actually, she could wear it while conversing with the Moon.

Hilda Effania decided to chance fate & spend the rest of the morning in her fancy garb from Cypress. The girls were silent when she entered the parlor in black lace. She looked like she did in those hazy photos from before they were born. Indigo rushed over to the easy chair & straightened the pillows.

"Mama, I have my present for you." Hilda Effania swallowed hard. There was no telling what Indigo might bring her.

"Well, Sweetheart. I'm eager for it. I'm excited, too."

Indigo opened her new violin case, took out her violin, made motions of tuning it (which she'd already done). In a terribly still moment, she began "My Buddy," Hilda Effania's mother's favorite song. At the end, she bowed to her mother. Her sisters applauded.

Sassafrass gave her mother two things: a woven hanging of twined ikat using jute and raffia, called "You Know Where We Came From, Mama"; & six amethysts with holes drilled through, for her mother's creative weaving.

"Mama, you've gotta promise me you won't have a bracelet or a ring or something made from them. Those are for your very own pieces." Sassafrass wanted her mother to experience weaving as an expression of herself, not as something the family did for Miz Fitzhugh. Hilda Effania was still trying to figure out where in the devil she could put this "hanging," as Sassafrass had called it.

"Oh, no, dear. I wouldn't dream of doing anything with these stones but what you intended."

When the doorbell rang, Hilda Effania didn't know what to do with herself. Should she run upstairs? Sit calmly? Run get her house robe? She had no time to do any of that. Indigo opened the door.

"Merry Christmas, Miz Fitzhugh. Won't you come in?" Hilda sank back in the easy chair. Cypress casually threw her mother an afghan to cover herself. Miz Fitzhugh in red wool suit, tailored green satin shirt, red tam, all of Hilda's design, and those plain brown pumps white women like, wished everyone a "Merry Christmas." She said Mathew, her butler, would bring some sweetbreads & venison over later, more toward the dinner hour. Miz Fitzhugh liked Sassafrass the best of the girls. That's why she'd sponsored her at the Callahan School. The other two, the one with the gall to want to be a ballerina & the headstrong one with the fiddle, were much too much for Miz Fitzhugh. They didn't even wanta be weavers. What was becoming of the Negro, refusing to ply an honorable trade.

Nevertheless, Miz Fitzhugh hugged each one with her frail blue-veined arms, gave them their yearly checks for their savings accounts she'd established when each was born. There be no talk that her Negroes were destitute. What she didn't know was that Hilda Effania let the girls use that money as they pleased. Hilda believed every family needed only one mother. She was the mother to her girls. That white lady was mighty generous, but she wasn't her daughers' mama or manna from Heaven. If somebody needed taking care of, Hilda Effania determined that was her responsibility, knowing in her heart that white folks were just peculiar.

"Why, Miz Fitzhugh, that's right kindly of you," Hilda honeyed.

"Why, Hilda, you know I feel like the girls were my very own," Miz Fitzhugh confided. Cypress began a series of violent *ronds de jambe.* Sassafrass picked up all the wrapping papers as if it were the most important thing in the world. Indigo felt some huge anger coming over her. Next thing she knew, Miz Fitzhugh couldn't keep her hat on. There was a wind justa pushing, blowing Miz Fitzhugh out the door. Because she had blue blood or blue veins, whichever, Indigo knew Miz Fitzhugh would never act like anything strange was going on. She'd let herself be blown right out the door with her white kid gloves, red tailored suit & all. Waving good-bye, shouting, "Merry Christmas," Miz Fitzhugh vanished as demurely as her station demanded.

Sucha raucous laughing & carrying on rarely came out of Hilda Effania's house like it did after Miz Fitzhugh'd been blown away. Hilda Effania did an imitation of her, hugging the girls.

"But Miz Fitzhugh, do the other white folks know you touch your Negroes?" Hilda responded, "Oh, I don't tell anyone!"

Eventually, they all went to their rooms, to their private fantasies & preoccupations. Hilda was in the kitchen working the fat off her goose, fiddling with the chestnut stuffing, wondering how she would handle the house when it was really empty again. It would be empty; not even Indigo would be home come January.

"Yes, Alfred. I think I'm doing right by 'em. Sassafrass is in that fine school with rich white children. Cypress is studying classical ballet with Effie in New York City. Imagine that? I'm sending Indigo out to Difuskie with Aunt Haydee. Miz Fitzhugh's promised me a tutor for her. She doesn't want the child involved in all the violence 'bout the white & the colored going to school together, the integration. I know you know what I mean, 'less up there's segregated too.

"No, Alfred, I'm not blaspheming. I just can't imagine another world. I'm trying to, though. I want the girls to live the good life. Like what we planned. Nice husbands. Big houses. Children. Trips to Paris & London. Going to the opera. Knowing nice people for friends. Remember we used to say we were the nicest, most in-teresting folks we'd ever met? Well, I don't want it to be that way for our girls. You know, I'm sort of scared of being here by myself. I can always talk to you, though. Can't I?

"I'ma tell Miz Fitzhugh that if she wants Indigo in Difuskie, that tutor will have to be a violin teacher. Oh, Alfred, you wouldn't believe what she can do on that fiddle. If you could only see how Cypress dances. Sassafrass' weavings. I wish you were here some-times, so we could tell the world to look at what all we, Hilda Effania & Alfred, brought to this world."

Once her Christmas supper was organized in the oven, the frigerator, the sideboard, Hilda Effania slept in her new negligée, Alfred's WWII portrait close to her bosom.

Afterword

I
What Are Occasional Stories?

Christmas stories belong to a category or subgenre of art called occasional art. Most of us are familiar with occasional art, although the name for it isn't as familiar as the fact of it. Works of art created to celebrate or commemorate some public event are works of occasional art. A painting celebrating Easter is an occasional painting. It will also be an example of a particular school of art (for instance, representationalism or cubism), a particular technique, (for instance, impasto) and a particular medium (for instance, oil or water colors); the painting is also a sample of the work of a particular artist and therefore represents the vision of a single individual.

Funeral masses and wedding processionals are occasional music.

Everyone is familiar with the office of "poet laureate" but few realize that it is a *job*. Poet laureates are poets who have agreed to compose poetry for special events. This is occasional poetry, poetry that can be read as part of some great public happening.

The occasional short story, a subgenre of literature as well as a subgenre of occasional art, has been particularly popular in the United States in the last two centuries. And its development has been mainly in the hands of women, although men have written their share as well.

Occasional stories, when they become well enough known, often cease to be known as a work of fiction by an individual author. They enter the realm of cultural myth and sometimes even achieve the status of history.

For instance, many people believe that Abraham Lincoln wrote the Gettysburg Address on the back of an envelope while riding on a hot, dusty train to deliver the speech.

But that isn't how it happened. It's a story. It's a story called "The Perfect Tribute," written by Mary Raymond Shipman Andrews in 1906. It was written as an occasional story, to be published for Memorial Day. Because we no longer have enormous mass public celebrations of this holiday, because it has in fact lost its status as an important public occasion, the origins of this story have been lost, have gone unnoticed.

II
Why Don't Occasional Stories Get Serious Literary Critical Attention?

Because the market for occasional stories is great, the quality of those that get published is more various than other stories, which have fewer limitations on their subject matter. Because so many of these particular kinds of stories are written and published—Christmas stories, Passover stories, Memorial Day stories, Thanksgiving stories, and so on—that are of a quality deemed less "artistic" than more idiosyncratic stories, literary critics tend to judge the entire subgenre of occasional stories by the worst examples of them. Judging the entire genre by its worst examples leads them to dismiss the entire subgenre as mawkish, whorish, trite, formulaic, and "subliterary."

That is a foolish way to arrive at a judgment of a type of anything. It is no different from the type of judgment that leads the person who has studied criminal psychology to assume that the most basic nature of the human is the criminal nature. It is the reductio ad absurdum of pessimism.

If we can free ourselves from those who counsel us about occasional stories from the perspective of that sad pseudophilosophical position, then we can look through unbiased eyes at the stories written to celebrate or commemorate some aspect of an event or a person who has been raised to heroic or monstrous status by the members of a community.

When we look at women's Christmas stories through unbiased eyes, we discover some examples of carefully crafted and brilliantly realized works of literary art. These stories are not less great art because they move us. In fact, if a story has the power to elicit strong emotional responses from us it has met a necessary (though not sufficient) criterion for being judged great art.

III
Can Occasional Stories Be Great Art?

Conforming a work of art to an inherited set of conventions does not predispose the work of art to mediocrity. Some of the best poems ever written are sonnets. And the form of the symphony certainly makes *its* own formulaic demands. The demands of the occasional work of art are those of *subject matter* rather than *style*. The subject matter of a Christmas story is *Christmas*. But the writer can use that subject matter in any way she or he chooses. Christmas can be the theme, provide the motivation for the action, cast influence in the form of ironic juxtaposing of apparently contradictory realities; it can simply be used to provide atmosphere or it can explain the occasion of the meeting of characters. There are as many ways to write a Christmas story as there are ways to write a *story*.

And just as some poets and most composers produce their best work when they work within the constraints of an inherited form—like, for instance the sonnet or the sonata—so do some short story writers produce *their* best work when they are working within the constraints of the occasional story.

IV
What Does All This Have To Do with Christmas Stories?

Editors of magazines want good Christmas stories for their December issues. Christmas sells well in the periodical business, as in most other business. Good Christmas stories and Christmas stories by beloved and well-known authors are part of what help the issue sell well. So there is an unusually large market for stories that touch on Christmas.

This annual demand for Christmas stories has two consequences. First, magazine editors are willing to pay higher rates than usual for such stories. Second, they sometimes accept fiction that isn't quite up to their usual literary standards. They seem to reason that a less-than-prize-winning Christmas story is better than no Christmas story at all.

I have discovered that some writers wrote at least one Christmas story every year for many, many years. Some of these productive celebrants of the Christmas season are Elizabeth Stuart Phelps, Mary E. Wilkins (Freeman), Harriet Prescott Spofford, Fannie Hurst, Zona Gale, Bess Streeter Aldrich, and Pearl Buck. These writers were not only otherwise prolific, but each was, in her day, an extremely popular writer with a large and devoted following. So, for instance, a story by Pearl Buck that was less than her literary finest would sell more magazines than a story of greater artistic merit by a complete unknown.

A magazine editor, given a choice between the two might refuse to choose, reasoning that the Christmas issue would be even better with both stories. Hence, the abundance of Christmas stories by both known and unknown writers—and, too, the great number of writers whose first publication was a Christmas story—or some other occasional story.*

---

*But of course the Buck story would be better paid, because after a certain time what writers are selling first of all is the name and not the material. When the name stops selling magazines, a writer once accepted for name-recognition value will begin to have work rejected.

However even those writers who are past their peak of popularity, those writers who have lost their "box office" draw (so long as they haven't become box office poison), will

V
Who Are Women's Christmas Stories Written for?

American women have written hundreds of stories over the last 120 years to be read at Christmas time. Most were published in the Christmas issue of a popular magazine or newspaper to be enjoyed as part of the readers' holiday. They were written for the audiences dearest to a serious writer's heart: the nonprofessional reader.

The nonprofessional reader is the person who reads because she or he *likes* to read. There will be no tests on the stories. There will be no rewards for reading the stories except the pleasure of reading them. The nonprofessional reader chooses and often spends hard-earned money and another precious commodity—discretionary time—engaged with the product of a writer's imagination and craft. The nonprofessional reader could be doing any of a million other things but chooses to read.

No other reader is so coveted or so cherished by writers. And no other reader is so disdained or so scorned by writers who fail to attract their attention. These Christmas Stories were all written for the nonprofessional reader.

---

continue to sell their Christmas stories. One explanation for this might be that those who buy issues of magazines *because* they are Christmas issues tend to be traditionalists. Traditionalists are notable for the characteristic of loyalty (known by some, and in some situations, as stubbornness). So these traditionalists are apt to buy an issue advertising a story by Mary E. Wilkins (Freeman) years after she has ceased to have a growing audience of readers.

Susan Koppelman is an independent scholar who lives in St. Louis, Missouri, with her husband, her son, and their cats. She received her formal education at Cleveland Heights High School, Barnard College, Western Reserve University, the Ohio State University, and Bowling Green State University. Her previous anthologies include the first collection of third wave feminist literary criticism, *Images of Women in Fiction: Feminist Perspectives* (1972), *Old Maids: Short Stories by Nineteenth Century U.S. Women Writers* (1984), *The Other Woman: Stories of Two Women and a Man* (1984), and *Between Mothers and Daughters: Stories Across a Generation* (1985).

The manuscript for this anthology was prepared for publication by Michael Lane. The book was designed by Joanne Kinney. The typeface for the text and the display is Garamond Light. The book is printed on 55-lb. Glatfelter text paper and is bound in Holliston Mills' Roxite Linen over binders boards.

Manufactured in the United States of America.